Research with
CHILDREN

SAGE has been part of the global academic community since 1965, supporting high quality research and learning that transforms society and our understanding of individuals, groups, and cultures. SAGE is the independent, innovative, natural home for authors, editors and societies who share our commitment and passion for the social sciences.

Find out more at: **www.sagepublications.com**

Connect, Debate, Engage on Methodspace

Connect with other researchers and discuss your research interests

Keep up with announcements in the field, for example calls for papers and jobs

Discover and review resources

Engage with featured content such as key articles, podcasts and videos

Find out about relevant conferences and events

www.methodspace.com

brought to you by

Research with CHILDREN

Theory & Practice

Michelle O'Reilly · Pablo Ronzoni · Nisha Dogra

⑤SAGE

Los Angeles | London | New Delhi
Singapore | Washington DC

Los Angeles | London | New Delhi
Singapore | Washington DC

SAGE Publications Ltd
1 Oliver's Yard
55 City Road
London EC1Y 1SP

SAGE Publications Inc.
2455 Teller Road
Thousand Oaks, California 91320

SAGE Publications India Pvt Ltd
B 1/I 1 Mohan Cooperative Industrial Area
Mathura Road
New Delhi 110 044

SAGE Publications Asia-Pacific Pte Ltd
3 Church Street
#10-04 Samsung Hub
Singapore 049483

Editor: Jai Seaman
Assistant editor: Anna Horvai
Production editor: Nicola Marshall
Copyeditor: Gemma Marren
Proofreader: Sharon Cawood
Indexer: Martin Hargreaves
Marketing manager: Sally Ransom
Cover design: Jennifer Crisp
Typeset by: C&M Digitals (P) Ltd, Chennai, India
Printed by: MPG Printgroup,

© Michelle O'Reilly, Pablo Ronzoni and Nisha Dogra 2013

First published 2013

Library of Congress Control Number: 2012942123

British Library Cataloguing in Publication data

A catalogue record for this book is available from
the British Library

ISBN 978-1-4462-0848-9
ISBN 978-1-4462-0849-6 (pbk)

MIX
Paper from
responsible sources
FSC
www.fsc.org   FSC® C018575

Contents

List of Figures

List of Boxes

About the Authors

Dr Michelle O'Reilly (BSc, MSc, MA, PhD, PGCAPHE, Cert Management) is a Senior Lecturer in Psychology at the Greenwood Institute, University of Leicester. Following training in counselling and child protection Michelle has pursued an academic career. During her research career she has undertaken research in qualitative research ethics, family therapy interactions, child psychiatry assessments, child mental health and homelessness. Michelle is trained in discourse and conversation analysis and is the director of a research group, LIRA (Language and Interaction Research Assembly).

Dr Pablo Ronzoni (MBBS, MPH, MRCPsych) is a Speciality Registrar (ST6) in Child and Adolescent Psychiatry at Leicestershire Partnership NHS Trust. Prior to starting his speciality clinical training in child and adolescent psychiatry, he completed a Master's in public health and then became an Academic Clinical Fellow in Psychiatry. His academic interests are centred around mental health inequalities, quality in healthcare and children and their families' experiences of mental health services.

Professor Nisha Dogra (BM, MA, PhD, FRPsych) is Professor of Psychiatry Education and Honorary Consultant in Child and Adolescent Psychiatry at the University of Leicester. She undertook some training in paediatrics before training in psychiatry and then as an academic child psychiatrist. In her clinical role, she works as a generic child and adolescent psychiatrist within a multidisciplinary team. In her academic role she has undertaken educational research and research in her clinical discipline. The latter has involved direct research with young people and their families in clinical and educational contexts.

Michelle and Nisha are affiliated with the Greenwood Institute, University of Leicester, and Pablo is affiliated with Leicestershire Partnership NHS Trust.

Acknowledgements

We would like to thank Claire Bone and Nadzeya Svirydzenka for their comments on earlier chapter drafts. We would also like to thank Nick Taub for his support in writing Chapter 10. Thanks also to other colleagues at the Greenwood for their interest at different stages of the project, and we appreciate the support offered by friends and family.

Abbreviations

AAA	American Association of Anthropology
AAS	Australian Anthropology Association
ACA	American Counselling Association/Australian Counselling Association
AMA	American Medical Association/Australian Medical Association
APA	American Psychological Association
APS	Australian Psychological Society
ASA	Association of Social Anthropologists of the UK and Commonwealth
ASEE	American Society for Ethics in Education
BACP	British Association for Counselling and Psychotherapy
BPS	British Psychological Society
CAMHS	Child and Adolescent Mental Health Service
CCPA	Canadian Counseling and Psychotherapy Association
CEA	Canadian Education Association
CMA	Canadian Medical Association
CPA	Canadian Psychological Association
CSAA	Canadian Sociology and Anthropology Association
ESRC	Economic and Social Research Council – funding body for social research
GMC	General Medical Council (UK)
IRB	Institutional Review Board – ethics committee in the US
NEA	National Education Association (UK)
NHS	National Health Service – state funded and run healthcare in the UK
NRES	National Research Ethics Service – governing body for health ethics in the UK
R&D	Research and Development – a department in all UK NHS Trusts
REC	Research Ethics Committee – ethics committee in the UK
SRA	Social Research Association

Preface

How to use this book

We begin with some advice regarding how to get the best out of this book before setting the context. This book has been written to support researchers who are new to research with children. Some of you may be familiar with research but less used to working with children and some of you may be very experienced with children but less confident regarding research. We have used our own academic and clinical experience of working with children and doing research with children to develop the chapters. After the overview of research with children, Part 1 begins by considering diversity and cultural issues. These are areas where we need to be aware of our own perspectives as these influence how we conduct any research we are involved in. We then move on to consider the origin and importance of ethics in research. Part 1 concludes by considering children's development and their ability to make decisions and why this is relevant in research. In Part 2, we begin by covering a range of issues you need to consider to plan research and to get started, followed by some attention to the different groups of children that are represented in research. We provide a chapter highlighting recruitment issues and communicating with gatekeepers as both these are a key component of research with children. Part 3 introduces you to the main methodologies and has chapters on quantitative and qualitative research respectively to enable you to gain a better understanding of these methods as well as analysis of data collected from them. The book concludes with a chapter on dissemination. Throughout the book we have included exercises so you can reflect and consolidate your learning. For those exercises that have specific responses these are given at the end of the book.

You may find it useful to read through this book as a whole to obtain a broader perspective, before focusing on getting started in which we discuss the function of a research protocol. To be able successfully to write a research proposal you need to have a sound understanding of research methods, which are covered in later chapters. This book may help you identify areas for further training and if it does, that is positive. Don't worry if, on initial reading, there are more questions than answers as this is usually the case. The book is achieving its aim in helping you design and undertake better research with children. If you have any feedback we would be grateful to receive it.

Terminology

In order to avoid the use of clumsy sentences throughout this book we have used terms in the following ways for convenience, rather than to imply that these terms are preferred or better than any alternatives.

In this book, when appropriate and talking in very general terms we simply use the word children/child/childhood as a way of encompassing children of all ages, when there is no need to differentiate the different ages and when treating the group as a whole. This saves us saying 'children and young people' each time children are referred to generically.

When necessary to differentiate different ages of children we have mostly used the terms children/child and young people/young person to refer to the groups described. When we use the terms children or child we are generally referring to those occupying a younger developmental and chronological age category. When we refer to young people/young person we are generally referring to older children. Occasionally in the book we use the terms 'teenager' or 'adolescent' to refer to this older group. We use the term adolescent only when part of an institutional name, or if the study we are citing specifically used this term. We use the word teenager when the use of the word young person is inappropriate for context or grammar.

When referring to the legal guardians of children we use the term 'parents' to encompass the adults who care for the children. Again this is to save using multiple terms each time we refer to the legal guardians of the children. We do acknowledge that there is a range of terms such as 'carer', 'guardian', 'parent' and so forth, but simply use the term parent for convenience.

1

Introduction: Setting the Context

Learning outcomes

By the end of this chapter you should be able to:

- Identify the ways in which society has changed how it views children and their place in society
- Critically appraise the new sociology of childhood
- Reflect on the role of children in research

Key words: childhood, children's rights, children's welfare, society, sociology

Introduction

The term childhood is non-specific and relates to a varying range of years in human development in different contexts. Developmentally, it refers to the period between infancy and adulthood, but it has been argued that it is a sociological concept rather than a natural phenomenon and thus accordingly has changed over time as views of children have changed.

In this chapter, we provide a very brief history of children and childhood to explore their place in society to set the context for the book. First, we describe the theory of childhood and signpost you to a range of sources that provide a comprehensive discussion of the theories and views. We present a timeline to highlight changes in the concept of childhood over the centuries and illustrate how this has affected the development of legislation around children's rights. Second, we explain how the concept of childhood has moved from a position where children were perceived as vulnerable, incompetent and passive recipients of adult care, to competent social actors shaping their place and role in society; and we outline the interactions with legislation, which is mainly approached from a generational order (when members of a group are categorised by age and legal rights). Finally, we discuss how the process of researching children has evolved in parallel to the changing social, political and legal views about children.

The sociology of childhood

As our understanding of children and childhood is historically, culturally and politically influenced, it is useful to consider the concept of childhood as a dynamic process. That is to say that the concept of childhood changes in response to societal changes and also that the perspectives of society change in response to new ideas or findings. The perspectives and views of children held within any given culture are important as they influence whether and how children are understood and prioritised by politicians, health providers, lawyers, social workers, educationalists, families and other parties, including researchers.

Concepts of developmental age as opposed to chronological age and the meanings given to these age-related groupings are neither fixed nor universal. Childhood as a definition and its components is subject to the changing values, definitions and expectations within any society. Over time our understanding of children and childhood has changed quite considerably and these changes are briefly outlined in Figure 1.1.

During the last century there has been a growth in interest in treating children as a distinct **population** that warrants inquiry in its own right. Initially there was a surge of looking at children's development and their abilities, which was later criticised for treating children as objects. However, historically, society's interest in children's roles began well before this time.

If you are interested in this topic then we recommend you source one or more of the following textbooks which provide a good comprehensive discussion of the debates, issues, theories and developments in this field.

- Corsaro, W. (2011) *The Sociology of Childhood* (3rd edn). Thousand Oaks, CA: Pine Forge Press.
- James, A. and Prout, A. (eds) (1997) *Contemporary Issues in the Sociological Studies of Childhood*. London: Falmer Press.
- Jenks, C. (2005) *Childhood*. London: Routledge.
- Woodhead, M. and Montgomery, H. (2003) *Understanding Childhood: An Interdisciplinary Approach*. Milton Keynes: Open University.
- Wyness, M. (2011) *Childhood and Society* (2nd edn). Basingstoke: Palgrave Macmillan.

Please note that this is not an extensive list and there are lots of other good textbooks on this issue, but this should help you to get started.

Activity 1.1

There is a long history to the concept of childhood and how it is encapsulated. What are your views on children? Are they mini adults or are they not? Write down a few of your preconceptions about childhood and children. Think about how your own perception of childhood and your own experiences as a child might influence how you undertake your research with them.

We provide some discussion of this issue for you to refer to when you have completed the activity at the back of the book. You might want to compare your ideas with these.

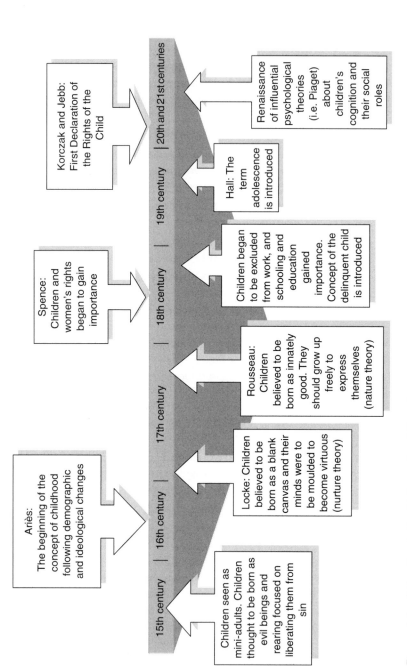

Figure 1.1 A timeline in the history of childhood

Children's rights

The contemporary sociology of childhood is organised around two central discussions, namely the child as a social actor and the generational view. We do not go into detail here as this is beyond the scope of this book, but rather provide a brief introduction to the issue.

The social actor approach: The concept of childhood has evolved from children being a uniform group perceived as vulnerable and irrational, to the view that children actively operate in their environments and are able to make sound decisions on a daily basis, as competent social actors that define their sense of self through interactions with others. In other words, this social actor approach focuses on children's everyday life and the ways they orientate themselves in society, engaging with the cultural performances and the social worlds they construct and take part in.

The generational view: The second approach that has shaped the sociology of childhood is called the generational view. This centres on socio-structural and socio-theoretical questions concerning social equality and social order, which categorises their members by age and segregates them in many respects (rights, deeds, economical participation, ascribed needs and so forth). This generational view of social groups underpins the traditional way in which the law understands children.

History is not always coherent or neatly organised and frequently the social actor and generational views of children clash. Those who contributed to shape the modern concept of childhood have postulated the idea that children should be entitled to socio-cultural rights and moral rights. In other words, the fact that children belong to an identifiable group allows them to be considered by society as a group with particular rights and worthy of moral consideration (Paul, 2007). However, having a moral right does not necessarily mean that one is entitled to legal rights and although attempts are made to incorporate moral and socio-cultural rights into the law, this is not always possible and significant differences between the rights of adults and children, which can be thought as unfair, become evident.

For instance, children have specific moral rights (such as enjoying the right to be safeguarded) precisely because they constitute a distinct vulnerable group. This contrasts with the legal age of criminal responsibility, which in some countries, such as India, starts at 7 years old. On the other hand, children and adults share the same status of personhood, as they have civil, political, social and economic rights, which in theory enable them to practise their citizenships. Yet, legally, children are not considered citizens in so far as they do not have the right to vote and their rights are limited by age.

Activity 1.2

Do you think children should have rights? What would be the justification for your perspective? Note down some of the reasons why you think children should or should not have rights. What do you think are the pros and cons of these rights in today's society?

   We provide some discussion of this at the back of the book to help you balance your perspective.

Research

The views of children and childhood, children's rights and children's abilities inevitably have an influence on the way **research** is conducted. The way in which children are positioned in society will affect the way researchers carry out their projects and therefore it is important that we consider how this is influenced in practice.

Research 'on' children

It is tempting, but unfair, to judge how unfavourably children have been perceived in the past compared with how they are viewed today, given the vast amount of literature that is currently available to us. However, it is important to remember that what is known about children and young people today is because they have been made participants of a systematic process of observation and interpretation.

   Over the past two centuries, the view of children has changed dramatically. It is now widely accepted that childhood is a special, eventful and unique period through which skills are acquired to achieve full potential by adulthood. It is now clear that there is a division between childhood and adulthood in terms of roles and expectations. While this is the majority view, there are those who would argue that children should be treated as adults. This position has been reached because of research that has been previously undertaken.

Activity 1.3

Make a list of all the reasons you can think of why it might be important to consider how children feel about being studied. We provide some additional information at the back of the book to help you develop your list.

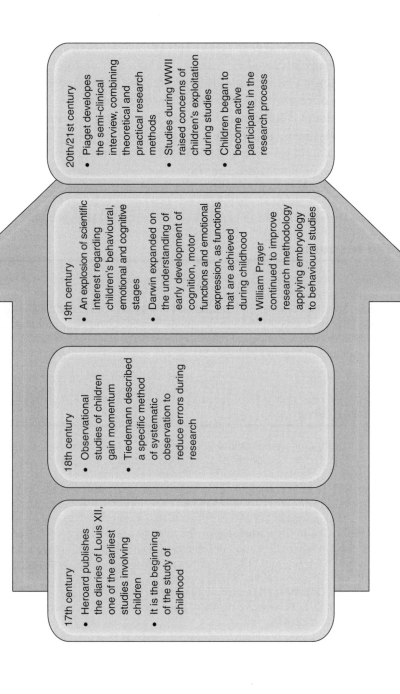

Figure 1.2 The history of research with children

Research 'with' children

The transition between research 'on' children, as passive participants, to research 'with' children, where participants' rights are respected and taken into account, began towards the latter end of the twentieth century. Following the death of many involved in research, adults and children, as a result of Nazi **experiment**s conducted during World War II in concentration camps, the protection of research participants gained relevance.

As attitudes about childhood and children began to change, including the idea of children as research participants, it became more common to include them in the planning stages of research and to consult with them on core research issues. We consider this in more depth later in the book as we discuss the reasons why researchers do research with children in a range of different disciplines.

Useful resources

Avert (2011) *Worldwide Ages of Consent*. www.avert.org/age-of-consent.htm (accessed 21/12/2011).

Interagency Working Group on Children's Participation (2008) *Children as Active Citizens*. http://sca.savethechildren.se/upload/scs/SEAP/publication/publication%20 pdf/child%20rights%20programming/Children%20as%20Active%20Citizens%20 A4%20book.pdf (accessed 29/12/2011).

Further reading

Archard, D. (1993) *Children, Rights and Childhood* (2nd edn). London: Routledge.

Corsaro, W. (2011) *The Sociology of Childhood* (3rd edn). Thousand Oaks, CA: Pine Forge Press.

Grieshaber, S. J. (2007) 'The sociology of childhood', in R. New and M. Cochran (eds), *Early Childhood Education: An International Encyclopedia*. Westport, CT: Greenwood Publishing Group, pp. 871–874.

Hart, R. (1997) *Children's Participation: The Theory and Practice of Involving Young Citizens in Community Development and Environmental Care*. London: Earthscan.

James, A. and Prout, A. (eds) (1997) *Contemporary Issues in the Sociological Studies of Childhood*. London: Falmer Press.

Jenks, C. (2005) *Childhood*. London: Routledge.

Matthews, S. (2007) 'A window on the "new" sociology of childhood', *Sociology Compass*, 1 (1): 322–334.

Morrow, V. (2001) 'Using qualitative methods to elicit young people's perspectives on their environments: some ideas for community health initiatives', *Health Education Research: Theory and Practice*, 16 (3): 255–268.

Woodhead, M. and Montgomery, H. (2003) *Understanding Childhood: An Inter-disciplinary Approach*. Milton Keynes: Open University Press.

Wyness, M. (2011) *Childhood and Society* (2nd edn). Basingstoke: Palgrave Macmillan.

PART 1

PRELIMINARY ISSUES

2

Cultural and Diversity Issues

Chapter outline

Learning outcomes

By the end of the chapter you should be able to:

- Provide a range of definitions of culture and justify the definition you use
- Recognise your own biases and their potential impact on your research
- Anticipate potential conflict and make plans to overcome or address it
- Ensure that you have a framework to consider the possibility of bias at each stage of the research process

Key words: biases, conflict, culture, diversity

Introduction

In this chapter we will consider the range of cultural issues that you need to be aware of. We provide a working definition of culture and consider the way cultural aspects may influence the research process. We also highlight specific issues of communication that may be affected by cultural factors. We will not attempt to provide an overview of how different cultural groups view research or the research process, as it would be erroneous to assume that people with similar cultural characteristics necessarily hold the same views about a particular topic. We would argue that any researcher working with children in any context or country needs to be mindful of the issues we raise in this chapter.

Activity 2.1

Write down how you define race, ethnicity, culture and diversity. Then as you read the next few pages compare your definitions with those we have collated. How do your definitions compare? A reference to this activity is positioned at the back of the book.

Definitions of culture and associated terms

There are many definitions of culture, race, ethnicity and diversity. These are no different when working with children so we will discuss them more generally. It is beyond the scope of this book to explore the complex terminology in this area so we justify the definitions we advocate rather than attempt to critique the many other definitions. We highlight the need to be aware of assumptions researchers may make about different cultural groups such as ethnic minorities and disabled people.

The purpose of providing a range of definitions is so we can illustrate the variation that exists rather than to critique each definition, as in different contexts their meanings will vary. Additionally, as such there is no right or wrong definition and all serve some function.

The rationale for providing examples from a Google search is that these are the definitions that are most widely used, hence their inclusion. As you read through the definitions provided, think about which ones you use or prefer and what might be the reasons for your preferences (do you go for those that fit your world view and on what factors is your world view based?). We now present a range of definitions to illustrate the point.

Ethnicity

Some definitions of ethnicity include:

- 'A term which represents social groups with a shared history, sense of identity, geography and cultural roots which may occur despite racial differences' (Race Relations, 2009).
- 'An ethnic quality of affiliation from racial or cultural ties' (The Free Dictionary, 2009).

Race

Some definitions of race are:

- 'Human population considered distinct based on physical characteristics ... race is predominantly a social construct' (Race Relations, 2009).
- 'A local geographic or global human population distinguished as a more or less distinct group by genetically transmitted physical characteristics.
- A group of people united or classified together on the basis of common history, nationality, or geographic distribution.
- A genealogical line; a lineage.
- Humans considered as a group' (The Free Dictionary, 2009).

The Free Dictionary includes a usage note highlighting that 'The notion of race is nearly as problematic from a scientific point of view as it is from a social one ... Many cultural anthropologists now consider race to be more a social or mental construct than an objective biological fact' (The Free Dictionary, 2009).

Culture

Some definitions of culture are:

- 'Culture refers to the perspectives, practices and products of a social group' (Race Relations, 2009).

- 'Culture is the totality of socially transmitted behaviour patterns, arts, beliefs, institutions, and all other products of human work and thought.
- These patterns, traits, and products considered as the expression of a particular period, class, community, or population' (The Free Dictionary, 2009).

Diversity

Some definitions of diversity include:

- 'The quality of being different or varied or a point of difference' (The Free Dictionary, 2009).
- 'The concept of diversity encompasses acceptance and respect. It means understanding that each individual is unique, and recognizing our individual differences. These can be along the dimensions of race, ethnicity, gender, sexual orientation, socio-economic status, age, physical abilities, religious beliefs, political beliefs, or other ideologies. It is the exploration of these differences in a safe, positive, and nurturing environment. It is about understanding each other and moving beyond simple tolerance to embracing and celebrating the rich dimensions of diversity contained within each individual' (http://gladstone.uoregon.edu/~asuomca/diversityinit/definition.html).

In much of the research undertaken, it is often unclear as to how the terms are being used thereby making it difficult to translate the research into practice. Cultural definitions are an issue, for example, if one believes that there are biological differences between people on the basis of their skin colour, the biological construct around race is likely to be acceptable. However, if one believes that skin colour is more about social reflections than biology, the use of it as a biological fact is unlikely to be acceptable. If you believe that ethnicity is the defining feature of someone's identity, then you may overlook other important factors in designing your research as your bias may lead you to focus on investigating ethnicity as the key factor. Research questions should be clearly specified, and ethnicity needs to be defined and measured in the context that is relevant for the research question and should be explicitly described. In this way, any potential conflict is transparent, without hindering the translation of evidence into service models for children and young people. To help clarify we present a number of examples here:

1 In investigating the relationship between ethnic and other identities that children and young people may have about themselves and their school performance, the participants themselves are asked to decide how they view their ethnicity so there is no need for the researcher to define it. However, it is worth bearing in mind that research participants may also have diverse views about how they define ethnicity.

2 If establishing the prevalence of mental health problems in Indian children in Leicester, the fact that a child is Indian or not is highly relevant. However, in trying to ensure you capture all those who may belong to this category, you need to be

aware that while the census may see them as 'Indian', the participants may view themselves differently, and your research may need to account for this. Children who are Indian are most likely to be Hindu, however, it does not exclude those that may not be Hindu but may still be Indian.

3 Because of the variation in the demographic characteristics and prevalence of mental health problems among different ethnic minority groups, the use of broad groupings and collective terminologies for these groups should be discouraged. Data from minority groups should not be merged, as at this point there is no evidence that we are dealing with homogenous populations.

Suggested definitions to use dependent on context

Rather than think about culture and cultural identity being based on ethnicity alone, we would like to suggest that for the purposes of thinking about research participants it is more useful to think about culture being dependent on many different factors which certainly include ethnicity. A suggested working definition is shown in Box 2.1.

Box 2.1 Working definition of culture

'Culture may be best defined by each person in relationship to the group or groups with whom he or she identifies. An individual's cultural identity may be based on heritage (by factors such as race, ethnicity, language, country of origin) as well as individual circumstances (age, gender, sexual orientation, socioeconomic status, physical ability) and personal choice (religious/spiritual beliefs). These factors may impact behaviours such as communication styles, diet preferences, health beliefs, family roles, lifestyle, rituals and decision-making processes. Culture, while not always tied to race or ethnicity, defines how we interpret and interact with others through these and many other factors' (extracted from the Association of American Medical Colleges (AAMC), 1999).

The justification for the definition suggested is that it is centred on how individuals define themselves rather than how others define them. It also suggests that individuals draw upon a range of resources and that, through the interplay of external and internal meanings, they construct a sense of identity and unique culture. It is also useful because it recognises that both parties bring a complex individual self to the encounter. Finally, it acknowledges that people are not neat packages who reach decisions through a necessarily similar process. This applies equally to children as well as adults, and the important role that children play in the family or social subsystem is relevant in how they see themselves and also how they are seen by others (as discussed in

Chapter 1). For children in new cultures there may be additional components of identity to consider.

However, in public health type research it may be more useful to use demographic characteristics (such as, for example, ethnicity using census criteria, gender or socioeconomic status) albeit with limitations, as public policy and service developments are not based on individual perspective but wider populations needs. The challenge is to consider how policies can then be implemented to have meaning for individuals. Bradby (2003) is one of many that has highlighted the complexities and inconsistencies of how researchers use terms such as ethnicity.

Multiculturalism

An online dictionary defines multiculturalism as 'the state or condition of being multicultural' or the preservation of different cultures or cultural identities within a unified society, as a state or nation (http://dictionary.reference.com/browse/multiculturalism) and some argue that one interpretation of it is 'diversity'. However, when 'multiculturalism' is used it often lacks clarity as its use is widely varied in different contexts (for example, http://news.bbc.co.uk/1/hi/uk/3600791.stm shows how varied the use is depending on your own perspective). The context is usually that different ethnicities and different cultures (usually linked to skin colour and different nationalities) lead to differences in the overall group, for example, people of different cultures will share the same beliefs, dress in the same way and so on. The concept of multiculturalism is often ideologically and/or politically defined. It is usually used in a quite restrictive way and not a term that we would advocate in research unless it is clearly defined and the limitations recognised.

A second concept relating to multiculturalism that is often used in research is 'cross-cultural'. This means research across different cultures and culture is used in the traditional sense of groups sharing characteristics based on ethnicity, nationality and heritage as opposed to other variables such as gender, sexuality and disability (and similar factors). Often comparisons between different nationalities are presented in cross-cultural research journals, for example, in *Cross-Cultural Research*, a paper by Jankowiak, Joiner and Khatib (2011) described Chinese children's play patterns in two different Chinese capitals. The study was based on naturalistic observations of children in different age cohorts interacting in a variety of social contexts. It draws on a social ecology approach to examine the role of social setting, social class and regional variation on children's interaction style. The authors wanted to link their findings to previous studies in different contexts. They sought to identify the frequency of particular types of children's interactions that ranged from types of aggressive and dominance displays, cooperative and altruistic acts, to the frequency of acts of retaliation to aggressive act(s). One can argue this is cross-cultural because the authors compared patterns of play across different cultures. However, as becomes immediately evident, there are limitations in this approach as the premise assumes homogeneity between populations. There is also an assumption that a similar behaviour has the same meaning in different contexts.

This is evident in a study in which Aycicegi-Dinn and Kagitcibasi (2010) argued that the value that children have for parents (i.e. social/traditional, economic/utilitarian and psychological) is important in shedding light on parental goals and expectations regarding children, intergenerational relationships and a host of related factors that reflect the place of the child in family and society. So in their study they focused on Turkish and American emerging adults, the former residing in urban/metropolitan and rural settings, the latter university students in a metropolitan area. Students' attitudes and values were compared to their perceptions of the attitudes and values of their parents.

Minkov and Hofstede (2012) stated that although many cross-cultural studies have used nations as the units of analysis, the concept of national culture has been challenged on various grounds. One objection is that there may be significant cultural diversity within some countries and similarities across national borders, compromising the concept of national culture. Based on their work in World Values Survey data, they found that 299 in-country regions from 28 countries in East and Southeast Asia, sub-Saharan Africa, Latin America and the Anglo world overwhelmingly cluster along national lines on basic cultural values, cross-border intermixtures being relatively rare. This is true even of countries such as Malaysia and Indonesia, or Mexico and Guatemala, despite their shared official languages, religions, ethnic groups, historical experiences and various traditions. Even the regions of neighbouring African nations, such as Ghana, Burkina Faso and Mali, do not intermix much when they are clustered on the basis of cultural values. On this basis they concluded that there is little evidence for the objection to be maintained. It is arguable though, how often is it that only basic cultural values are being studied? As we have already discussed in research with children, there is often so much more to take into account.

In considering research in different contexts, it might be worth looking at what factors need to be taken into account when working with different groups. In different contexts there may need to be a different emphasis, but good practice means that every time there should be a process of reflection and an examining of the research question from several perspectives. When one of the authors undertook some work on stigma related to mental illness with Nigerian school children, while there needed to be an awareness of cultural factors (for example, Nigerian schoolchildren have more didactic teaching than in the UK so may need more encouragement to participate in the group work that was planned) it was important not to assume that no child would want to participate.

Why does culture matter in research?

Researchers are often and sometimes fairly criticised for only undertaking research on those samples that are readily available. 'Hard to reach groups' are often not accessed. However, the matter is not usually that straightforward. It is worth asking: are these groups hard to reach because one is not using appropriate mechanisms or processes to reach them, or are they hard to reach because they are insufficiently engaged or invested in the work?

The term 'hard to reach' is broadly used to apply to most minority or vulnerable groups (this includes minority ethnic groups, black and otherwise, children with disabilities, looked after children, chronically ill, young offenders, refugees and asylum seekers to name a few). However, it is self-evident that it is unlikely that using previous approaches that have failed to engage these groups would make them more reachable unless researchers explored what the barriers may be.

The researcher's cultural identity and how it may influence the research process

There are three major issues to consider in relation to the researcher's role. First is the way that the researcher's own perspectives may colour the research. Then there are issues of how the researcher is perceived, and also how that perception influences the research process. These are now discussed in turn but before that, you should complete the exercise below to help begin to identify potential researcher bias.

Activity 2.2

Read the case scenario below and write down which of the researcher's characteristics might influence the research process and how.

Case scenario

The research aim is to identify how children feel their cultural needs have been met by staff working in a Child and Adolescent Mental Health Service (CAMHS). This research was undertaken by a female, of Indian origin, aged 40, brought up and educated in the UK, who works as a senior clinical academic in child and adolescent psychiatry at an East Midlands medical school. She has undertaken the development of a module in 'cultural diversity', so has some professional familiarity and experience with the topic. Her experience suggested that much of the training given to clinical staff was deemed to be irrelevant and marginalising and makes little difference to clinical practice.

We make some suggestions regarding how the researcher may have influenced the research process at the back of the book. Have a look at these when you have developed your answer and see if you were able to come up with anything different.

Planning to take into account potential bias

Reflexivity is an attitude of attending systematically to the context of knowledge construction, especially to the effect of the researcher, at every step of the research process (Robert Wood Johnson Foundation, 2008). To be reflexive means that the researcher should reflect on the way in which the research is carried out and think about how the process of doing research in itself can shape the outcomes (Hardy et al., 2001).

It is a useful way for the researcher to identify potential biases and consider how to address them. The first step would be to write down your personal perspectives in undertaking the research, the assumptions associated with gender, race, socioeconomic status and the political milieu of the research, as well as where the power is held in relation to the research, and where you are placed within the power hierarchy. You should also identify **gatekeepers'** interests and consider the extent to which they are favourably disposed to the project. Gatekeepers are those third parties that you need to communicate with to be able to access your population; we return to this issue later in the book.

The issues of reactivity and respondent bias also need to be addressed. Reactivity refers to the way in which the researcher's presence may interfere in some way with the setting, which forms the focus of the study, and in particular the behaviour of the people involved. Respondent bias is always a potential problem and the relationship between the researcher and respondent needs to take into account aspects of human relationships such as power differentials, professional roles and/or hierarchies or social expectations and so forth.

Research can be strongly influenced by a range of external factors and resources which may affect how the research is subsequently utilised. For example, a piece of research undertaken with Gujarati young people and their parents (Dogra et al., 2007) explored their understanding of child mental health and the services they were aware of to address such problems. The findings were used locally in service development as it became evident that the young people and their families understood the issues differently from what was being assumed by local services. They were also used to identify the work that was required to develop more effective strategies to ensure the local community were actually aware of the local service. This different use of the same findings highlights that it is important to:

- Recognise the political climate in which the research is taking place as it may strongly influence not only the research that is prioritised but also how the findings are used.
- Recognise that funding bodies may want to influence the research process and design and how they want the findings to be shared.
- The preceding two points raise ethical issues and it is important that the researcher is mindful of this.

Some such as Seale (1999) and Finlay (2002) have argued that there can be a tendency for reflexivity to be self-indulgent but that is an issue the researcher needs to be aware of rather than a reason for not engaging in reflective practice in research.

The researcher and participant relationship

The relationship between the researcher and participants brings in many potential variables that may influence the research process. Holliday (2002: 148) described what could happen when two groups of people such as researchers and participants from different backgrounds come together. He used the analogy of tourists and local people, where the researcher is the tourist and the research setting is the tourist business set up by the villagers. It could also illustrate the everyday clinical encounter. Holliday (2002: 148) considered three issues:

1 A specialised culture of dealing between the tourist and the villager is set up.
2 The dealing is influenced by and to some extent a product of the complex cultural baggage that each of the involved parties brings.
3 What is perceived by each party of the behaviour of the other party or parties, and is influenced by 1) and 2), is easily prone to essentialising cultural over-generalisation.

The second point implies that the researcher's culture has significant influence on the research setting making **qualitative** research impossible if the aim is to see, naturalistically, what was there before the researchers arrived. Holliday (2002: 149) believes that within the third point lies the seeds of 'otherising' or reducing whole swathes of people to deterministic description. For these reasons, it is important to be aware that for some organisations it may have been difficult to decline to participate in the research because of the impression this might have given to external observers. Individuals may decline to participate if the research questions their positions or roles. A junior researcher may have less success in engaging very senior respondents, although sometimes they may collect some fascinating information especially if they are perceived as unknowledgeable. This may relate to the perceived research outcomes, which participants may feel are more likely to be disseminated than if undertaken by a senior member of staff.

Sometimes it can be easier to access those from similar backgrounds and disciplines as there may be some sympathy for the researcher. Another technique to help access relevant participants is 'snowballing'. This is when those who have already been recruited to participate in the research suggest other potential participants and they in turn may suggest others. This can be helpful as, if suggested by a colleague, people may respond more positively as they do not want to let down the colleague who has recommended them. Also those who are interested in the research subject area may be more likely to respond because they want to share their own experience and views. Often direct contact by the researcher with potential participants can improve recruitment. Responses may be less favourable when letters are circulated to a professional committee from their chairperson as the personal touch is lost and potential participants may not identify with the researcher or project.

Participants may have concerns about what judgements are being made about them, especially if being interviewed by staff from psychology or psychiatry, as there can be misperceptions that they are being analysed. For some participants, disclosure of sensitive information or acknowledging that they did not know may make them feel vulnerable or increase their discomfort. However, this can be negated to some extent by how the interview is set up. Careful thought about how the interview is set up and being aware of the interviewee's perspective may also dispel doubts about whether or not perspectives are really valued.

As many factors may influence the individual's understanding of research, at the outset of any project it can be useful to check out what potential participants think your role or job is and what they think is going to happen (consenting to participate does not always mean that the information about the project has been fully understood or has removed anxieties). This may be reassuring and help put them at ease. It also enables them to clarify anything they may be concerned about.

It is also important to clarify personal value systems and acknowledge areas of greater **subjectivity**. These are sometimes the subjects of research interest for us for those very reasons. It is important to reflect on how your own communication style might hinder or help the research process. For example, if you have a tendency to interrupt and reason out loud (as does one of the authors) this can be distracting for interviewees. So when you undertake research interviews you might want to make a more concerted effort not to interrupt. Scribbling down notes, even if the interview is being taped, can be helpful as you will be less likely to fidget and distract the interviewee.

It is important to describe areas of potential role conflict and be aware of what kinds of situations and people might increase frustration, anxiety or bias towards preferred positions, as unless these are clear there is potential for bias. There is also a need to recognise when there is a lack of neutrality and how that is approached. Take, for example, an individual who has open and easy to read body language and facial expressions. While that can be positive in conveying enthusiasm and warmth, it can also convey surprise, disappointment or disapproval. It is, therefore, important in research interviews to check your reactions to comments that evoke a strong response. For example, if interviewing parents who have authoritarian views of parenting that are different to your own, you need to ensure you do not convey judgement that inhibits them from saying what they really believe.

With young people it is equally important to remain aware of how your body language is being received. Shock at a young person's sexual behaviour may stop them from disclosing any more information. Another example is how to manage parents who are very negative about their children in the child's presence; as a researcher you might find that very uncomfortable (for yourself and the child). You might feel quite angry with the parent but you need to be aware of how you convey this. The action you take may depend on what you intend to do next, for example, if you were also planning to interview the child and have 'allowed' the parent to criticise without challenge, this might reflect on the interview with the child themselves. They may be less engaged and interested in participating.

In summary, any researcher characteristic can positively or negatively influence the research process. It is important to recognise how our own perspectives might be influencing the process, especially when we also need to take into account that participants bring their own baggage to the research process.

Issues to consider when undertaking research to ensure it is sensitive to cultural issues

Sensitivity to cultural issues needs to be considered at each stage of the research process from undertaking the literature review, establishing the research question, developing the appropriate methodology, to carrying out the research, analysing the data and disseminating the findings.

It is probably more effective to have a principle based approach (Dogra, 2003). A principle based approach is one which does not attempt to identify cookbook-type solutions for all potential situations. Instead it relies on helping the researcher identify the areas and issues that the researcher needs to address to minimise the chances of problems arising. This will ensure that cultural issues are taken on board for all families and not just those from minority 'ethnic' groups or those that are perceived to be from non-mainstream populations, as the latter are not homogenous. A principle based approach:

- Prevents facts relevant to one individual being assumed to be relevant to others that may appear to be from a similar background.
- Should prevent stereotyping of any groups.
- Enables the researcher to see participants as whole people who are more complex than a series of variables.
- Works with the central philosophy that children/young people and their families all bring perspectives which need to be taken into account.

It should be emphasised that currently there is no strong evidence that one type of approach is more effective than another in encompassing all perspectives. However, it is known that much of what has been done to date has not been effective (Anderson et al., 2003) or has been insufficiently evaluated (Bennett et al., 2007). A principle based approach using the above suggestions is less likely to lead to assumptions about children and their families than approaches which list how people from particular 'ethnic' groups may behave.

As a potential researcher, the following practical points may be useful:

- Reflect on your own biases and prejudices to ensure that these do not consciously or subconsciously influence the research question without you being aware of how the process might be being affected.
- Remain constantly open to the idea that subjective perspectives can be hard to abandon.
- Critically consider whether the evidence in the literature really supports the analysis or whether it just reflects the researcher's personal biases.
- Supervision sessions are an opportunity to consider whether all aspects of the issue have been considered, even those that you may find uncomfortable.
- Don't be afraid of asking if you are not sure – just ask respectfully without judgement.
- Don't be intimidated into avoiding difficult questions just because someone is from a visibly different background.
- Don't assume that because the last family from a similar background had a particular perspective this will be shared by others from the same community. There may be different factors at play.
- If there are a number of options, don't assume what the child or young person will choose. Discuss all the options and ensure the child/young person is able to make an informed choice (which depending on their age may need parental input). Different children will need different levels of explanation and time so be prepared for that when undertaking research with them.
- Parents will be as diverse as children and young people so avoid making assumptions about them too.

In considering the research process, it can be useful to ask yourself whether the research you are reviewing was explicit about how it addressed some of the above issues. These issues also warrant consideration when using questionnaires developed for a different audience or context as you will need to think about how this might influence the research.

Activity 2.3

What cultural factors and biases do you need to consider before being able to investigate how children and young people view their peer relationships?

We provide an answer to this exercise at the back of the book.

To avoid repetition Chapters 9, 10 and 11 deal with these issues in more detail. However, to ensure we present an integrated view of this in practice, the exercise at the end of the book looks at the research process as a whole, once you have been familiarised with all aspects of it, and provides the opportunity to revisit this.

Summary

In this chapter we have highlighted how important it is for the potential researcher to be self-aware and reflective in order to identify how personal perspectives may bias all aspects of the research process. We have identified ways in which diverse communities can be researched using a set of principles to avoid stereotyping or discriminating any particular group. The process needs regular revisiting as our world views continue to develop as we have new experiences.

Further reading

Anderson, L., Scrimshaw, S., Fullilove, M., Fielding, J., Normand, J. and The Task Force on Community Preventive Services (2003) 'Culturally competent healthcare systems: a systematic review', *American Journal of Preventative Medicine*, 24 (3S): 68–79.

Bennett, J., Kalathil, J. and Keating, F. (2007) *Race Equality Training in Mental Health Services in England: Does One Size Fit All?* London: The Sainsbury Centre for Mental Health.

Bradby, H. (2003) 'Describing ethnicity in health research', *Ethnicity and Health*, 8: 5–13.

Dogra, N. (2003) 'Cultural competence or cultural sensibility? A comparison of two ideal type models to teach cultural diversity to medical students', *International Journal of Medicine*, 5 (4): 223–231.

Finlay, L. (2002) 'Negotiating the swamp: the opportunity and challenge of reflexivity in research practice', *Qualitative Research*, 2 (2): 209–230.

Holliday, A. (2002) *Doing and Writing Qualitative Research*. London: Sage.

Hutchinson, G. and McKenzie, K. (1995) 'What is an Afro-Caribbean? Implications for psychiatric research', *Psychiatric Bulletin*, 19: 700–702.

Seale, C. (1999) *The Quality of Qualitative Research*. London: Sage.

3

Ethics in Child Research

> ### Learning outcomes
>
> By the end of this chapter you should be able to:
>
> - Evaluate the importance of ethics in research
> - Differentiate particular ethical sensitivities when doing research with children
> - Appreciate the history and development of ethics committees
> - Recognise the core principles involved in ethical decision-making
> - Illustrate how the core ethics of informed consent, confidentiality and the right to withdraw are relevant to research with children
>
> **Key words:** autonomy, competence, confidentiality, ethics committees, informed consent, philosophy

Introduction

This chapter is designed to help you understand some of the complex ethical issues when doing research with children and to give you some practical advice for writing ethics applications and dealing with ethics committees. It is designed to guide you through the minefield of ethics and to help you appreciate some of the ethical complexities of doing research with children by providing you with some context about how ethics committees obtained their regulatory powers. The chapter will help you to recognise the core ethical principles that you are likely to have to consider in designing your child-focused research project and highlight other pertinent issues such as your own safety in the field.

Why are ethics important?

Ethics are the guiding principles which are based on what is believed to be right or wrong. Most people learn what they believe to be right or wrong, moral or amoral during their childhood years and it is easy to fall into the trap of believing that ethics are just common sense. While your moral code might seem like common sense to you, the ethics of research are not straightforward and have prompted considerable debate over the decades.

Ethics in the research context are especially important and they link in with a professional code of conduct and contribute to the broader reputation of various disciplines such as medicine, education, sociology and psychology. This reputation is important to build trust between institutions to promote collaboration, and with the general public to promote participation. Public support for research is important for political, financial and informational reasons. The ethical rules help promote the aims of research, to produce knowledge and truth. Ethics are important in research as they are the mechanisms to protect participants in research projects from coming to any harm, or being exploited during the research process. Currently, participants generally enter voluntarily into research projects and thus trust the researcher to be mindful of their welfare. Researchers have a responsibility to act in an ethical way during the research and attend to the needs of their participants. By questioning the ethics of your research you are likely to make your research methods better, the design stronger and improve the project.

It is easy to think that your project is small and insignificant in the grand scheme of research. You may think that what you are doing does not have potential to cause harm and that there are few if any ethical issues to consider. However, the size of a project does not determine the potential ethical issues. Even if the risks are small, if you are doing research with children there will always be some risk and you need to think about this before embarking on your project. The nature of their **vulnerability** means that even if you are only observing their behaviour in the playground, asking them a few questions about a general topic or giving them a sheet of problems to solve, there will be some ethical considerations for you to address.

You may feel that you do not really need to think much about ethics in your research because you are an ethical person and you would never fabricate data, put children at risk or cause them harm. Fortunately, most researchers have ethical integrity and protect their participants in the research process. An ethical researcher is one who is aware of all of the issues and takes practical steps to ensure the physical and psychological safety of their participants. If you do not take ethics for granted, you are much more likely to act ethically.

Research with children and adults requires several ethical considerations relating mostly to their **autonomy** to make their own choices based on a reasonable understanding of the commitment involved. Before we start exploring ethics on a general research basis we first briefly consider the history of the development of ethical principles, codes and practice. A significant reason for ethical regulation and attention to ethical practice has resulted from several highly publicised research scandals, particularly in the medical field, and many of these breaches involved vulnerable populations. Of course these are extreme cases and it is unlikely that you will be taking on research projects like these. It is important, however, to contextualise ethical developments as these types of scandals have informed the ethical codes which you now have to follow when doing research with human participants. When people think of extreme ethical scandals, typically they associate them with the field of medicine. This is because medicine has the highest potential to cause physical harm and even death, and also because of the trusting nature of the relationship between doctors and patients. Note, though, that ethical scandals are not confined to medicine and we draw your attention to scandals from the social sciences following this initial discussion.

Examples of historical medical scandals

Example one

The Syphilis scandal – in the 1940s US researchers deliberately infected Guatemalan prisoners and soldiers with syphilis and gonorrhoea. Around 1500 participants were involved and none were told the purpose of the study and consent was not sought.

Example two

The Nazi experiments – the Nazis performed a number of experiments on adults and children. They performed experiments on twin children to look at similarities and differences in genetics which involved injecting them with chemicals, they tested treatments for hypothermia by submerging people in ice cold water and they injected prisoners with a range of bacteria to test interventions. Unsurprisingly, many of their participants died.

Example three

Alder Hey – this became a public scandal when it was revealed that Alder Hey hospital was retaining patients' organs and tissue without prior consent. There was a public inquiry in 1999 which found that dead children's organs were being retained without consultation with parents.

Examples of scandals in other areas

Example one

The Stanford Prison experiment – conducted in 1971, Zimbardo and colleagues conducted a psychological study of responses to captivity as they were interested in the behavioural effects on both inmates and guards. Those in a prisoner role became traumatised and emotional and those in a guard role became abusive and anti-social and the experiment was forced to cease.

Example two

The Monster study – conducted in 1939, 22 orphan children were experimented on. Some children were given positive speech therapy which involved praising the fluency of their speech and rewarding them, whereas others were given negative speech therapy which included inducing speech problems and belittling the way they talked. Those normal-speaking orphans who received negative speech therapy suffered psychological effects and retained some speech problems into adulthood. None of the orphans were told the purpose of the study and believed they were receiving speech therapy.

Example three

Milgram's obedience study – conducted in 1963, Milgram wanted to test the effect of authority and power on obedience and set up an experiment whereby participants administered electric shocks to a stooge. This experiment caused extreme emotional distress to participants and had a number of ethical flaws.

While there are many more historical cases of research abuse, or reflections on unanticipated ethical consequences, an increase in regulation, an abundance of ethical literature and a greater awareness of ethical issues is pushing researchers to take more care in research. Across the globe complex regulatory frameworks have been put in place as a way of preventing further research scandals and protecting potential participants from harm and/or abuse of power by researchers, and all researchers, including students, have to show that they are acting responsibly. Ethics, however, are not only important to satisfy regulators, but also for the credibility of the researcher and research teams. It should be a priority for any researcher to treat participants with respect and consider their welfare during the research process to prevent them from coming to any harm.

The three philosophies of ethics

There are three core approaches to ethics in philosophy which inform research practice.

1 Consequentialism – this approach to ethics focuses on the consequences of actions. It is less concerned with the motives of researchers and places more emphasis on outcomes and harm caused to participants.

This philosophy of ethics thus relates the rightness or wrongness of a piece of research in relation to the consequences of the research. If one returns to the ethical problems in Milgram's obedience research one can see that this is a consequentialist judgement of ethics. Milgram intended to test obedience and, unforeseen to him, his participants became significantly distressed following their actions and required counselling to help them overcome the effects of the experiment. The consequences, therefore, were negative psychological harm and the project is viewed as unethical because of this.

2 Deontology – an approach which attempts to generate a universal code and guide
   to ethics by generating moral rules and principles for all to follow. This is a duty
   based or rule based approach to ethics and is less concerned with consequences
   and more concerned with the nature of the actions.

The deontological approach is the one that tends to be adopted in research
contexts. This means that most researchers use a guiding set of principles (discussed later in the chapter) to determine whether their research is ethical. If
one returns to the Monster Study conducted in 1922 on speech therapy it can
be seen that many of the moral principles were not followed. The children were
not treated autonomously as they were not consulted about their participation,
the parents and children were not fully informed on the nature of the project
and the principles relating to harm were not followed. You may want to read
the later section in this chapter on principles and then return to this section.

3 Virtue ethics – places emphasis on the individual and sees the researcher as a moral
   agent, thus the researcher needs to be capable of moral reasoning.

This philosophy of ethics is more concerned with who you are as a researcher,
your moral compass and ethical practices. This philosophy maintains that an
ethical researcher will engage in ethical practice by virtue of their character.
Note, although Milgram did not set out to harm his participants, his research
programme did lead to unintended harm.

Why are ethics important in research with children?

```
       ┐  Activity 3.1  ┌

Before proceeding with the chapter any further, have a think about your own
ethical frameworks. Consider the following two vignettes and answer these two
questions:

•  Why is this research important?
•  What are the key ethical issues raised?
```

Vignette 1

Lucy is dying from cancer. She is 8 years old and her parents are distraught. She
is expected to live for six more months and is in and out of hospital. Her consultant has secured funding to look at a newly available drug that may be beneficial.
As yet, the drug has only been tested on animals and therefore human studies,
through clinical trials, are needed. The doctor will do a randomised control trial.
One group will have the normal available medication and the other will have the

new drug. This drug is unlikely to save Lucy's life as her disease is so far progressed but the results do have the potential to save other children if the trial is successful. The doctor wants to ask Lucy's parents to allow her to participate in the trial. This will mean additional blood tests and additional visits to the hospital in her final six months.

Vignette 2

Claire is a researcher in the Department of Education. She has two children of her own and noticed that her children were not eating well in school. She wondered whether this was due to their choices or the food available. She wondered why her children seemed happy to eat lots of junk food despite her actively encouraging them to eat healthily. After some thought she secured funding to interview children about their eating habits in school and at home and explore their perceptions of healthy eating. She wanted to make this part of a healthy eating study more generally and to look at obesity and exercise. She wants to interview 20 children from the ages of 4 to 16 years old.

We provide a comprehensive overview of the issues you should have noted at the back of the book. Take a look at these now and see what you managed to consider.

You will hopefully have noticed two things from doing this vignette activity. You will notice, first, that doing research with children raises some special ethical issues and, second, that different research questions can raise slightly different ethical concerns.

Researching children raises particular ethical concerns due to the vulnerable status that children are afforded. Children are vulnerable in two ways. First, there are those that would argue they are inherently vulnerable because of their more limited knowledge and physical weaknesses that render them dependent upon adults, although the extent of vulnerability changes as they develop. Second, they are structurally vulnerable because of a lack of economic and political power (Lansdown, 1994). Particular ethical attention has been paid to this research group, therefore, and ethical guidelines have been heavily influenced by the development of policy such as the Children's Act, the UN Convention on the Rights of the Child (UNICEF, 1989; 2012) and the Economic and Social Research Council (ESRC) ethics framework.

The Children Act 1989 (HM Government, 1989), with its heavy emphasis on child protection, has influenced the protection of children in the research setting, helping to position them as vulnerable and highlighting them as a special group in need of particular ethical attention. Think back to the material you read in Chapters 1 and 2 about children's position in society and the relationship you have with different groups of children in the research context. The UN Convention on the Rights of the Child has been heavily influential in shaping our attitudes towards children to viewing them as agentive, with particular rights, and this is accounted for in contemporary ethical frameworks. The ESRC is a large-scale body that funds social research, and through the power of funding has shaped the way researchers do research with children. Changes in how ethics are seen in research with children reflects broader changes in the way one views children, not as passive objects of research but as active agents, which was discussed in detail in the introduction of this book.

History and development of ethics committees

Broadly speaking there are two types of ethics committee: those regulating health and medical research, and those regulating other research including educational and social science. The National Ethics Research Service (NRES) governs ethics in the UK National Health Service (NHS) (equivalent bodies are set up internationally), and universities tend to have ethics committees to govern any other research involving human participants that are not from a health context.

The development of research ethics committees in health

Health research ethics committees (RECs) have an interesting history. In most Western countries (for example, the USA, Canada, Australia, the UK) it is mandatory for research related to human subjects to be reviewed by an ethics panel before the researcher can proceed. Review by committee in the UK is now mandatory for research involving any aspect of the NHS. These committees have an important regulatory function to protect participants and maintain public trust. Initially research ethics committees were set up in America, and Britain followed suit shortly afterwards along with other countries (Hedgecoe, 2009). In 1973 the Royal College of Physicians requested more formal supervision of research and in 1991 formal committees were established (Hedgecoe, 2009).

Ethics committees are groups of volunteers and consist of a range of people with varying expertise and knowledge, and it is required that a minimum of one layperson will represent the public view. Members of ethics committees judge the formal application submitted through an online system and present either a favourable or unfavourable opinion. During the course of their decision-making they may make recommendations or request changes in the application.

When an application is received by the ethics committee it is checked by an administrator and passed to the committee to deliberate (Ashcroft, 2003). The main purpose of the ethics committee is thus to agree a decision regarding the ethical feasibility of a proposed project (Dixon-Woods et al., 2007). In the UK once a project has been granted a favourable opinion by a committee the applicant must apply for R&D (Research and Development) approval from the local NHS Trust. This is because it is thought that a general ethics committee is unable to comment on specific local issues which may vary nationally.

It can take considerable time to complete the application form and then a further 12 weeks for the committee to reach a decision. It can then take several weeks for R&D approval of local issues to be granted. It is therefore important that you are sensible about how much time to allow for this element of the research. This is also true of other countries as time needs to be given for reviewing protocols and discussing decisions.

The development of ethics committees in universities

The development of ethics committees within universities has been on a more ad hoc basis and each individual university has its own guidelines, forms and procedures. More recently universities have been developing governance systems to review applications. This has been driven by the ESRC insisting on ethical review before funding, and increasing pressure from journals to report ethical procedures (Hunter, 2008).

Currently researchers need to consult the individual guidelines of their university and fill in an application indigenous to that university. This means that there is little standardisation across universities within any country or across countries. It would, however, be sensible for universities to agree on an acceptable model of ethics with formalised procedures (Hunter, 2008). Research governance frameworks require there to be clear processes in how research with human subjects is approved.[1]

Obtaining ethical approval from universities tends to be less time-consuming than when going through health ethics. The forms tend to be shorter and decisions tend to be reached more quickly. Nonetheless it is still a stringent process and university committees are concerned with similar issues to health committees.

In practice this means that you need to be aware that you will need to seek approval to collect your data from some ethics committee, whether it is through health or the university. You will need to factor this into your timescale and allow the committee time to review your research plan. You will need to ensure that you submit all the appropriate documents and that they are child friendly. There are many resources out there to help you do this so make good use of them.

---

[1]Please note that while we appreciate that animal welfare and the ethics of research on animals is important it is not relevant or related to the issues in this book and therefore we do not extend our discussions or arguments to research of this kind.

Lessons to be learned about ethics applications

There has been some research which looks at the actual practice of ethics committees and considers some of the core issues that they highlight. O'Reilly et al. (2009a) found that ethics committees highlighted particular ethical issues in the application, noted when mistakes were made by applicants, and noticed missing information. We recommend that you read this paper in conjunction with this chapter to help you better appreciate the role of the ethics committee. After reading the paper it should be clear that there are several practical steps you need to take when developing your research proposal. We provide you with a checklist in Box 3.1.

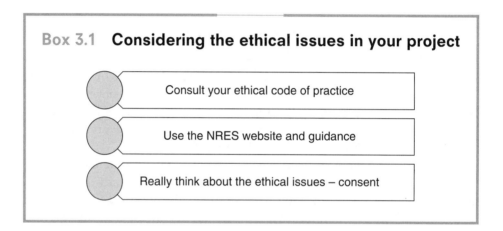

Box 3.1 **Considering the ethical issues in your project**

Consult your ethical code of practice

Use the NRES website and guidance

Really think about the ethical issues – consent

After reading this paper you should see how easy it is to make simple mistakes in your ethical application. Ideally once you have completed your ethics application we suggest you take the steps in the checklist in Box 3.2.

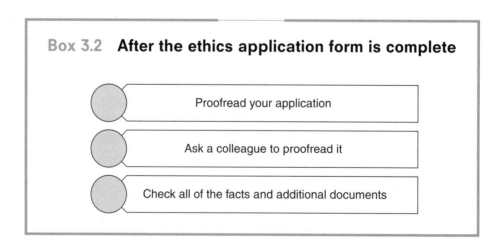

Box 3.2 **After the ethics application form is complete**

Proofread your application

Ask a colleague to proofread it

Check all of the facts and additional documents

When you are going through your ethics application you need to be mindful that you are supposed to attach further documentation with it (see Box 3.3). Do not omit mandatory appendices.

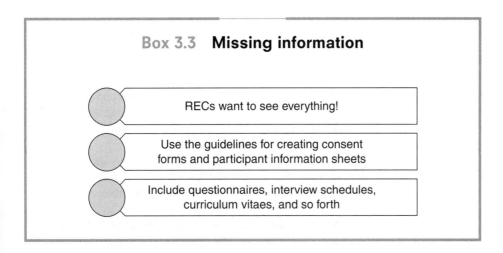

Box 3.3   **Missing information**

RECs want to see everything!

Use the guidelines for creating consent forms and participant information sheets

Include questionnaires, interview schedules, curriculum vitaes, and so forth

The likelihood is that the REC will find something in your application that concerns them or that they want further information about. Do not encourage it, however, by missing out important information, making mistakes or not following the guidelines. Key ethical concerns seem to be **informed consent**, **confidentiality** – particularly data storage, using laptops, passwords and so forth, and **coercion** – particularly related to the clinical role.

Practical guidance for developing ethics applications

There are several factors that you might want to consider when you are in the process of developing your application to any ethics committee. First, you should consult your code of ethics for guidance. Each discipline has an ethical code and this should be the first thing you look at. See Box 3.4 for some examples.

Box 3.4   **Some examples of ethical codes of practice**

- If you are doing psychological research your first consideration should be the code of ethics of the BPS (British Psychological Association), APA (American Psychological Association), CPA (Canadian Psychological Association), APS (Australian Psychological Society) and so forth.

(Continued)

(Continued)

- If you are doing medical research consult the GMC (General Medical Council), AMA (American Medical Association), CMA (Canadian Medical Association), AMA (Australian Medical Association).
- If doing counselling research consult the BACP (British Association for Counselling and Psychotherapy), ACA (American Counseling Association), ACA (Australian Counseling Association), CCPA (Canadian Counseling and Psychotherapy Association).
- If doing anthropology research consult the ASA (Association of Social Anthropologists of the UK and Commonwealth), AAA (American Association of Anthropology), CSAA (Canadian Sociology and Anthropology Association), AAS (Australian Anthropology Association).
- In education, consult the NEA (National Education Association – UK), Code of the Australian Association for Research in Education, CEA (Canadian Education Association), ASEE (American Society for Ethics in Education).

(It is not possible to list the codes for all countries across the globe and therefore we provide these only as an example. You will need to search out the relevant bodies for your own country and use those.)

Second, we recommend that you use the internet to help you. The ethics committee will have a website with substantial guidance – use it! For example, in the UK the NRES website has clear guidance for each question and if you read these sections carefully and follow the guidance properly you should be able to submit an application that can be properly reviewed. Remember that the ethics committee to whom you are applying will have its own application form for you to fill in. You will need to download a copy of this from the relevant website and follow their specific guidance in doing so.

Third, we recommend that you allow yourself plenty of time to fill in the application form adequately. When you have filled in your application make sure you proofread it thoroughly. Ask a colleague to comment on it before you submit it and get it proofread again.

You may find it useful to seek some further advice about ethics, or about the particulars of your project. In some countries, for example the USA, all investigators involved in the research project have to undertake training in ethics to be approved by Institutional Review Boards (IRBs) to conduct the research. Even if training is not mandatory, you may benefit from undertaking a short course on research ethics to help you appreciate the implementation of an ethics framework.

Example of experiencing an ethics committee

Nationally and internationally, ethics committees have to deal with a huge number of applications every year. It is perhaps unsurprising then that different researchers have different experiences. Many of these are reported in the literature in a number of ways and there is a large volume of papers that present complaints about the ethics process. Here we present two types of experience to demonstrate the variability that can exist.

Box 3.5 A difficult experience

Project one

An MSc student of ours proposed to interview clinical professionals about ethnicity issues in practice. The purpose of the study was to look at how professionals worked with children from minority groups and to seek their perspectives on an important child-focused issue. Because the sample was to be obtained through a health organisation, it was necessary for the student to fill in an online ethical application form through the governing body NRES.

The project only required competent, educated, professional adults and although the point of discussion was children, it was adults who were actually participating. It was therefore anticipated that, provided he consider the core ethical issues and address them, approval should be relatively straightforward as no patients were taking part.

Despite this, however, the student had a number of difficulties in obtaining ethical approval and did not secure approval for over six months. This was not due to ethical sensitivities in the project, but rather to a number of administrative errors and misunderstandings.

As the student had not filled in an ethics application previously he telephoned NRES to seek guidance and was given some comprehensive advice which he followed. Unfortunately each time he submitted the application new changes were required. Furthermore he encountered contradictory advice from different personnel each time he made a further telephone call.

The final problem encountered related to his student status, with NRES finally arguing that the supervisor must take responsibility for the project and that the student could not be chief investigator.

Each time a further administrative issue, contradictory advice and a further submission was made, significant time passed and this resulted in a lengthy delay for approval.

The example in Box 3.5 is not meant as a criticism of NRES, as the second example in Box 3.6 will show they can be a particularly helpful body of people who enhance research projects. However, no matter how frustrating the process is, as a researcher you need to be aware that this is unavoidable and you must comply with the regulations. The example is included to show that despite anticipations about limited ethical sensitivity, administrative errors and organisational problems can mean that your project gets delayed by the ethics process. When you plan your project you need to build in time for obtaining ethical approval and you need to build in contingency time for any delays.

Box 3.6   A more positive experience

Project two

A research team within our institute planned a research project with patients of a Child and Adolescent Mental Health Service. Due to the nature of the methodology it was considered imperative to video-record naturally occurring therapy sessions of families attending their first appointment in the service.

A project of this nature of course raises a number of ethical sensitivities, too many to write about here. Because of the involvement of children in the project, patients from the health service and the method of data collection, the researchers spent considerable time thinking about the ethical issues and the necessary strategies required to protect the participants from any harm.

The form was submitted and a meeting scheduled. It was at this meeting that the researchers were afforded the opportunity to discuss with the ethics committee any troubling issues and were able to seek guidance in relation to their proposed strategies. Approval was granted and the advice given by the committee was followed. Attending the meeting and discussing any concerns was particularly useful in helping the researchers conduct a stronger and more ethical project.

Remember that although it may seem like an administrative hurdle and is likely to take up much of your time, you can find that the ethics committee will help you to really think about how you conduct your project. They are not there to stop you doing your research, they are there to ensure you consider the welfare of your participants and safeguard people. If you engage with the committee, ask them questions about your work and respect them they can be a very useful source of support for your project.

Activity 3.2

Reflect on the two experiences in Boxes 3.5 and 3.6 and think about what the core issues are in applying for ethical approval. What do you see as the main challenges as a researcher and how might you overcome them? Think reflexively about how you feel about the ethics process and write down your expectations. It may be useful to revisit these when you have gone through the experience.

Core ethical principles

There are four core guiding principles which have informed the complex ethical frameworks for all research with human participants. These are respect for **autonomy**, **justice**, **beneficence** and **non-maleficence.**

Respect for autonomy

A central principle guiding ethics is the need to respect participants' autonomy. This means that the participants in the research are required to make active decisions regarding whether they want to participate in the research project or not. In practice this means that you should consult your participants and engage them in the process.

In relation to children, therefore, you need to recognise that they do have autonomy to make their own decisions. In research it means that you should respect their choices even if they do not make sense to you. You should also respect the autonomy of the parents. If a parent decides not to allow you access to their child this should be accepted; there is no need to seek out reasons.

Justice

The principle of justice has guided our understanding of our moral obligations to participants. Justice means that you need to treat your participants fairly and equally. There are three main types of justice: distributive justice, which means a fair distribution of resources; rights based justice, which means a respect for people's rights; and legal justice, which means a respect for morally acceptable laws.

At the centre of the notion of justice, therefore, is equality. In research it is important that you treat your participants equitably and justly. When doing research with children you need to recognise that they are not a homogenous group and that you need to treat all different types of children without prejudice or discrimination. It may be useful to reflect back on Chapter 2 concerning culture.

Beneficence

Researching children will always carry some degree of risk and therefore it is important to consider beneficence, which means to do 'good' either for the participants in the study or for the wider society more generally. This means that you will need to define any potential benefits of your research and be clear about how the outcomes of your research might usefully be translated into tangible benefits. These benefits will be weighed against potential risks. While you should aim for your research to have tangible benefits, you should be aware that it is possible that there will be no change as a result of your findings. You need to be careful not to make promises to your participants which are beyond the scope of what you can really achieve.

Non-maleficence

Non-maleficence means to avoid doing harm. Together with the principle of beneficence it means that you should aim to produce net benefit and reduce risk of harm. This includes psychological as well as physical harm. This means that when you are planning your project you need to perform a risk assessment and you need to provide a rationale showing how the benefits outweigh any possible risks or harms.

Think about whether the children or parents will be distressed by participating in your study, whether they might be offended by any of your actions or questions and consider whether there are any physical risks that you are exposing them to and how these risks might be mitigated. For example, you may think that interviewing children about their eating habits is not particularly risky. You may, however, inadvertently cause a child to worry about their size or weight; you may find that the child you are interviewing has an eating disorder and becomes upset by the questions, or is being bullied for being overweight. You cannot anticipate all harms, but by being prepared, and putting contingency plans in place, you can minimise any risks.

Overview

These four core principles have thus been translated into key guidelines for researchers so that they may engage in research in an ethical way. Four of the main ethical issues that are considered of utmost importance in research with human participants are the need to obtain informed consent, the need to assure **anonymity** and confidentiality, a necessity to offer the right to withdraw, and the usefulness of debriefing participants at the end of the research. This is not to dismiss the relevance or the importance of other ethics, but rather to give you a starting point to think about the ethical issues in your project.

A research principles example: The Willowbrook experiment (Rothman and Rothman, [1984] 2005) is a good example to explain ethical conflicts when researching children. In this study, mentally retarded children housed at the Willowbrook State School in New York were intentionally given hepatitis in an attempt to develop a vaccine against the viral infection. The study began in 1956 and lasted for 14 years. As DuBois (2008) discusses, this experiment clearly shows the conflict of the ethical principles. First, beneficence, as the study aimed at enhancing public health through the development of a vaccine. Second, justice, because institutionalised populations are often overlooked and tend not to enjoy the benefits of research. Third, autonomy, because these children were unable to give consent, and only those whose parents consented to the experiment were included. Finally, non-maleficence, as the researcher (Krugman) justified the deliberate infections and exposures by claiming that given that there was a high rate of infection in the institution it was practically inevitable that the children would become infected. Krugman's intentions of including marginalised vulnerable children for the good of all children were clear. Though important and useful scientific outcomes were obtained from the Willowbrook experiment, the principles of beneficence and non-maleficence were in clear tension and this was the main criticism that today makes it unethical.

Applying the principles in practice

While the four core principles provide researchers with a framework for undertaking their research it is important to consider how these are realised in practice. Researchers ensure that participants are assured autonomy by allowing them to make informed decisions regarding whether to participate through informed consent and the right to withdraw, protecting them from harm through anonymity and confidentiality, assuring justice through recruitment strategies, and facilitating beneficence through incentives for participants, and quality research findings which benefit society. We focus here on the main ethical concerns raised by research participation.

Applying the principle of respect for autonomy

Respecting autonomy is realised through a range of ethical practices. It is necessary to obtain the informed consent of the child and their parents as a way of acknowledging their capacity to decide for themselves about participation. This is not a simple issue and while we introduce it here in the context of ethics, we consider the issue in more detail in the next chapter. Furthermore, to respect your participant's autonomy means that you must not deceive them about your research and must allow them to withdraw should they choose to. It is important that you communicate effectively and efficiently with all parties in your research. Good communication is essential to help the children in your research understand the research commitments required of them and to ascertain their willingness to participate. We focus now on the most prominent aspects of autonomy – informed consent and the right to withdraw.

Informed consent

Obtaining informed consent is very important but with younger children or those who are especially vulnerable it is complex and challenging for the researcher. While it is advocated that you have to obtain the consent of parents before you can recruit children to research, there are rare exceptions or challenges to this. There are some cases where it is not in the child's interest to obtain parental consent or it is more difficult to obtain parental consent.

Example one

Children and young people who are homeless, living on the streets or in shelters may not know where their parents are, may not care, or may have very strong objections to you contacting them.

Example two

You may be undertaking research on a particularly sensitive topic and the child/young person may not wish the parents to know about their condition. STDs and drug use are particular examples whereby asking for parental consent may compromise the child.

Example three

Children in foster care, orphans, or unaccompanied refugee minors can be difficult to engage in research because of their legal guardian status. Usually in these cases an institutional representative such as social services will need to provide consent instead of the natural parents. In the case of foster children whose biological parents are accessible there are a number of dilemmas surrounding whether their consent is sought.

It is now accepted that you will need to acquire the informed consent or assent from the child, or at the very least check for active dissent. After providing the children with a clear information sheet outlining the required commitments and information about the project, the child will be expected to complete written evidence of consent/assent.

Activity 3.3

Cathy is a PhD sociology student. She has done considerable planning for her project and has secured ethics approval. She is planning to do a qualitative interview study looking at the experiences of young people who become pregnant before the age of 16 and their coping strategies. She has identified a charity group who run peer support groups for pregnant girls and has consulted the group leader. On her first visit to the unit she hands out information sheets and presents her proposed research. During her presentations, she states that she will need parental consent as all of the potential participants are under the age of 16. After six weeks she has not recruited any young people and no one has agreed to provide her with parental contact details. Several of the young people were considering abortions and all present in the group said that their parents were currently unaware of their status.

What should Cathy do?

We provide some answers to this activity at the back of the book but before you look at this try to have a go at answering the question yourself.

An important part of the consent process is the consent form. It is a good idea to have a written consent form for your participants to sign. You may need to read this to younger children and it is a good idea if you are available to answer any questions they have relating to it.

Activity 3.4

Have a look at the two consent forms produced overleaf (in Box 3.7) and think about what is good and bad about them. What do you notice about these consent forms and what recommendations would you make to the researchers? Remember, you don't have to recommend changes for the sake of it.

Box 3.7 **Consent forms**

[*University logo here*]

Form for young people

[*Researcher's name here*]

Child/young person to circle all they agree with:

1 You should have been afforded the opportunity to consider   Yes / No
   taking part in our research and you should have had a chance
   to look at the information sheet that came with this form.
   Have you had this opportunity?

2 The researcher should have provided you with some time to   Yes / No
   ask questions about what it means to participate in the research
   and should have given you the chance to raise any queries you
   have about it. Has the researcher given you this?

3 You have the right to withdraw your consent from this research   Yes / No
   at any time during the research process. Has this been
   adequately explained to you?

4 This is an important study on bullying. Do you understand   Yes / No
   what bullying is?

5 You are being asked to participate in this study because you   Yes / No
   are eligible and meet the criteria. Are you willing to participate
   in this very important study?

To take part in our research please complete below:

Your name _____

Date   _____

The teacher who explained this project to you needs to sign too:

Print name _____

Sign   _____

Date   _____

[University logo here]

Assent form for young people

(To be completed by the child and their parent/guardian)

[Address, telephone and e-mails of the researchers here]

Centre number:
Study number:
Family identification number:

[Title of the project here]

[Names of the researchers here]

Child (or if unable, parent on their behalf)/young person to circle all they agree with:

1	Has somebody explained this project to you?	Yes / No
2	Have you asked all the questions you want to ask?	Yes / No
3	Do you understand it's OK to stop taking part at any time?	Yes / No
4	Are you happy to take part?	Yes / No

If any answers are 'no' or you **do not** want to take part, **do not** sign your name!

If you **do** want to take part, you can **write your name** below:

Your name _____

Date _____

The doctor who explained this project to you needs to sign too:

Print name _____

Sign _____

Date _____

Thank you

It is clear from these forms that one is more child friendly and written in accessible language whereas the other one is much more adult centred. In form one the sentences are long and unwieldy, they contain a lot of information and use long complex terms which children, particularly younger children, are unlikely to understand. In the second form the sentences are much shorter, using shorter words and phrases which most children will be familiar with. Some guidance is given at the end of the chapter and you may want to refer to this now.

Right to withdraw

All participants have the right to withdraw from the research at any point in the process; they have the autonomy to do so. The asymmetrical relationship between the researcher and the child, however, may make it virtually impossible for the child to actively request to withdraw once they have committed to take part. It is your responsibility to keep reminding the child at various junctures during the research process that they have this option.

You may find it difficult to keep reminding the child of this. This is partly due to the fact that you will be busy and preoccupied with all of the research activities you are undertaking and partly because you have a vested interest in keeping the child in the study. Managing this can be difficult.

Example one

During a period of study (O'Reilly (1999) MSc in social psychology) the author interviewed children aged 4 to 11 years old about children's conflict. At this point the author was fairly new to research and had not undertaken interviews with children before. Twelve interviews were carried out as part of the dissertation and during one interview a child aged 9 years kept becoming distracted from the interviewer. He looked uncomfortable with the video camera and kept looking out of the window. It took the interviewer (O'Reilly) over 20 minutes to realise that the child was not sufficiently engaging. At this point the child was offered the opportunity to stop and go back to class. He took this opportunity and the interview stopped. The author decided to delete the short interview and not include the child in the study. With hindsight and experience the author should have given the child the opportunity to stop much sooner. Following discussions with the teacher later it became evident that the child was not uncomfortable participating, but was missing out on a fun activity with friends in the classroom and therefore timing was the main problem.

Example two

In a research project on family therapy (conducted by O'Reilly) there was an instance of one of the parents requesting that the recording device was stopped. This project involved video-recording actual family therapy sessions and at this point the father requested that the recording ceased so that they could talk to the therapist about a sensitive issue without the researcher being privileged to it. Analysis showed how difficult this was for the father to implement (please see O'Reilly et al., 2011 for a full discussion) and therefore illustrates the importance for researchers to allow space for parents or children to withdraw or suspend participation. In this case consent was simply suspended and then resumed.

When children withdraw from **quantitative** research it can bias the results and make them less meaningful; when children withdraw from qualitative research such as focus groups it can render the whole activity useless and you may have to start again. Although this is not an outcome you want as a researcher it is important that you maintain your ethical integrity and allow the child space to reflect on their willingness to participate.

Applying the principle of non-maleficence

Confidentiality and anonymity

Central to research with children are the notions of anonymity and confidentiality. While sometimes thought of as synonymous, they are actually different concepts.

Anonymity: Anonymity means the removal of all identifying features from dissemination and representations of the data. This means that people's names and identifying characteristics do not appear in print in any form. Anonymity is one of the mechanisms through which confidentiality is realised.

Data management and protection is vital and needs to be clear when discussing concerns about confidentiality with potential participants and their families. The Data Protection Act (HM Government [1984] 1998), which primarily applied to electronic data, states that information must:

• be processed fairly and lawfully in accordance with the individual's rights
• be obtained and processed for specified purposes
• be relevant and not excessive, and kept no longer than necessary
• be kept safely and
• not be transferred without adequate protection.

During research, data anonymisation can be achieved in several ways. One of the most popular is by allocating codes to each participant and keeping identifiable information separate. In this way, the data regarding personal information is correctly protected as stipulated by the Data Protection Act (HM Government, [1984] 1998), but you can ensure that if serious events occur during your research, the anonymisation is reversible. Moreover, in some cases, if anonymisation is used effectively, such as in public health research, data can even be used without explicit consent (Medical Research Council, 2004).

Confidentiality: Confidentiality is, however, more than just keeping data anonymous. Confidentiality is the means of assuring privacy to participants. This means protecting the raw data, keeping confidential identifying information such as names and addresses and maintaining secrets told outside of the research.

Confidentiality is regulated though the mechanism of informed consent described above, in other words ensuring that no data is disclosed for research purposes without consent of the individuals involved (Biggs, 2010). It becomes clear that reassurances about confidentiality need to be spelled out in the consent form. The concept of confidentiality lies in the principle of individual autonomy, providing people with the right to control information about themselves, who it can be shared with and under what circumstances they are entitled to access it. Keeping sensitive information confidential and private is a cornerstone of healthcare law, mainly the common law of equity but also of ethical codes and professional guidelines.

Protecting participants is a primary concern for researchers and confidentiality has the visible advantage of minimising some risks (Giordano et al., 2007). Research evidence shows us that parents and children have different views of anonymity and confidentiality. Parents seem less concerned about being identified and see benefits to research, benefits to others and positive aspects of being open and honest (O'Reilly et al., 2012a). Children, however, have been shown to prefer secrecy, as they fear the consequences of being identified and do not always understand what confidentiality means. Evidence suggests that children find it difficult to define confidentiality and hold false beliefs that researchers will share information with their parents and teachers (Hurley and Underwood, 2002).

It is clear that you need to spend some time with your child participants explaining what you mean by confidentiality and anonymity. You need to explain that their information will not be shared with others, especially people close to them. You need to build a **rapport** and relationship with your research participants and show them that they can trust you. It is possible that parents may ask you lots of questions after you have collected your data and you will have to manage your relationship with them professionally. They need to understand that they cannot have access to information that is shared with the expectation of confidentiality.

When doing research with children there are likely to be limits to confidentiality. The Children Act 1989 and 2004 (HM Government, 1989; 2004b) stipulates that there are occasions where confidentiality must be breached. If you suspect that the child is at risk of any type of abuse or their safety is at risk, you will need to breach confidentiality and report your suspicions.

For example, if the child reports being touched inappropriately, you need to report the issues to the relevant authorities or at least discuss them with those staff responsible for safeguarding. You do need to be careful here, however, as there will be consequences. Before you make the decision make sure you consult colleagues, your research team members and/or your supervisor. Do not make the decision alone. It is very important that the limits of confidentiality are explained and understood by the child or young person and the parents before the data is collected. This is often explained as partial confidentiality. One retains the trust of young participants by being transparent about the process and letting them know that one will discuss breaches with them before they are made but that legally there may be no other option.

Activity 3.5

Why do you think that keeping information confidential is important? Consider whether there are any exceptions to your view. Is your position different when considering research than any other area of your work? We provide some additional information at the back of the book which may help you to formulate your answer. Have a look at this now and then try to write down your ideas.

Debriefing

An important part of the data collection process is to debrief the child/parent after you have collected data from them. It is necessary to thank them for their participation, reflect with them on their contribution and give them the opportunity to ask any questions. You can use this space to ensure that the participants have not been adversely affected by the research process.

Applying the principle of beneficence

The principle of beneficence relates to an ethical obligation to act for the benefit of others. In the case of research it is possible for the children who are participating in the research to benefit in some way, and/or for the research to benefit wider society. Children may benefit directly, for example, by receiving new treatments in healthcare, or being part of new educational packages which improve their learning. Alternatively they may not benefit directly from their participation, and therefore their involvement in the research may benefit children in society more generally. You need to remember that research will not necessarily bring about change and may simply build on the evidence base and therefore you need to be careful what you promise your participants. The main issue for beneficence in terms of the participating children relates to inducements.

Inducements

An important question when implementing the principle of beneficence relates to whose interests are being served by the research (Farrell, 2010). If the child participating in the study is going to directly benefit from participating, through developing their social or intellectual skills or being given a more effective intervention for their mental or physical health, it may be more justified to include them in the study. If, however, the child will not gain any direct benefit then it is possible to compensate their participation by offering an inducement. Paying research participants is quite common but it is a contentious issue ethically as it leads to a risk of coercion (Grady, 2005). 'Coercion is paradigmatically a case of the denial of autonomy, since it consists in the deliberate imposition of one person's will on another' (Wilkinson and Moore, 1997: 378). This is particularly problematic with children who are more susceptible to being coerced into research due to power differences.

Applying the principle of justice

The principle of justice requires that researchers ensure an equal distribution of the benefits and risks that participating in a study brings. To apply this principle means that the researcher cannot expose one group of people to the risks of research solely for the benefit of another group. So, for example, a researcher could not experiment on young offenders in prison for the sole purpose of benefitting children in society. The main practical implementation for justice relates to the equal recruitment of participants and avoiding coercion (note that coercion also links to autonomy as a person should be free from coercion to exercise their autonomy).

Coercion

To implement the practice of justice requires an equitable selection of participants which in reality means that researchers should take additional care if recruiting participant populations that may be unfairly coerced into participating such as prisoners and institutionalised children. Researching young offenders or populations in prison can be challenging because of this ethical consideration and the challenge is not to further marginalise these groups by excluding them from research (Moser et al., 2004).

When researching children additional care should be taken to ensure justice by not coercing children to participate. There is a difference between explicit coercion, which is easy to recognise as the assertion of power over a child, and implicit coercion, which occurs in the quiet space of relationships (Singh, 2010). For example, a parent may pressurise a child to participate in your research outside of your presence and knowledge. It is imperative therefore that you allow the child space to withdraw, reassure the child (and parent) that there are no consequences of this and actively look for signs of dissent, particularly in younger children.

Furthermore you may want to think more about the ways you might influence a decision. Your title, your age, your authority, your role may all be things that inadvertently coerce a child into participating. Think about the following example.

Example one

One of the authors (O'Reilly) was involved in a sociological health study looking at decision-making in child psychiatry. This meant video-recording initial child psychiatry consultations of the child and their family. Consent was required from the clinical professionals, the parents (and extended family members involved), and the children. Because the research team consisted of an academic psychologist (O'Reilly), a psychiatrist and a professor of sociology, the team had concerns about the professional titles unduly coercing families into agreeing. To counter this possibility it was agreed that the research assistant would do this. Although less experienced, this person was younger and did not have the title doctor or professor. Liaising with clinical professionals meant that children and parents were assessed for capacity and competence properly and the researcher was trained by the team in taking consent.

Summary

In this chapter we have introduced you to some of the core ethical principles for doing research with children. We have highlighted that ethics are important for doing research with children to prevent research participants from coming to any harm. We have considered the role of the ethics committee and the issues that they concern themselves with. It is clear from this chapter that you need to be cautious when doing research with children and that you need to respect them as participants. You need to think about how you obtain their consent and ensure that they are comfortable.

Useful resource

The National Research Ethics Service website is a useful resource. This is a UK based website with considerable guidance relating to ethics, designing consent forms and designing information sheets for children. This will be useful for anyone in Western countries designing a research project with children. See www.nres.npsa.nhs.uk.

Further reading

Alderson, P. (2004) 'Ethics', in S. Fraser, V. Lewis, S. Ding, M. Kellett and C. Robinson (eds) *Doing Research with Children and Young People*. London: Sage, pp. 97–112.

Alderson, P. and Morrow, V. (2004) *Ethics, Social Research and Consulting with Children and Young People*. Barkingside: Barnardo's.

Carter, B. (2009) 'Tick box for child? The ethical positioning of children as vulnerable, researchers as barbarians and reviewers as overly cautious', *International Journal of Nursing Studies*, 46: 858–864.

Giordano, J., O'Reilly, M., Taylor, H. and Dogra, N. (2007) 'Confidentiality and autonomy: the challenge(s) of offering research participants a choice of disclosing their identity', *Qualitative Health Research*, 17 (2): 264–275.

Grodin, M.A. and Glantz, L.H. (eds) (1994) *Children as Research Subjects: Science, Ethics, and Law*. Oxford and New York: Oxford University Press.

Hoagwood, K., Jensen, P. and Fisher, C. (1996) *Ethical Issues in Mental Health Research with Children and Adolescents*. London: Routledge.

Kodish, E. (2005) *Ethics and Research with Children: A Case-Based Approach*. Oxford: Oxford University Press.

O'Reilly, M., Dixon-Woods, M., Angell, E., Ashcroft, R. and Bryman, A. (2009a) 'Doing accountability: a discourse analysis of Research Ethics Committee letters', *Sociology of Health and Illness*, 31 (2): 246–291.

4

Children's Capacity to Make Decisions

Chapter outline

- Introduction
- Children's development
- The basic principles of consent
  - Autonomy
  - Children's capacity to make decisions
  - Factors that affect children's capacity to make decisions
  - The concept of capacity from different points of view
- Informed consent
- Understanding informed consent
- The legal framework of consent
  - Assent
  - Refusal
  - The process of obtaining consent
- Summary
- Further reading

Learning outcomes

By the end of this chapter you should be able to:

- Describe the skills needed to assess capacity in children
- Identify the implications of Gillick competence on the ability to consent
- Differentiate between consent and assent
- Outline or describe the legal framework underpinning informed consent and confidentiality
- Design a consent form appropriate for a specific age group

Key words: autonomy, capacity, competence, Gillick, informed consent

Introduction

This chapter explores the issues and debates that deal with the child's capacity for providing informed consent to participate in decisions that affect them. This refers to the child's mental, cognitive, emotional and physical ability to provide informed consent. In the previous chapter we introduced you to the ethics of informed consent for research, but as this is such an important issue in research with children we consider it in more depth here. We explore the issues related to children with and without capacity and the issues that arise for researchers when taking consent from members of vulnerable groups, and we give additional attention to particularly sensitive forms of research such as medical. The chapter will cover Gillick competence, child development and capacity and provide some practical tips for taking consent.

Children's development

National and local governments, agencies and children's services invest significant amounts of resources in consulting children and inviting them to participate in services planning, evaluation and delivery (Alderson and Morrow, 2011), as children are granted rights for their views to be taken into account, respected and included. In that way, children's rights to be properly researched means that they should be encouraged to participate by the use of scientific, systematic and appropriate methods ensuring that researchers behave ethically (Ennew, 2009).

As stated earlier in the book, children are not just miniature adults, so research needs to take into account their differences. Involving children raises ethical questions as you will need to think about their developmental ability, and therefore the research question and framework need to consider the child's stage of development and the relative contributions that they can make. A significant contributor to our understanding of children's cognitive development was Jean Piaget ([1936] 1963). As you read this section, therefore, please refer to Box 4.1 that shows Piaget's stages of cognitive development. In addition to universality, stages are characterised by qualitatively different cognitive structures (and modes of reasoning). Each stage has specific sub-stages and is not only derived from the previous stage (incorporating and transforming it) but also follows an invariant sequence. That is, stage 1 always comes before stage 2 and so on; regression is not possible. Children's thinking differs from stage to stage in a steady progression towards logical reasoning (Harris and Butterworth, 2002).

While there are many critiques of Piaget's work, in general it remains a helpful way of understanding how children think and their ability to understand. The importance of this as a researcher is evident when it comes to deciding relevant research questions and in considering how children might think about such issues as consent and also how they understand information presented to them about any particular study.

Box 4.1 **Piaget's stages of development**

Sensory motor

At 0–2 years, the child gains motor mastery, understanding the world through perception and action. Thought is not only independent of language, it is a sensory motor activity that occurs before language, leading to representations of experience which children then label using words.

Concrete pre-operational

At 2–6 years, the child is now able to make mental representations of objects, and imagine actions related to them. They are, however, still very egocentric and see the world as relating to themselves with an inability to distinguish other people's viewpoints from their own. Egocentrism may lead young children to attribute their own thoughts and feelings to other people, and even to inanimate objects. Piaget called this tendency *animism*.

Concrete operational

At 7–11 years, the child is able to think logically, but only in concrete terms, and should be less egocentric at this stage. During this stage thought is logical, flexible and organised, but still tied to concrete information. Children are no longer

(Continued)

(Continued)

egocentric. Nevertheless, according to Piaget, the capacity for *abstract* reasoning is still lacking.

Formal operational

From 12 years onwards, the child moves beyond their concrete experiences and begins to think in abstract and logical ways. During this stage adolescents are able to represent and manipulate thought processes in three ways. They become:

- able to combine ideas logically and use deductive reasoning to find explanations for problems
- systematic problem solvers through using scientific reasoning
- able to think about possibilities rather than just reality, to think abstractly, and to consider the consequences of their actions, making long-term planning possible.

The basic principles of consent

Autonomy

We first introduced you to the concept of autonomy in Chapter 3. The concept of autonomy underlies the principle that all have a right to self-determination and a choice in relation to our personal and physical integrity. One of the most important elements of autonomy is the respect for individual liberty and this underpins the reason why asking children for their consent to participate in research projects is important. Autonomy is an essential concept guiding research ethics. It has long been recognised in medical law, and in fact is a basic principle of common law, as a way for an individual to have the freedom to 'deal with his body as he [sic] sees free' (Kennedy, 1991: 320).

Autonomy extends beyond the research context and is used in order to allow people to make free, informed choices about their lives and it is not, therefore, sufficient to ask whether or not someone is willing to receive medical treatment, or take part in a research project. Rather more importantly, the key is whether they have agreed to it after having received sufficient and accurate information that makes the risks and advantages clear and is delivered in a way that participants are able to understand, thereby making such consent legally valid. In simple terms, asking for informed consent means that someone authorises another person to have physical contact or access to private information in a way that protects the participant, allowing them to retain control and exercise their own autonomy.

From the above, there are two aspects when working lawfully with children that you will need to consider. First, the concept of autonomy for children is dependent on the cultural perspective about children's place in society as discussed in earlier chapters. In most Western contexts, respect for children's autonomy is paramount, stemming from the idea that children have rights. This means you need to ensure that the children you are intending to do research with receive sufficient information about your research project and what you expect of them, to be able to make an informed decision about what is going to happen to them. However, before you can do that, it needs to be determined whether they are legally competent to provide you with that consent: that is, the child has the 'capacity' to consent. From this, it becomes clear that the concept of capacity is central to the law's approach to consent.

Activity 4.1

Before reading any further, based on your professional or personal experience, reflect on and write down those elements that you consider important to determine whether children are able to make decisions about themselves.

You might find some of the following questions helpful to start your list:

Is age important? If so, why?
Is there anything other than age that needs to be taken into account? If so, what?
Do parents have a role to play? If so, why?
Do cultural factors play a role in children's ability to make decisions? If so, what factors and why?

We provide some suggestions at the back of the book. You might find it useful to refer to these when you have had an opportunity to answer each of the questions posed.

Children's capacity to make decisions

As children are developing, their capacity to make decisions is constantly changing. A typical measure of children's capacity relates to Gillick competence, which was developed in relation to children consenting to medical treatments, and has been used as a measure for medical research and other types of research, such as social science and educational research, since.

A child who is 'Gillick competent' has the ability to understand information about the proposed treatment, including the nature and objective of the treatment (refer to Box 4.2), likely beneficial and adverse effects and risks, available alternatives and so forth. This measure of competence is based on age, maturity, understanding and intelligence (Cocks, 2006). In research terms therefore, the child must be able to understand the nature of the research project, the commitments they need to make if choosing to participate and the ethical protection they are afforded. It is therefore necessary that you perform an assessment of the child's intelligence and understanding prior to engaging them in research and seeking their consent (Balen et al., 2006).

Box 4.2 Gillick competence

The term 'Gillick competence' refers to a legal case which looked specifically at whether doctors should be able to give contraceptive advice or treatment to under 16-year-olds without parental consent (Taylor, 2007). In 1982, Victoria Gillick took her local health authority and the Department of Health and Social Services to court in an attempt to stop doctors from giving contraceptive advice or treatment to under 16-year-olds without parental consent.

The above judicial process, which included the High Court, the Court of Appeal and the House of Lords, determined that a child's capacity for giving the necessary consent will depend on their maturity and understanding and the nature of the consent needed. It required that the child be capable of making reasonable assessments of the advantages and disadvantages of the treatment proposed so the consent, if given, could be described as true consent.

Since the ruling, the notion of Gillick competence has been more widely used to help assess whether a child has the maturity to make their own decisions and to understand the implications of those decisions. In research terms therefore, you need to determine whether the child has the maturity to make their own decision to agree to participate.

The ruling, which was delivered by Lord Fraser (so is also known as 'Fraser competence'), is particularly significant for the legal rights of minors in England, although this has been taken up by other countries such as Scotland, Canada, Australia and New Zealand. As we will discuss below, the scope of Gillick competence extends beyond that of prescribing contraception and applies to all cases where consent from a child is required, including research. The underlying principle is that the authority of parents to make decisions for their children is not absolute; rather, it diminishes with the child's evolving maturity.

In the same way that applies to adults, the legal test for competence is set out to ensure that individuals, first, comprehend and retain the information given, second, are able to weigh up the information to arrive at a choice and, third, communicate their wishes. This is especially important for research and thus one can learn from the medical world about children's capacity to make decisions (see Box 4.3).

Box 4.3   Recommendations for assessing competence to participate in research

The assessment of competence with respect to research should consider a young person's:

1 Ability to understand that there is a choice to participate and that each choice has consequences
2 Willingness and ability to make a choice (including the option of choosing that someone else makes the decision about participation)
3 Understanding of the nature and purpose of the research
4 Understanding of the risks and side-effects of the research
5 Understanding of the alternatives to the procedure and the risks attached to them, and the consequences of no treatment
6 Freedom from pressure or coercion

Adapted from British Medical Association and the Law Society (1995)

Factors that affect children's capacity to make decisions

There are several factors, in addition to the above recommendations, that need to be taken into account when assessing children's competence for providing informed consent to participate in your research project.

Being competent to make decisions is not a permanent state. In other words, being incompetent today does not mean that a person will remain that way, as this can also change over time, and in fact does so as children mature. For instance, if you consider what we have previously discussed about Piaget's theory of cognitive development and the changes that occur as children develop, to expect young school children to be competent to decide whether or not to participate in a research project may be unfair. On the one hand, their capacity to memorise, retain and balance all the information may be limited, but on the other, they would struggle to foresee alternative options to their participation due to their unidirectional way of thinking (concrete operational stage). However, as children mature and achieve the ability to think more logically in terms of cause and effect relationships, they are better suited to understand what the project is about, the benefits of participating based on a balance of risk and possible alternatives.

In a similar way, being competent does not apply to all domains of life simultaneously. For example, one can be competent to make decisions about one thing, such as how to keep safe, while being incompetent regarding others, like refusing a specific medical treatment. The latter requires different and perhaps more complex knowledge and hence the criteria for being competent may not be met.

Competence also varies in the presence of temporary factors that may erode our mental capacity. Examples of these may include considering how tired, agitated or excited (i.e. fight or flight response) a child is when assessing their competence, which may affect their ability to concentrate or level of understanding. For example, imagine that you want to recruit children with untreated Attention Deficit Hyperactivity Disorder (ADHD). Some of the main features of this condition are forgetfulness and short attention span. Therefore, it would be logical to question whether these children are competent to consent to their participation, as they might not be able to retain the information you provide. On the other hand, this scenario can significantly change if, for instance, you decided to recruit children undergoing treatment for ADHD, because as their ability to concentrate and retain information improves with treatment, so does the likelihood that they will be able to meet the competence criteria we discussed above. However, we cannot emphasise enough the importance of considering children's capacity on an individual basis rather than based on generalisations, for example, not all children with untreated ADHD will present with forgetfulness!

Other factors to consider when assessing capacity are the possible side-effects of medication for an underlying medical condition, that may not be related to your research project, but that may affect their cognitive abilities. The following example may sound obvious, but think about a social research project in which a large number of children need to be recruited to explore the impact of poverty on social development. It is likely that some of them will suffer from non-serious, common medical conditions, for example, hay fever. Some medications used to treat hay fever commonly also cause drowsiness. In this case, it is easy to see how your assessment of capacity may be affected by the side-effects of medication. Hence, you may need to arrange to see the child when they are free of hay fever medication.

The concept of capacity from different points of view

It may be tempting to assume that older children are more likely to be Gillick competent and therefore researching older children will be simpler from a legal and ethical perspective. However, making such assumptions could mean that you are not allowing younger children to participate, thereby potentially discriminating against them by underestimating their abilities. For example, Weithorn and Campbell (1982) compared decision-making in four groups of healthy individuals aged 9, 14, 18 and 21 years old. They concluded that the 14-year-olds showed a level of competence that was similar to that of the adult groups. It is important therefore that young children are included in research if researchers are to understand their worlds better, inform their treatments, improve their school lives and so forth. Excluding young children on the basis of capacity would limit the evidence base and thus reduce our knowledge about this important group.

Gender and children's life experiences may also influence the ability to make decisions. Assumptions may lead to over-estimating the ability of some and under-estimating the ability of others. For instance, Alderson (1993), in a study of children aged 8 to 15 years old undergoing orthopaedic surgery, reported that children and their parents agreed that the mean age at which children could decide about their treatment was 14 years old, concurring with Weithorn and Campbell's findings. However, there were differences based on sex, as girls and their parents reported a younger age of about 12, whereas boys and their parents said that they expected to be competent at the age of 15. This was slightly lower than the age given by ordinary school pupils (a mean of 15 for girls and 17 for boys). Interestingly, when Alderson asked health professionals, they recommended a mean age of 10.3 years, much younger than their patients or the parents.

Decision-making processes can vary in different cultures, and it is worth keeping in mind that the concept of capacity to make decisions finds its roots within Western societies and tensions within multicultural societies are unavoidable. For example, while an essential element of consent is to be free from coercion, in other societies, such as the Arab, Hispanic or traditional African communities, decisions are taken collectively or even led by older members, where community norms may take precedence over individual autonomy (Del Carmen and Joffe, 2005).

Moreover, in some cultural settings, homosexuality is still considered a deviant and illegal behaviour, which is punishable by prison or even death (Crompton, 2003). It would therefore be reasonable to assume that sexual preferences in these settings could be perceived as affecting people's capacity, in a similar way as disabilities (both mental and physical) used to be perceived as sufficient reasons for the lack of capacity to make autonomous decisions (Braddock and Parish, 2003).

Informed consent

Again we introduced you to the notion of informed consent in Chapter 3. Consent involves the voluntary agreement of an adult or competent child to participate in an intervention, based on adequate knowledge and understanding of relevant information (Shaw, 2001). The issue of informed consent has gained importance in recent years following cases in which failing to obtain consent (usually with regard to medical treatment), led to potential criminal and civil liability. An example of this would be touching a patient or administering a treatment without obtaining consent, which theoretically might be seen as battery in terms of criminal charges, or trespass, resulting in punitive charges. However, this is an uncommon situation and more frequently the cases where consent was questionably obtained tend to be brought under negligence (Biggs, 2010). Essentially, negligence means failing to meet professional duties, and even though it may seem more obvious in clinical practice, it also applies to the area of research.

For example, a breach of duty in the research context might be a failure to protect potential participants from the reasonable foreseeable harms that may result from it. Someone participating in the research can only make an informed decision if they are made aware of the potential risks. Remember that the risks in social science research may not be physical as in health research, but do not forget the importance of psychological risks such as distress and anxiety. This demonstrates why so much emphasis is given to ensuring that consent is made on the basis of being appropriately informed.

Activity 4.2

Do you think that parents have the right to consent on behalf of their children? Justify your perspective but also try to think of reasons against it as exceptions to your views. We provide some additional information at the back of the book. You might want to formulate your own answer before referring to this.

Understanding informed consent

Much of our understanding of informed consent for research purposes stems from the discipline of medicine and there are three leading international codes of ethics for biomedical research involving human subjects: the Nuremberg Code, the Declaration of Helsinki, and the International Ethical Guidelines for Biomedical Research Involving Human Subjects.

The Nuremberg Code of 1947 represented the first code of conduct governing the ethical aspects of human research. Among other important contributions, it placed special emphasis on individuals consenting to their participation. For instance, the Code established the voluntary consent of all human subjects as an essential aspect of research. In practice, this means that participants are able to exercise free power of choice without any form of constraint or coercion and that they have sufficient knowledge and comprehension to make an informed decision. Some interpreted the voluntary consent as an 'absolute', and forbade research with children and the mentally ill as they were assumed to be incapable of consent. Consequently, research with children was felt to be unethical or even illegal (Brierley and Larcher, 2010) because of this uncertainty regarding their capacity to consent (Annas and Grodin, 1995).

Attempts to address the need for children to give consent first appeared in the Declaration of Helsinki of 1964. This was an important document as it was the first significant effort of the medical community to self-regulate research. It developed from the Nuremberg Code's principles and tied them to the Declaration of Geneva of 1948, a statement of doctors' ethical duties. It also specifically addressed clinical research, and in particular it provides a relaxation of the conditions of consent. These were modified from 'absolutely essential' (Nuremberg Code) to obtaining consent 'if at all possible', for example by allowing proxy consent from a responsible relative. However, during the second revision of the Declaration in 1983, it was recommended to seek **assent** from children 'where possible' (discussed later in the chapter) (Article 25). In that respect, the Declaration recognised the increased vulnerability of some individuals and special groups (Article 8), stating that surrogate consent from someone acting in the subject's best interest should be obtained when dealing with research participants who are minor or incompetent (physically or mentally incapable of giving consent) (Articles 23, 24).

Finally, the International Ethical Guidelines were created by the Council for International Organizations of Medical Sciences (1982) to ensure effective implementation of the Helsinki Declaration, particularly when research is carried out in technologically developing countries by sponsors and investigators from developed countries. Therefore while Nuremberg and Helsinki strive for ethical universality, the International Ethical Guidelines implicitly acknowledge the legitimacy of some degree of cultural pluralism.

Despite such resistance to the universalisation of research guidelines, they have provided a framework for individual countries to develop their own regulations, which were thought to better fit particular circumstances. In the UK, the National Health Service Research Ethics Committee (NHS REC) emerged in 1974 following the National Research Act. It established that researchers were obliged to apply for initial and subsequent amendments to gain ethical approval of their proposals and protocol. Other pieces of legislation have followed to regulate different types of research, such as the Clinical Trials Regulation (HM Government, 2004c) or the Human Tissue Act (HM Government, 2004d). However, a common denominator of these is that consent needs to be obtained as the norm, unless there are transparent and vital reasons that it cannot be obtained.

The legal framework of consent

So far, we have established that although the law in different parts of the UK developed differently, and across countries may vary, generally, when minors have sufficient understanding, intelligence and maturity to understand what the project proposes and involves, their consent as well as parental consent should be obtained. It is generally agreed that for research in any discipline, parental consent for those under the age of 18 is required in addition to the young person's own consent.

The legal aspects for children's consent are mainly covered by the common law. This states that children between the ages of 16 and 18 are competent to give consent. Until the Gillick case discussed earlier, there was no statute to govern the rights of those under 16 years old to give consent. In Gillick competent children, although involvement from parents is encouraged, this is not legally necessary. This means that children under 16 years old who are deemed competent are able to consent, but parental consent, or consent of those with parental responsibility, should also be sought; if incompetent then parental consent is sought instead (Shaw, 2001). Shaw notes that in older children, those aged 17 to 18 years old and competent are able to consent for themselves without the need for parental consent, but if incompetent then parental consent should be sought.

The law also differentiates between therapeutic research (treatment research) and non-therapeutic research (non-treatment research). In the former, a competent child or a person with parental responsibility can give consent. For the latter, the procedure cannot go ahead if the child withholds consent, irrespective of their age and parental consent. This predominantly relates to research in health.

More recently, the Convention on the Rights of the Child (1989) added an essential element to consent, which stated that a child not only has to be competent to understand what is proposed, but also the intervention needs to be in his or her best interest (the best interests principle). The term 'best interest' implies ensuring the well-being of children, which is determined by several individual circumstances, such as age, level of maturity, presence or absence of parents, the child's environment and their experiences. In other words, acting in children's best interests should ensure that child protection practices are in place, preventing child abuse, neglect, exploitation and violence, avoiding discrimination and assuring that children are free to express their views in matters affecting them (United Nations High Commissioner for Human Rights, 2002).

Box 4.4   Exceptions to traditional consent

It is worth noticing that there are some exceptions to the above. For example, for clinical trials, the Clinical Trial Regulation and the Medicines for Human Use Regulations, rather than the Gillick case law, apply. As opposed to the common law, where legal adulthood is not reached until the age of 18 years old, the Clinical Trial Regulation considers as minors those under the age of 16. Under these legal principles, minors (under 16 years old) can consent to participate should they have the capacity; however, parents or legal guardians must also give informed consent and may withdraw the young person from the trial at any time. This is especially relevant when the potential stakes are high.

Other exceptions apply, for example in the case of non-therapeutic procedures, such as organ donation. Here, the assumption of automatic competence of 16- and 17-year-old young people does not apply, and competency tests should be carried out in all children irrespective of their age.

Assent

So far, we have discussed cases of children that are considered competent to consent to participate in research. If the child does not have capacity, then a person with parental responsibility could legally consent on an incompetent child's behalf. This does not mean that the child should not be consulted. It is expected that when the parent provides consent for their child to participate in a research project of any nature the child should assent to participate. This may not be fully informed but does mean that the child agrees to take part when asked. If the child actively dissents (that is, shows signs of distress or clearly does not want to participate) then the child should not be included as a participant in your research.

Although legally the researcher only needs consent from one person with parental responsibility, it is recommended that consent from a second parent is obtained and hence the child can be included in the project should agreement between both parties be reached (Medical Research Council, 2004). Again, although not legally required, it is considered good practice to exclude from the project those children for whom both parents have not agreed to their participation.

In some research contexts, for example studies in which very young children are the ideal subjects, the parents themselves may be under the age of 16. It is agreed that in these cases, parents can only consent to their children's participation if they are competent themselves to take that decision (Medical Research Council, 2004). This is because, as we previously discussed, the law (in the UK) presumes that only those young people aged over 16 years old are competent, regardless of whether they are parents or not. Therefore, when children or under 16s are to be recruited, an assessment of their capacity to allow their children's participation in the study needs to be undertaken.

Generally, consent by proxy needs to be avoided and you will find it very difficult, though not impossible, to get your project successfully passed through a research ethics committee. The key aspect of this type of research is to be able to demonstrate that there is no alternative to your project and that, given the child's condition, the intervention will be of direct benefit. However, if the research does not offer potential benefit to the child, the parents can still consent provided the risks are small enough not to go against the child's best interests. In fact, a study in the USA showed that most parents were willing to let their children participate, even without the prospect of direct benefit, providing the children were at no risk (Wendler and Jenkins, 2008). Some argue that the justification for this type of research is that children may have benefitted from previous research in which other children may not have obtained a direct benefit and that if their participation is analysed in detail, perhaps the development of altruism may represent an important gain (Lo, 2010).

In any case, what is important here is that the project ensures that risks are minimal, such as in observation studies, questionnaires on non-sensitive topics or interviews. Here, you will be required to obtain assent from the child in addition to the consent of the legally authorised representative, which should be respected. That is, if the child does not assent, it would not be ethical to proceed with their participation.

Refusal

Refusing to participate in research is clearly different from children's rights to refuse medical treatment. For instance, regarding treatment, based on The Children Act 1989 (HM Government, 1989), competent children cannot refuse an intervention that is thought to be in their best interest and may therefore have their views overruled by those with parental responsibility, or even the courts in the case where their parents also refuse such intervention. A good example of this is the case of Jehovah's Witness children in need of a blood transfusion. As opposed to adults, where the law supports respecting the wishes of those who have made their treatment choices clear, for children the situation is very different, as a doctor can administer a necessary blood transfusion against parental wishes with a specific order from the High Court under the Children Act 1989 (HM Government, 1989) (Cretney et al., 2003). Even Gillick competent young people will find the courts still instructing the administration of a transfusion, as being Gillick competent only allows the child to opt in to treatment, and not to opt out of it.

On the other hand, when considering research, children's wishes to decline participation must be respected, regardless of their parents' or legal guardians' views.

Box 4.5 **Legal advice**

The issues surrounding consent and competence are controversial, advice can vary and the legal aspects are complex. As a researcher, you will be expected to consult your organisation's legal team to seek clarification in difficult cases.

The process of obtaining consent

The process of obtaining informed consent consists of two elements. First there are the information sheets given to parents and children, which should be presented in different ways. Second, is the informed consent form, sometimes also called the consent certificate (we introduced you to this in the previous chapter). Examples of information sheets to parents and children are presented below, and they are followed by a typical consent form.

Box 4.6 **Example of an information leaflet for parents/carers about a research project**

Dear Parent/Carer,

You are being invited to take part in a research project. It is aimed at finding out how children generally feel about themselves. This research is needed because we lack this information, which prevents us from developing the right kinds of services. These will help develop children's sense of well-being and help them to achieve their full academic and personal potential. This project is being carried out by the [*insert name*] and has received ethical approval from the University of [*insert name*].

You were previously asked about your child taking part in this research and you chose not to opt out. Now we ask for your participation in the same study.

What do I have to do?

You are being asked to fill out a questionnaire. For the most part you will be asked to answer a number of questions by ticking an appropriate box. Questions should not be too difficult and we do not expect that they will upset you.

Do I have to take part?

No, you do not have to take part. You are free to decide on your own whether or not you would like to take part. Not taking part does not affect the current or future care of you or your child.

(Continued)

(Continued)

What about confidentiality?

Whatever answers you provide in the questionnaire will be kept anonymous. This means we will not be able to link what you say to your name. Your child or teachers at the school will not see your answers. We do hope that if you agree to participate, you will give full and honest answers.

What are the benefits of taking part?

There may be no immediate or direct benefit to you personally. However, you will be helping us assess the needs of children and their parents as well as telling us how best we can help children achieve their full potential in school and in life.

I would like to help and to take part. What do I have to do now?

If you would like to participate, please sign the Consent Form that follows and fill out the questionnaire to the best of your knowledge.

After you complete the questionnaire, put it in the provided envelope and seal it. Then either give it to your child to return to the teacher or put it in the post. It will go straight to us at [insert name] (the envelope is addressed and no additional postage needs to be added).

If in a few days or weeks after the study is finished you have any questions, please contact Dr [insert name] on [insert telephone number] or [insert email address].

Please feel free to keep this information sheet.

Box 4.7   Example of an information letter to children about a research project

This survey will ask you how you and your classmates have been feeling and behaving lately and if you have been experiencing any difficulties. We would also like to find out whom it is that you go to for help or advice when you are feeling down or upset. This information will help us develop programmes and services that will help you or other young people deal with upsetting emotions, should they occur. Having as many young people as possible fill out this survey will help us do a better job of getting a more accurate picture.

For the most part you will be asked to answer a number of questions by ticking an appropriate response box. However, sometimes you will be asked to give brief answers to questions in your own words.

In either case, the questions should not be too difficult and we do not expect that they will upset you. However, if you find that you are struggling with the questions for any reason you can ask for our help.

Whatever answers you provide in the questionnaire will be kept anonymous. This means we will not be able to link what you say to your name. Your parents and teachers know that you are being asked to take part in the survey, but they will not see your answers. We do hope that if you agree to participate, you will give full and honest answers. However, if you decide on your own to give us information other than what we have asked for in the questionnaire, and we are worried that you or someone else may not be safe, we might not be able to guarantee complete anonymity in those particular instances.

You do not have to take part in this survey. You can also stop your participation at any time or not answer some questions without being penalised. If you would like to participate, please sign the Consent Form that follows.

If in a few days or weeks after the survey is finished you have a question about the study, please contact Dr [*insert name*] on [*insert telephone number*] or [*insert email address*] for answers.

Please feel free to keep this information sheet.

Box 4.8   Example of a consent form for parents/carers

Please complete this form after you have been read the Information Sheet explaining the research.

By signing below you are agreeing that you have been read the Information Sheet and that you fully understand the information it contains: (i) that any questions you may have in the course of the survey or afterwards will be answered by the researcher Dr [*insert name*] and (ii) that you don't have to take part in the study and are free to discontinue your participation at any point without penalty.

_____   _____
Participant's signature   Date

_____
Participant's name

_____
School

_____

                                                                  (Continued)

(Continued)

Printed name of person obtaining consent

[*University logo here*]

[*Names and contact details of research team here*]

Child (or if unable, parent on their behalf)/young person to circle all they agree with:

Has somebody else explained this project to you?	Yes / No
Do you understand what this project is about?	Yes / No
Have you asked all the questions you want to ask?	Yes / No
Have you had your questions answered in a way you understand?	Yes / No
Do you understand it's OK to stop taking part at any time?	Yes / No
Are you happy to take part?	Yes / No

If any answers are 'no' or you **do not** want to take part, **do not** sign your name!

If you **do** want to take part, you can **write your name** below:

Your name   _____

Date   _____

The doctor who explained this project to you needs to sign too:

Print name   _____

Sign   _____

Date   _____

Thank you

You might want to compare these to the ones presented in Chapter 3 and think about how differently they are laid out. There is no prototype for developing a consent form for children but they should be accessible, child friendly and clear.

Summary

Decision-making about enrolling children in research needs to be based on: (a) an informed consent process that involves giving children and their parents enough opportunity to ask the researchers questions and to communicate with one another; and (b) giving children the opportunity to exercise their right to refuse participation without parental influence. This process should be tailored to the child's maturity level and style of communication in the family.

Further reading

Alderson, P. and Morrow, V. (2011) *The Ethics of Research with Children and Young People: A Practical Handbook*. London: Sage.

Biggs, H. (2010) *Healthcare Research Ethics and Law: Regulation, Review and Responsibility*. London: Routledge-Cavendish.

Braddock, D.L. and Parish, S.L. (2003) 'An institutional history of disability', in G.L. Albrecht, K.D. Seelman and M. Bury (eds), *Handbook of Disability Studies*. London: Sage.

Cretney, S.M., Maisson, J. and Bailey-Harris, R. (2003) *Principles of Family Law*. London: Sweet and Maxwell.

Crompton, L. (2003) *Homosexuality and Civilization*. Cambridge, M: Harvard University Press.

Del Carmen, M.G. and Joffe, A. (2005) 'Informed consent for medical treatment and research: a review', *The Oncologist*, 10 (8): 636–641.

Ennew, J. (2009) *The Right to Be Properly Researched: How to Do Rights-based, Scientific Research with Children. A Set of 10 Manuals for Field Researchers*. Oslo: Black on White Publications.

Homan, R. (2002) 'The principle of assumed consent: the ethics of gatekeeping', in M. McNamee and D. Bridges (eds), *The Ethics of Educational Research*. Oxford: Blackwell Publishing, pp. 23–40.

Lo, B. (2010) *Ethical Issues in Clinical Research: A Practical Guide*. Philadelphia: Wolter Kluwer.

Shaw, M. (2001) 'Competence and consent to treatment in children and adolescents', *Advances in Psychiatric Treatment*, 7: 150–159.

Tinson, J. (2009) *Conducting Research with Children and Adolescents: Design, Methods and Empirical Cases*. Oxford: Goodfellow Publishers.

Wendler, D. and Jenkins T. (2008) 'Children's and the parents views on facing research risks for the benefit of others', *Archives of Psychiatry and Adolescent Medicine*, 162: 9–14.

PART 2

STARTING A RESEARCH PROJECT WITH CHILDREN

5

Planning to Do Research with Children

> **Learning outcomes**
>
> By the end of the chapter you should be able to:
>
> - Evaluate the rationale for undertaking research with children and families
> - Differentiate between research and audit
> - Describe the reasons children and families cooperate with research
> - Identify factors that facilitate and inhibit effective supervision and research in teams
> - Identify your research skills, limitations and training requirements
> - Highlight the steps you need to take to ensure your own safety in the research process
> - Reflect on personal barriers to starting research, especially addressing your own anxieties about the research process
>
> **Key words:** anxiety, audit, motivation, research researcher safety, supervisor, training, training skills

Introduction

In this chapter we begin by thinking about why there is a need to undertake research with children and/or families and clarify what research actually is. We take a practical and reflective look at the factors you need to consider in deciding whether you are ready to undertake research and the preparation you might need to ensure you are. By the end of the chapter you should be able to identify if there are specific skills that you need to acquire or some particular processes you need to complete before progressing with your plans. We begin the chapter with Activity 5.1.

> **Activity 5.1**
>
> We begin this chapter by asking you to identify three reasons why it might be useful to undertake research with children. Write these down and then compare them with our reasons below. We also provide a summary at the end of the book to help you compare your answers. Did you manage to identify anything not on our list?

Why do research with children?

Chapter 1 highlighted that there has been more recognition of the importance of children and their perspectives. In line with changing views of children, it has become much more common for children and young people to participate in policy decision-making and be more generally consulted on issues that are relevant to them (Tisdall and Davis, 2004). It is also being increasingly recognised that children are active participants in their lives and in some situations children are better placed than adults to produce knowledge about themselves (Balen et al., 2006).

Tisdall and Davis (2004) suggest that research with children requires celebration as it enables them to have a voice. They do caution, however, that children and young people can become professionalised 'experts' and then are no longer able to fulfil the role they were initially recruited to do, which is to provide an independent perspective. It is important that if one does research with children, all children have the opportunity to participate and not only those from specific groups. Sharing and acknowledging children's part in the research process can encourage others to want to contribute to the research process.

No one can tell us better than children themselves about what childhood at any given point feels like. Asking them directly about the issues that are important to them helps us understand their lives and also determine whether any interventions are required. Children can also provide solutions or ideas about interventions that are acceptable to them. These interventions can be in any arena of the child's life such as social, educational, health or environmental settings.

Why do research with families?

In some areas of research with children it is more appropriate to research the child and their family, to better understand processes within the family as they may relate to the child or wider issues. Families are not simple straightforward institutions (Hutchby and O'Reilly, 2010) and there is limited agreement on what the family is (Greenstein, 2006).

If you want to do research with families it is essential that you are clear about how you define the family and how your definition relates to your research question. Remember that in family research the focus is not on particular individuals, rather a group of people functioning as a unit. Family members occupy multiple roles and statuses simultaneously (Greenstein, 2006). Parental perspectives may be given more weight than the child or young person's perspective, however, and this should be guided by the research question and the child's developmental stage. The area of study may be the relationships between different members of the family unit and the research may warrant seeing them together and separately to effectively answer the research question. Consider the following two examples related to the usefulness of giving children curfews.

Example one

If you were interested in families' views and feelings about giving children curfews you might want to interview the family together as a group to ascertain a better idea about the process and how that particular family arrives at their decision. Seeing them together enables you to get a family view and understand differences of opinions between members, contradictions in views and the hierarchical structure of the family.

Example two

If you were interested in individuals' opinions of curfews and you wanted to do a later comparison of views then you might want to interview each family member separately. This would reveal different responses as the views of the children, particularly, would be less inhibited.

Sometimes the context or setting of your research may dictate whether you research families or individuals. For example, O'Reilly (see 2006, 2007, 2008) studied family therapy and thus the inclusion of the whole family was dictated by the context of the research. On the other hand, Dogra (in a new project) explored the prevalence rate of child mental health problems in the Gujarati population and therefore questionnaires for individuals were sent out to ascertain the numbers needed.

Why do health and/or medical research with children?

Health research explores children's physical and mental health. Not all health research is medical research; indeed much of our understanding of children's health relates to non-medical interventions, their experiences of health and illness, their potential marginalised status in a medical encounter, communication between child patients and their physicians, counselling conversations and so forth.

Children are faced with many health-related encounters during their childhood: visiting doctors for minor ailments, visiting hospitals for more serious illnesses, and visiting mental health professionals if they encounter a mental health problem. Research in this area has the potential to illuminate their experiences, measure the effectiveness of different interventions and explore their role and status in the encounter.

Medical research deserves some particular attention as it is perceived to have greater risks, and therefore there is increased justification for seeking the child's perspective. Medical research with children can help us understand more about disease and illness from a child's perspective. It can also help us find out more about some of the adult diseases that begin in childhood. Research is also required because diseases and potential treatments in children often differ from those in adults. Additionally, many childhood problems can only be understood when growth and development are also taken into consideration.

Currently, many of the medicines given to children are only tested on adults, despite us knowing that children's bodies react differently to some medicine compared with adults. This means that considerably less is known about how drugs work on the young and there are fewer medicines that children can take. The ways that medicines are handled in children's bodies also varies with age and different doses are needed to treat children of different ages. All new medicines used in children must be properly tested through research to find out:

- Whether the medicine works better than the best current treatment.
- Whether the medicine is safe and what side-effects may be expected.
- What dose works best.
- The best way of administering the medicine for children.

Testing is carried out through clinical trials which usually involve testing a new treatment against the best currently available treatment to see which is better and safer. For the reasons highlighted above, it is important that clinical trials are carried out with children as well as adults. An example is the use of antidepressants. Trials were undertaken with adults and some antidepressants called the Selective Serotonin Reuptake Inhibitor (SSRIs). These were considered effective to treat depression in adults. When trials were actually undertaken with a younger age group only one called Fluoxetine was found to be effective in children. This led to the recommendation that the others should no longer be routinely used for children for depression, although they kept their license for some other conditions (Food and Drug Administration, 2005). The Medical Research Council's (2004) *MRC Ethics Guide: Medical Research Involving Children* offers some useful advice relating to clinical trials with children.

Why do social sciences research with children?

The social sciences include a range of different disciplines including (but not limited to) psychology, sociology, anthropology, law, political science, linguistics, criminology, economics and human geography. Although each of these disciplines has different purposes and fields of study, they are interested in the study of social groups, and children are a large part of this. The social and societal, as well as the psychological and legal aspects of children's lives are especially important. If children are to be understood then there is a need for an understanding of their psychological functioning, their social relations, their positions within a wider society and the ideological, economic and political issues that are embedded in their lives.

Social science research has a lot to offer the study of children and will be guided by the aims of the particular discipline that the researcher is operating under. By undertaking research in the social sciences, researchers are able to mobilise knowledge about important issues that affect children in today's society. To be able to develop, evaluate and implement policies, legislation and interventions which help children psychologically, socially, legally and economically an evidence base is needed to rationalise those developments and decisions.

Social science research with children has explored issues such as juvenile delinquency, the social welfare of children and families, the effect of poverty on children, the value of new technology in helping children learn, the impact of social networking, bullying and conflict and a range of other social issues. Social science research informs us of the effect of gender, age, ethnicity and other demographic factors which influence children's development, social positioning, social relationships and so forth. This information and understanding enables society to make improvements to children's lives and tackle some of the global economic and political issues affecting children and families worldwide.

Why do educational research with children?

Education is an important discipline for children as it involves the teaching and learning of specific skills. Policy-making and funding for education is continually evolving and is driven both politically and by changing ideas in research. The way in which education is delivered and funded varies across countries, but research into learning styles, cognitive developmental stages and the role of children in the classroom has contributed significantly to the types of curriculum that are delivered, teaching strategies and the use of new technologies.

In his presidential address, Mortimore (1999) argued that educational research has four major tasks. First, to conceptualise, observe and systematically record events and processes to do with learning. Second, to analyse those observations to accurately describe their conditions, implications and contexts. Third, to publish research findings drawing on existing theory and evidence to contextualise their importance and value and, fourth, potentially most importantly, to improve education.

Across many countries governments seek means for improving children's academic achievement and these are often measured through a variety of standardised tests. Research has potential not only to evaluate the effectiveness of these measures, but also to address other important questions regarding what constitutes good education and considering other factors such as intelligence and social skills which affect children's ability to learn.

Differentiating audit from research

Before embarking on your project you need to be clear whether you are engaging in an **audit** or undertaking a research project. Audits aim to establish the extent to which actual practice compares to best practice, whereas research tests what best practice should be and addresses questions about how to tackle problems (Closs and Cheater, 1996). Box 5.1 should provide some clarity regarding what research and audit are.

Box 5.1 Differentiating audit from research

	Research	Audit
What is it?	The systematic investigation into and study of materials and sources in order to establish facts and reach new conclusions	An evaluation of a person, organisation, system, process, enterprise, project or product
Aims	To discover new knowledge such as whether an intervention is effective, whether one intervention is better than another or whether an intervention is cost-effective	To ensure research findings are implemented to improve practice by monitoring or assessing practice. For example: assessing whether the right medicine (that has been found through research to be effective) for attention deficit hyperactivity disorder is being used in the right doses or assessing whether the criteria for educational standards are implemented

---

It is evident from this table that there are some similarities between audit and research which may make it difficult for you to differentiate between them. There are, however, some key differences and therefore you do need to be clear whether you are doing research or an audit. For example, in children's services (such as social services child protection) an audit may be carried out to see if child protection standards are being met, whereas research may be done to see which child protection strategies are better for children. It is important that you understand the similarities and differences between audit and research and this is now discussed.

Similarities between audit and research

For students and beginners, the similarities between research and audit can be confusing. For example, both audit and research begin with a question, both expect the answer to have some kind of influence in practice and both use similar methods and collect data from participants. Box 5.2, therefore, summarises the similarities between the two activities.

Box 5.2 Similarities between audit and research

	Research	Audit
Driver	Ultimately the driver may be to improve practice and individual experience, but that is usually through increasing knowledge and understanding. Change does not always come from one project, but potentially from a series of research projects when synthesised	To improve practice and individual experiences through implementation of research findings
Methods	Can use quantitative methods such as questionnaires or qualitative methods such as semi-structured interviews or mixed methods	Can use quantitative methods such as questionnaires or qualitative methods such as semi-structured interviews or mixed methods
Sample	Particular attention may need to be given to vulnerable groups, e.g. children	Particular attention may need to be given to vulnerable groups, e.g. children
Training	Formal training is usually helpful	Formal training is usually helpful

---

You should be able to see from this that the motivations behind conducting an audit and carrying out a research project can be similar. The reasons why these two activities are undertaken are to drive improvements in the real world. Notably, change can be slow and not all research or audit result in observable changes. It is also evident that both activities have a range of methods available to use and that they both may need to pay particular attention to vulnerable groups such as children. Although the similarities between the two may leave you wondering which activity you are doing, understanding the differences between them can help to clarify this (Dogra and Davies, 2010).

Differences between audit and research

Research is designed to build on existing knowledge and to create new knowledge. An example might be finding out what happens to children's attitudes towards learning, depending on whether they are given homework or not. Audit, however, aims to establish if best practice in any given context is being applied so that improvements can be made if this is not the case. For example, research might reveal that children's learning is facilitated if they have homework that takes an hour. An audit might establish if any specific school children were being given such homework. Box 5.3 summarises the differences, a major difference being related to purpose.

Box 5.3 Differences between research and audit

	Research	Audit
Purpose	'Research is concerned with discovering the right thing to do' (Smith, 1992)	'Audit is ensuring that the right thing is done right' (Smith, 1992)
	e.g. the effectiveness of a particular intervention	e.g. to measure the effectiveness of a particular service in delivering an intervention that is known to be effective
Methods	Can be experimental and may test a new practice, therapy or drug	Should not be experimental; that is, unproven treatments should not be tested for effectiveness under the guise of audit
Sample	Sample size and selection criteria are critical	Sample size is often not important
	Can involve anyone	Is likely to involve staff and those that have used services such as youth clubs, hospitals or schools

(Continued)

(Continued)

	Research	Audit
Outcomes	Generally, research aims to ensure that the results are generalisable to other contexts	Generally, findings are unlikely to be generalisable and will apply to a particular context. However, the methods for particular audits may be generalisable to other services, especially if they are looking at the same issue
	Feedback to individual participants is not usually indicated but may be part of good practice	Feedback to staff involved in audit should be integral to the process to improve practice or service delivery (whatever the nature of the service being provided)
Ethical approval	Always need to check if required or not	Usually not needed as data collection is an integral part of the other processes
Consent	Always needed	Broad consent is generally obtained when the person enters the service, and does not usually have identifiable data attached
Confidentiality	Usually required if assured at outset	Data not usually confidential or linked to individuals

Ultimately, therefore, audit is usually a local institutional practice to see if things are being done the way they are supposed to be. It is a way of checking that standards are being met in the way they should. Research, however, explores issues and tests what the best way of doing things should be.

How to decide between audit and research

If you are still unsure whether your work is going to be a piece of research or an audit, then consider these two examples to help you make up your mind.

Box 5.4 **Examples of questions**

Example of an audit question:

Are the children in Primary School X eating three of their five a day fruit and vegetables at school dinner time?

Example of a research question:

What are children's attitudes towards healthy eating?

By now you should have a clear understanding of whether you are going to do audit or research. If you are still unsure then it is useful to talk to your colleagues, or your supervisor. Remember that sometimes the boundaries between audit and research are a little blurred and positioning your idea firmly in one camp may not be straightforward.

Practical considerations

When you are confident that your work constitutes research there are several practical considerations to ponder on before embarking on your project. If you are a student then you will need adequate supervision; if you are a researcher it is likely that you will be working as part of a team. Either way, there are some child-specific issues that you will have to consider.

Identifying a supervisor

For some research projects you may have little or no choice about the supervisor. For example, if working as a research associate the supervision is likely to be undertaken by the lead investigator, and if working as a research student the supervisor is likely to be a course tutor. If you have the opportunity to choose your own supervisor, there are several factors you might want to consider.

An expert in your research topic

There are advantages in having a supervisor who is an expert in your research area as they can easily guide you towards the relevant literature. They will be familiar with what is innovative research. However, you do need to consider whether they will have the time and skills to guide you through the research process as expertise and knowledge alone do not necessarily make a good supervisor.

Local

It is useful to have face-to-face meetings with your supervisor as this gives you an opportunity to discuss the issues that are concerning you, and by having a local supervisor the potential for such face-to-face supervision is increased. There are options, however, for distant supervision, and technological advancements mean that you can do telephone meetings, Skype, MSN or email communication. Making the time to meet with distant supervisors can, however, be time-consuming and it may be difficult to develop an effective working relationship.

Approaching someone you do not personally know

It is perfectly acceptable to approach someone you do not personally know about the possibility of them acting as a supervisor. Remember though that you may need to impress them more as they will not know your strengths or have any knowledge of your working style and abilities. In such cases effective preparation is even more important. Have the courtesy to have found out about their research interests and make the initial contact personalised, rather than sending a round robin letter that has clearly gone out to many other people!

Working with a supervisor

No matter how isolated you may feel at times you should have people who are supporting the project. If you are a student registered on a research course you will have to have a supervisor, and you may also have a co-supervisor and possibly some administrative support that you can access.

The relationship and responsibility between researcher and supervisor is two-way and it is necessary to clarify expectations early on in the relationship. Remember that your supervisor will be a busy person, likely to be supervising more than one student and with other commitments, so use the time you have with them wisely. Have clear questions in mind before you go and do not be afraid to write things down or have a checklist of areas you want to cover. It may be useful to email an agenda to your supervisor in advance, or an outline of the key issues that you want to discuss. If you are handing in some written work and you require feedback then allow enough time for your supervisor to fit this into their working schedule; supervisors will not appreciate you sending something in on Friday evening when your meeting is on Monday morning.

The supervisor and you will need to decide how the meetings are recorded. It can be useful to take minutes and also add some reflective notes and submit these for approval to your supervisor after the meeting. This is very helpful if you have a supervisor who changes their mind from one session to another as it can help keep them on track and remind them of what has already been agreed. Take some responsibility for the process and think about what is helpful to you. Most supervisors want the same outcome as you which is high quality finished research, so do not be afraid to ask for what you need.

Most universities have a code of practice for supervision and it is helpful for you to understand the central features of those documents. Usually these are provided during your induction. If you do not have one then it is up to you to find out where you may get a copy (usually on the university website).

Supervision should be fairly regular and it is up to you and your supervisor to determine the frequency of such meetings. When you do meet with your supervisor remember to make notes of the key things said, decisions made and agreements reached.

Cautions

Although your supervisor is likely to be your first source of support, bear in mind that they are not trained counsellors and neither is it their role to be so. While it is useful to seek their advice and to be reflective with them, if there is something particularly distressing or something personal which impacts upon your research you are better to seek out the university counselling services or other equivalent body.

It is useful at the first supervision meeting to set the boundaries, clarify roles and negotiate responsibilities. At this point you and your supervisor may be able to anticipate potential difficulties which can be dealt with as they arise.

Working in a team

If you are a researcher then you should have a team of people to discuss problems and ideas with. You should have colleagues who are working on the project with you, possibly a line manager and some administrative support.

Different people within the team will have different values, beliefs, practices and attitudes towards children and towards each other. Before the project starts it is important to be clear who is leading the research, how decisions will be made and to agree the status and responsibilities of each team member. Do not leave this until later in the project as conflict is likely to arise and this is harder to manage. Be clear about who is doing what, how much time is needed for each task and what the deadline is for completion.

Have this in writing with all members of the team agreeing the objectives. It is also useful to think about how each team member sees children and about how their attitudes may impact on the way data is collected and interpreted.

If you are working as part of a team then it is important to have regular team meetings to track the progress of the research and agree phased objectives. Make sure that there are written minutes (including key action points and who is to take action and decisions) following meetings. Although you may have good working relationships with other members of the team, having clear, written notes from all meetings will help you track the progress of the project and ensure that all tasks are completed by the relevant team members. Written notes are crucial as they ensure the group and project moves forward and does not waste time constantly covering the same ground. As with any group situation, there is the possibility of conflicting opinions and you need to think about how you deal with conflict and whether this is appropriate.

Criminal Records Bureau (CRB) checks

Internationally the procedures for checking criminal records do differ, but generally it is accepted that your criminal background should be checked if you propose to work with children. Anyone working with children in the UK will need to have completed a CRB check (other countries have their own similar regulations). You will either need a Standard or an Enhanced Disclosure. If you will be working with children or vulnerable adults, in an establishment that is wholly or mainly for children, in healthcare, or if you have applied to be a foster parent, adoptive parent or child minder then an enhanced check is likely to be needed. Research with children requires Disclosure that may also be required for a range of other types of job or licences. You cannot work with children if you refuse to apply for a Disclosure, as this is a legal requirement and the process is in place to safeguard the interests of children. Standard Disclosures show details of any current or spent convictions. These are all held on the Police National Computer and cover all crimes, not just those related to children.

Safeguards and guidelines have been introduced to ensure that conviction information is not misused and that ex-offenders are not treated unfairly. Ex-offenders will retain the protection afforded by the Rehabilitation of Offenders Act (1974). This Act enables some criminal convictions to become 'spent' or ignored, after a certain amount of time. A person convicted of all but the most serious criminal offences, and who receives a sentence of less than 2.5 years in prison, benefits from the Act if they are not convicted again during a specified period. This is called the rehabilitation period. In general terms, the more severe a penalty is, the longer the rehabilitation period. Once a rehabilitation period has expired and no further offending has taken place, a conviction is considered to be 'spent'. Once a conviction has been spent, the convicted person does not have to reveal it or admit its existence in most circumstances, including, for example, when applying for a job. Most serious offences on the other hand, and this generally includes most sexual offences, can never be spent.

Organisations have different rules about whether a CRB check from one area is acceptable or not. As the checking process can take several weeks it is important to determine early on if you require further checks, even if you have already been checked. You will not be able to work with children without the checks having been made, and delays to short projects will make the project unworkable. When deciding whether an employee needs Disclosure even if already in place, the organisation will take into account the length of time that has elapsed since that Disclosure was issued, the level of Disclosure, the nature of the position for which the Disclosure was issued, and the nature of the position for which you are now applying. Ultimately, it will be the organisation's decision whether to accept it or not. The Code of Practice does not encourage the use of Disclosure from one organisation to another as this may potentially miss some individuals who would otherwise be identified.

Payment is required for the checks, but this will usually be covered by the employer. The nature of the role determines the level of disclosure and the process that the organisation has in place to apply for this. Organisations using the Disclosure service must comply with the CRB Code of Practice, which is there to make sure the whole process works fairly and that any information revealed is treated fairly and securely. Also, the CRB is committed to compliance with the Data Protection Act. This means that any personal information submitted for a CRB has to be protected. Under the provisions of the Code, sensitive personal information must be handled and stored appropriately and must be kept for only as long as it is necessary. The Code is published on the CRB website, or you can request a copy from the person who asked you to apply for the Disclosure.

In addition to ensuring that the Rehabilitation of Offenders Act (1974) is not misused, the CRB and the Chartered Institute of Personnel and Development (CIPD) have developed guidance information for employers on this matter. Disclosures are dated but do not have a pre-determined period of **validity** as a conviction or other matter may change the status. There are two specific child-related lists that will be searched as well – these are the Protection of Children Act 1999 (POCA) (HM Government, 1999) list and something called List99. List99 contains information held under section 142 of the Education Act (2002). The Criminal Records Bureau is part of the Civil Service. To complete a CRB check, contact can also be made with the police, the Department of Health and the Department of Education (www. crb.gov.uk).

Developing your skills base

If you plan on working with children, consider acquiring some basic knowledge about children and their development. Knowing the levels that children function at can help in areas such as questionnaire design. It is unwise to take an unplanned, ad hoc approach to your training. It may be useful for you, with your colleagues/supervisor, to perform a systematic Training Needs Analysis during the planning phase of the project, as this enables you to identify your basic and advanced training needs as well as how to manage your training time and budget and build in regular reviews of your training.

During the planning phase you will also need to identify any generic or specialised research training needs. Most university departments provide training in basic and general research/IT skills and offer courses such as: 'Working with long documents', 'Preparing for your viva', 'Managing the supervisory relationship', and 'Time management skills'. Many of these general workshops are helpful in developing your basic research and computer skills and provide a platform for undertaking research.

Data management and ethics courses are also useful activities to have undertaken so you are clear about your responsibilities as a researcher. Data management is essentially how to handle and treat data, especially data that contains sensitive information (such as age, ethnicity, medical history, sexuality) and/or confidential data. There are clear processes and guidelines about data storage and who can access the data. You need to ensure you follow the protocols within your organisation.

Doing research with children and families, however, is likely to require more specialised skills and therefore it is important that you really think about what types of specialised training you need. Identifying suitable training courses is not always easy and you may have to spend some time trawling the internet looking for workshops that suit your needs. Furthermore, some of these can be expensive and while your employer may help with funding in some cases, in others you may have to self-fund. You may also need to fund accommodation and travel costs as well as the fees. If you are applying for funding for a project do not forget to include a training budget. You may have to think creatively to find the courses that you need.

You should document your attendance on all courses, regardless of their length or speciality. It is useful to maintain a Training Passport, which is simply a document that stipulates the name of the course, the course provider, the date attended and basic notes from the course. You may want to include a reflective column where you can reflect on what you have learned from it. An example based on the one provided by the University of Leicester is shown in Box 5.5.

Box 5.5   Example of a training passport

[*University logo here*]

Student: _____ Email [*insert email address*]: _____

University department: _____ Degree (BSc/MSc/PhD): _____

Year of study: Year 1 ☐; Year 2 ☐; Year 3 ☐; Year 4 (writing up) ☐
(tick one box)

Supervisor: _____ Initial registration date (mm/yr): _____

Instructions to student

You should use this training passport to keep an up-to-date record of any con-
tinuing professional development and training courses that you undertake,
whether within the university or externally. It is useful to record on this form any
conferences or specialist courses you attend and any presentations or poster
presentations you give.

   This training passport should be kept with the rest of your course documentation. Each year of your course you should build up a complete record of your
training and your progress. This document will be useful when you write your
annual reports and will contribute to any Personal Development Plan.

Record of attendance at training in Year 1 ☐; 2 ☐; 3 ☐; 4 (writing up) ☐
(It is suggested that you use a new copy of this sheet for each year)

Training session   Date

Please include the name of the institution, the name of the
course and the date completed.

Please add rows if required.

Safety of the researcher

It is easy to forget that there can be risks to you as a field researcher. Ethics
tend to focus on the welfare of the participants, which is very important, but
it is also necessary to think about potential risks to you. The UK Social

Research Association (SRA) developed a series of guidelines for researchers to perform a risk assessment, consider their welfare and engage in safe working. Along with guidelines from the Health and Safety at Work Act (1974), these documents provide some useful advice.

Although some topics and environments pose obvious risks to the researcher and these are mitigated and planned for in advance, there are occasions where you may be exposed to unanticipated risk. Below is an activity to help you think about risks in different contexts.

Activity 5.2

We suggest you read the articles by Dickson-Swift et al. (2008) and Parker and O'Reilly (forthcoming) to help you with this activity (full references at the end of the chapter and in the references section of the book).

What are the risks of undertaking interviews in community settings?
What are the risks of interviewing children from vulnerable groups?

We provide some suggestions at the back of the book as well as developing a more comprehensive discussion of those issues below.

Researchers may be exposed to physical, psychological or emotional harm during the process of research and it is important to undertake a risk assessment prior to starting your project. Qualitative research particularly may expose the researcher to specific emotional distress through hearing traumatic stories or dealing with sensitive issues (Dickson-Swift et al., 2008). Some topics can be especially difficult to deal with; in particular hearing accounts regarding child abuse, suicide attempts or life-limiting conditions, for example, can sometimes be an emotional rollercoaster for the researcher. Furthermore, evidence shows us that researchers have been victims of threatening behaviour, violence, stalking or fear during data collection (see Parker and O'Reilly, forthcoming; Paterson et al., 1999). You need to take precautions to protect yourself. For example:

- Consult the SRA guidelines. There are numerous strategies in here that will help you plan your research.
- *Do not* make assumptions about any groups you are researching. Just because a group is vulnerable does not mean it is automatically safe. For example, they may have a violent family member, or they may talk about an experience unrelated to your research that is particularly traumatic or emotional.
- Think twice about the geographical location of the research. Are you likely to end up alone on a train platform late at night? Does the area you are visiting have a reputation for being 'rough'? Are you going to the participant's own home?

- Make sure you have a mobile phone with you and make sure someone knows where you are at all times.
- Learn some basic self-defence.
- Attend some training on how to handle difficult situations.
- Perform a risk assessment and think about all the issues involved, such as the possibility of catching an infectious disease.
- Consider having a research partner with you.
- Ensure your car is in good working order, with enough fuel for your journey, if you are going to use it.
- Be clear about the train/bus times and locations if using public transport.

Our advice, therefore, is to be alert and be prepared. Planning is paramount so make sure you consult the above list during the planning stages of your project, and use the SRA guidelines to help you think about the more pertinent issues. It is imperative you discuss your safety and planning with your supervisor or research team in advance of the data collection phase.

Staying motivated and staying on track

The idea of research with children may provoke anxiety. If you are fairly inexperienced with children or if you are a research student then the anticipation about conducting a research project may feel daunting. First, this is normal. Most people feel a bit daunted by the prospect of completing a project. Second, there are many different ways of managing such anxiety:

1 Recognise that the anxiety is normal and your peers probably feel the same way.
2 Be proactive and set up a support group among your peers to provide an outlet for the anxiety.
3 Use the forums online. There are usually lots of groups. A good example of this is Methods space (www.methodspace.com). This website contains a lot of useful information and discussion groups that will help you manage your anxiety and your project.
4 Discuss your feelings with your supervisor or line manager. They will expect you to feel this way and it is good to get it off your chest.
5 Find distractions when it all gets a bit too much. Go to the shops, have a tea break, spend time on Facebook and so forth; just be careful that these tasks don't stop you from working altogether.
6 Break the research down into organised and manageable chunks. Try not to think about it as a project as a whole but have daily, weekly and monthly targets. Make sure these are realistic and agree them with your line manager or supervisor.
7 Be realistic about the kind of person you are. If you are deadline-driven then get your supervisor to set you deadlines. If you are naturally disorganised then work with your supervisor to have short manageable activities with more flexible deadlines.

Remember that it is easy to procrastinate and spend too much time distracting yourself from the real work. Anxiety is a great cause of 'writers' block'. Try to recognise what your fears are and address them. It is okay to procrastinate for short periods, but when it starts to consume much of your week then something needs to be done about it. Remember that if you are genuinely struggling, or if external life events are getting in the way, you need to talk to your supervisor about it and avoid struggling on alone.

Summary

In this chapter we have covered aspects that require preparation before you can begin research. Box 5.6 summarises these points in a checklist.

Box 5.6   Checklist for preparing for research

- Identify whether you are planning research or audit.
- Identify a research supervisor if you are undertaking research that is not part of a course or a supervised research project.
- Ensure you have your CRB disclosure in place (or equivalent).
- Acquire some basic understanding of child development and the levels at which children of different ages function.
- Familiarise yourself with the research governance policies of the organisations you work for.
- Identify courses to meet any specific basic skills deficits (some of this will become more apparent once you get under way).
- Address any anxieties you have.
- Set a timeline for achieving certain targets.

Useful resources

The Social Research Association has some useful resources and guidelines for thinking about your own safety. These can be accessed at www.the-sra.org.uk.

The Health and Safety at Work Act also provides some useful guidelines for your safety. This can be accessed at www.hse.gov.uk.

Further reading

Closs, S. and Cheater, F. (1996) 'Audit or research – what is the difference?', *Journal of Clinical Nursing*, 5: 249–256.

Dickson-Swift, V., James, E., Kippen, S. and Liamputtong, P. (2008) 'Risk to researchers in qualitative research on sensitive topics: issues and strategies', *Qualitative Health Research*, 18 (1): 133–144.

Dogra, N. and Davies, D. (2010) 'Clinical governance, audit and supervision', in N. Dogra and S. Leighton (eds), *Nursing in Child and Adolescent Mental Health*. Maidenhead: McGraw Hill, pp. 155–166.

Greenstein, T. (2006) *Methods of Family Research*. London: Sage.

Harris, M. and Butterworth, G. (2002) *Developmental Psychology: A Student's Handbook*. Hove: Psychology Press.

Parker, N. and O'Reilly, M. (forthcoming) '"We are alone in the house": a case study addressing researcher safety and risk', *Qualitative Research in Psychology*.

6

Getting Started in Research with Children

- Introduction
- Choosing a topic and an overall research question
- Developing a research proposal: planning the project
  - The title
  - Background/introduction/literature review
  - Aims and objectives
  - Methods and design
  - Recruitment and ethics
  - Benefits and outcomes
  - Timescales and time management
  - Costs and funding
  - Dissemination
- Keeping a research diary
- Effective preparation/planning: how to do a literature search
- How to critically appraise a paper
- Summary
- Useful resource
- Further reading

┌─────────┐ Learning outcomes ┌─────────┐

By the end of this chapter you should be able to:

- Choose a topic
- Produce a research diary
- Develop a research proposal
- Undertake a literature search
- Critique a paper

Key words: critical analysis, literature searching, planning, proposal, research diary

---

Introduction

This chapter is designed to provide you with knowledge and understanding to plan a research project with child participants. It will guide you through some of the important decisions that you will need to make as your research ideas unfold. During this chapter we introduce you to techniques and strategies for thinking about the nature and progress of your project to help you appreciate the progressive and reflective nature of research.

Choosing a topic and an overall research question

All research starts with a focus on a particular area and from this a general question is created. Choosing a topic can in itself be quite a challenge. Some researchers come into research with a clear idea of what they are interested in, while others only have a vague notion of a topic. Students particularly may be required to undertake a piece of research for educational purposes but feel in the dark about how to get started.

The best way to choose a topic is to brainstorm your ideas and then discuss them with colleagues or supervisors. Have a look through your brainstorm to see if there are any connections between the topics of interest and start to narrow down what it is about that area that really intrigues you. See Figure 6.1, developed by O'Reilly for her MSc dissertation (1999), for an example. By visualising all of the related issues it may help you identify the area of greatest interest.

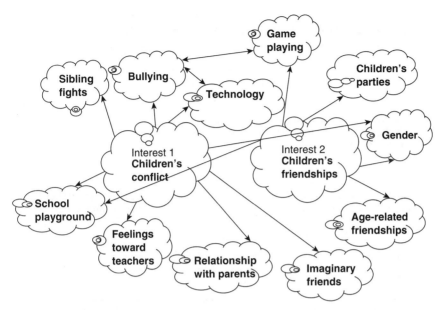

Figure 6.1   Brainstorming

Activity 6.1

Ask yourself these questions:

What contribution do I want to make to our understanding of children?
What aspect of children's lives interests me?
What setting will I be using to research children in?
What fascinates me about children's behaviour?

Answering these questions should help you make a start on your own brainstorm. Hypothetically, imagine you are interested in children's friendships as a topic. You need to develop a question about children's friendships. Remember that the overall research question is simply the question that reflects the research agenda and will need to be refined in relation to the broad methods you adopt (covered in the next chapter). So you are interested in something broad, for example: what makes children's friendships different from adult friendships? What kind of friendships do children have? Are there gender differences in children's friendships? Have a look at Figure 6.2 to help you develop your main question and research agenda.

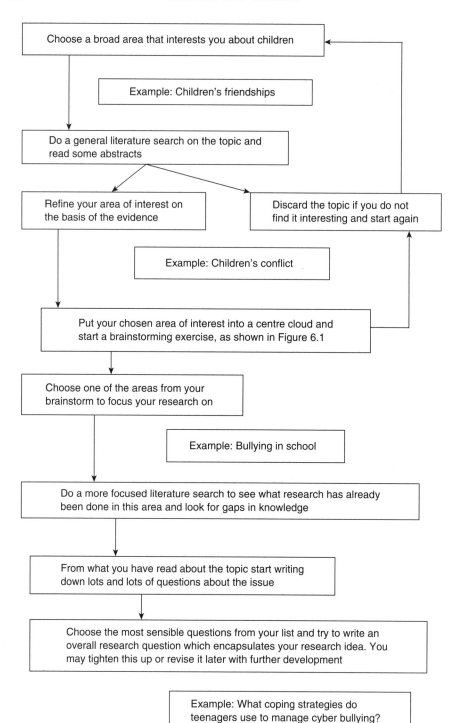

Figure 6.2   Developing areas of interest

When developing your overall research question you need to think about practical issues. Sometimes the research question is more about what can be more easily done than what is needed. One could argue that studies that are repeated without sub-stratifying their sample serve only those that are part of the larger groups and thereby the needs of smaller groups may be less well identified.

Sometimes the issue is that a theoretical model has arisen from studying one group but is then applied to another without testing whether it is equally valid in the next sample. A good example of this is attachment. Ainsworth et al. (1978) identified types of attachment behaviour through observations of US samples. The styles of attachment derived in this group have been applied as though these apply in all contexts. While this may be the case, research was undertaken to ensure that this was warranted.

Research has now confirmed that all infants develop attachment relationships with their caregivers and these may be secure or insecure. The number of children who develop secure relationships is proportionately similar across cultures at around two thirds. However, there is variability between those who are insecure-avoidant or insecure-ambivalent which may reflect differences as to how this behaviour is interpreted. Also different cultures may value different characteristics in children. At a very basic level it is often stated that Western cultures value independence, emotional openness and sociability and this is not necessarily the case in other cultures. So, if you were going to research any aspects of attachment, having some awareness of the different cultural perspectives would enable you to carefully consider how your research question might best be answered.

Developing a research proposal: planning the project

To plan a piece of research effectively it is essential to develop a proposal (sometimes referred to as a protocol) (Punch, 2000). This helps you to plan your project and is often used to convince others (such as a funding body or your supervisor) of the quality of your work (Rumsey and Marks, 2004). It is in the proposal that you show what you are going to do, how you are going to do it and what the expected benefits will be. During the proposal writing stage you need to make several important decisions and to achieve this will need to prepare by some extensive reading. You will not find everything in one place and will need to take a more diverse approach to learning. Box 6.1 provides you with an acceptable format for proposals.

Box 6.1   Layout for a proposal

- Title
- Background/literature review
- Aims and objectives
- Methods and design
- Recruitment and ethics
- Benefits and outcomes
- Timescale
- Costs and budgets
- Dissemination strategy

These vary slightly depending on where you submit your proposal, and you need to consult the appropriate guidelines when creating your proposal. Sometimes funding bodies have a particular layout that they want you to follow so adhere to it. If, however, there is no stipulated format, then the above format should cover everything that anyone might need to know.

The title

Developing an overall title for your research project can be challenging. The title needs to be eye-catching and original and capture the essence of what you are going to do. A useful way of testing your title is to ask people you know (such as your peers) if they can figure out what your research is about just by emailing them your title and seeing what responses you get. Remember, your title also needs to convey what you did in the project but be careful not to make it too long.

For example, my colleagues and I (O'Reilly et al., 2009b) wrote a paper related to perceptions of mental health among homeless young people. The title we eventually used was: '"Nuts, schiz, psycho": an exploration of young homeless people's perceptions and dilemmas of defining mental health'. Although the concepts used in the title are potentially stigmatising, they were the exact terms used by the young people in the sample, thus we started the title with a direct quotation as it is emotive, understandable and eye-catching, and reflects the actual words used by the young people. This helps to grab the attention of a reader but also grounds the paper in the data. We then followed this up with a clear representation of what the research was about – homeless young people and their views of mental health.

Think about how the paper might have come across if we had used this title instead: 'The paradoxes of suffering: research on kids without homes'. Ask yourself whether you could ascertain what this paper is about just from the title. This title fails to represent fully what the paper is about and it is less eye-catching and so is less likely to encourage the reader to bother going any further.

Background/introduction/literature review

An important aspect of the proposal is to situate your research idea into the broader context and evidence base. In the proposal you need to *critically* assess the existing knowledge about the subject area and identify an important gap in knowledge. It can be a struggle to keep this section brief, especially if you have done a lot of reading. But remember that the purpose of the reading is to prepare you for the research, not just to show how much you have read! Part of being critical is to positively appraise the contribution of work as well as consider its limitations. In this section you are trying to establish what one wants to know about this aspect of children's lives and why and how that is helpful and important to know. The idea is that you will then build upon this knowledge by filling in the gap with your research.

Aims and objectives

It is very important that you are clear about what you aim to achieve in your research, and what the key objectives are. People confuse aims with objectives so you need to really think about these. The aims of the project are what the project hopes to demonstrate and the objectives are what it hopes to achieve and these should reflect your overall research question. For example:

Research question: How do doctors communicate with children? 'This project aims to provide an understanding of how GPs communicate with children with an objective of developing a training course to help trainee doctors engage children in general practice'.

Research question: What are teachers' attitudes towards the National Curriculum? 'This research aims to identify what teachers think of the National Curriculum with an objective of developing a large-scale questionnaire for national distribution'.

Research question: Are children from lower socio-economic backgrounds less happy than those from wealthier backgrounds? 'This research aims to investigate whether there are differences in happiness levels between children from lower and higher socio-economic indices with an objective of developing parent information sheets to help parents recognise unhappiness in their children'.

In the proposal it is essential that you are clear about the aims and objectives of your research and you need to show how these relate to your research question. Of course it is likely that you will have more than one aim and more than one objective. It is preferable, however, not to have too many or to be overly ambitious with them. What is especially important in the proposal is that the aims and objectives should be achievable and that the methods adopted can meet them. Choosing a method is something we focus on later in the book and you will need to read this to help you develop your proposal fully.

Methods and design

Essentially methods are how you are going to do your project and achieve your aims and objectives. The first decision you need to make is whether you are going to utilise a quantitative, qualitative or mixed methods design to meet your aims and objectives as this will determine all of your methodological choices.

In this section you then outline the methodological aspects of the study by showing what method of data collection you are going to use, what method of analysis, and other design features such as information about your participant sample and sampling issues.

You will also need to think about how your methodology is going to be adapted to suit children. In the methods and design section you will also need to think about sampling. A sample is a subset of the broader population – this is typically a manageable size and represents the broader population from which it was drawn.

Example one

If you are interested in the levels of intelligence in teenage girls then you need a sample of girls to represent the broader population of girls.

Example two

If you are interested in why young people smoke then you will need to find those who smoke to form your sample. This sample will then represent smoking young people.

Recruitment and ethics

Accessing child populations is obviously essential for your research to work and in this section you need to outline the strategies for accessing the type of children you want to study. Think back to the different groups we considered earlier in the book and how and why it might be difficult to access some of those children.

In the proposal you need to outline the access and recruitment issues that you face and show what relationships you have already built. Having **stakeholder** involvement in the project will give it more credibility and will help you plan and design all aspects of your research, and we discuss how to do this later in the book.

An important part of this section will be the ethical considerations you are going to address. We do not go into detail here but refer you to Chapter 3 to help you think about the ethics issues you need to include in your proposal.

Benefits and outcomes

An important part of the proposal is to convince your audience that the research you are planning has some value, usually practical. You need to show that there will be some practical outcomes of the research and that you will be making a contribution to knowledge, practice and/or policy.

Timescales and time management

You need to think very carefully about how long it will take you to complete the different phases of the project. You need to plan the different tasks needed in the project and build in contingency time for when things do not go according to plan. See Figure 6.3 for an example **timeline**.

Remember when you are planning your time that there are certain times during the year when children may be less available. Children have summer holidays and Christmas breaks. They are at school during the working day. They may have hobbies or activities that they are committed to. It is up to

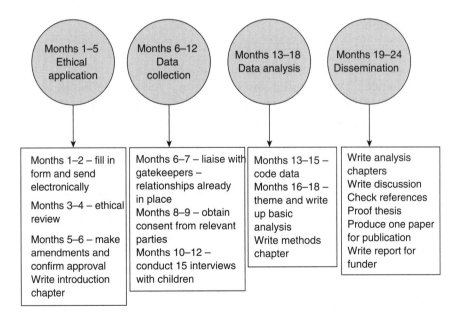

Figure 6.3 Timeline

you to work around their hectic schedules, not up to them to fit into yours. Talk to the parents and teachers about what the children's routines are. Think about when you have your own holidays planned and any special occasions on the horizon, and have contingency time built in for unexpected events such as illness and other life events. It is worth remembering that everything usually takes longer than planned or intended so contingency planning helps you set more realistic targets.

Costs and funding

Often the primary purpose of a research proposal is to seek funding for the project and it is important therefore to consider the large and the small costs. Think about how you might convince a funding body that your research is valuable (do this even if you are not applying for funding as you should be able to articulate the worth of your research). For your project you need to first think about which source of funding is most suitable for your project.

You need to think about whether you want to incorporate a reward system for the children that participate, such as gift vouchers, and you may need to think about reimbursing the parents for travelling to meet you. Think about the socio-economic status of the families you will be researching and remember that it is not fair for them to pay to come and see you. You may have to travel to them and include travel expenses. Small costs like tea and biscuits all add up.

Dissemination

In the proposal you will need to finish off by showing how you intend to disseminate your research so that the findings will be communicated to wider audiences. Typically this involves writing for publication in journals, reports for stakeholders, conference presentations and theses. This is discussed further in Chapter 12 on dissemination.

Keeping a research diary

A research diary is a useful aid throughout the research process. Keeping a research diary can help you to keep your decision-making transparent, will help with time management and help you write up the final report/thesis (Silverman, 2005). You can maintain your diary in whichever format suits you. You can keep written records in an exercise book or keep an electronic diary on a laptop or tablet (such as iPad or android). Whatever method you choose you need to record facts, dates, decisions, interpretations and reflection.

Example one

Factual information: Had a meeting with my supervisor today and it went well. He told me that he is pleased with my research questions but felt that my approach needed some work. He told me that I hadn't done enough reading and don't really seem to understand the qualitative approach yet. He recommended two good books – Silverman (2011) and Creswell (2002). Plan to go to the library on Friday afternoon.

Example two

Decisions: Because of the above supervision I have decided to use thematic analysis for my project. I have done quite a bit of reading about this subject. I have decided to use thematic analysis because I want to explore the language used by young children about bullying and look for the common things that they talk about. Other authors have used thematic analysis effectively to look at bullying in older children.

Example three

Reflection: During the supervision I reflected with my supervisor on a difficult interview I conducted yesterday. I interviewed an 11-year-old girl about her eating behaviours. She was painfully thin and made me feel really fat. Started to question whether I ought to drop a few pounds and had to remind myself that I have battled with eating all my life. It was very difficult not to let my own ideas about weight creep into the interview. I think it would be useful to talk to my supervisor about this.

From these examples you should be able to see that the research diary has many purposes and can be of use throughout your project. By recording factual information you can keep track of the important things that you have read or that your supervisor has told you. You can write down key references in this diary or helpful web pages that you might want to refer to. You can summarise your supervision or team meeting sessions and note anything particularly helpful that you have been told. It is necessary to record any decisions you make in the diary as you may need to refer to these during dissemination. By providing a clear rationale for your choices and directions you will have a benchmark for writing up later on in the project.

It is also important to be reflective in the diary. While this is absolutely essential for qualitative work it is also helpful for the quantitative researcher. Researching children can be hard work and some sensitive data may affect you emotionally. While offloading to supervisors is helpful, it is good to unburden yourself on paper. Furthermore there are limits to how much personal information you can or should disclose to your supervisor, so be careful not to rely too heavily on them, as you may actually need a counselling service. Use the diary to record your feelings and reactions to things and this will help you be a more reflexive researcher.

Effective preparation/planning: how to do a literature search

Doing an effective literature search is essential for research. You do not want to get half way through your project and find that it has all pretty much been done before. Although the literature on children is more limited than with adults (because of attitudes and ethics related to child research) there is a comprehensive research bank in some areas.

1 Identify the key words to help you find the key articles and books related to your topic. Write these down in a notepad, as you may need to use different combinations to reveal the relevant information.
2 Try to locate many references that relate to your chosen topic.
3 Read the abstracts to determine their relevance and usefulness, and only read the relevant papers in full.
4 Narrow down the large search to the most relevant articles and chapters.
5 Make your notes in your own words to ensure that you understand the broad issues and points.
6 Organise your notes and construct the introduction/literature review section of your proposal/report/paper/thesis.
7 When writing your notes, keep the full reference as you may need it later.
8 It is useful to import the abstract into your notes as this is a good summary of the paper and gives you the methodological detail that you may miss.
9 It is also useful to finish your notes on a particular paper with a general summary in your own words.

Remember that as you read through the articles the author may cite some useful papers that your search did not identify. This approach to searching can be a useful way of identifying further material. Google scholar can be a useful starting point for getting a general feel of the literature, but ultimately the academic databases are most helpful. The most relevant for health, social science and education are EBSCO, SAGE, SCOPUS, MEDline, ERIC, PSYCHinfo and PSYCHlit.

When undertaking a literature review you may also want to think about which journals are accessed. Is it only those in English? If you only include English journals this may exclude relevant research from other countries. Unfortunately, obtaining translated papers can be prohibitively expensive but it is the recognition of the limitation that is important.

Activity 6.2

Type the word 'Autism' into the EBSCO database and see how many articles and references are returned (when we did this (in 2011) we got 34,394).

By having a broad search term you return too many articles to go through so you need to have a more refined search. Type three words into the EBSCO boxes: 'Autism', 'Girls' and 'Treatments' (when we did this we got 252 returned). This is much more manageable and the focus allows us to search through the literature to determine which ones might be worth reading.

Try this now with your topic. Try just typing in the broad search term to see what you get. Now try narrowing down your search to be more specific. In your research diary, note down the combination of search terms that you have used and in what database to help you keep track of your activities.

How to critically appraise a paper

When making notes from the identified papers it is important that you write critically as this will help you write in a more academic style. When making notes from the literature it is important that you capture the key information to show what the problem was, the purpose of the study, the methodological information and the key results and implications.

Here we provide you with a step-by-step guide for developing a critical appraisal of a published paper.

Step 1

The first (very important) thing to do is to note down the full reference for the paper. You can either do this using computer software such as Refworks or you can type it out using the following information.

- The author's name (including initial).
- The date of publication in brackets.
- The title of the article.
- The title of the journal.
- The volume and page numbers.

If you cite a journal article in your work it needs to be fully referenced so do it early. You will be annoyed if a couple of months down the line you want to cite the paper but cannot find the full reference for it.

Step 2

Read the abstract and determine how relevant it is to your work:

- The abstract is an important feature of an article as it provides you with a summary of the study.
- In your literature searching you will read many abstracts but only go on to read a few of the whole articles.
- You should get a sense of the value of the study from this section and be able to make some critical judgements.

Step 3

Early on into the paper you should be able to identify the background of the research and determine what kind of evidence base is available on that particular issue:

- You need to read the literature review/introduction section of the article.
- This will provide you with the past research on the topic. Consider what other factors have contributed to a problem and how it has been studied.
- Consider the varied methodologies applied to the same subject matter and think about how the current authors align themselves with past research or how they critique past research.
- It will also help you identify any important articles, books or book chapters that you have missed from your literature search.

Step 4

What is the aim of the study? What are the main objectives?

- This is generally information you extract from the abstract and introduction sections of an article.
- Usually the aims of the study are given in the last one or two paragraphs of the introduction.
- It is a good idea to look at this bit first before reading the introduction as this will help you to actually read the introduction – knowing the point of the article helps you to read it.

Identifying what the aims of the paper are will enable you to determine whether those aims were met and how they were met and also if the paper is actually relevant to your planned work.

Step 5

Methodology section, which is often the easiest bit to appraise:

- What is the approach used? Quantitative or qualitative or mixed design?
- Were the methods used appropriate for the research question?

- Who were the participants in the study?
- What factors are considered? Age, gender and so forth are important for quantitative design.
- What was the data collection method?
- What was the analytic method?
- How are these advantageous or disadvantageous?

You may want to make some judgements about the **reliability** and validity of the project and the limitations inherent in the design.

Step 6

Ethics: the authors should provide some detail about the ethics of their research:

- In research with child participants, much of the research is likely to be ethically sensitive.
- Ethics committees should approve projects and, therefore, there should be some reference to ethics in the paper.
- Participants have to be protected in research and the authors need to show how they did this.
- Key ethical concerns include: informed consent, confidentiality, anonymity, right to withdraw, debriefing and coercion.

It is thus important that you spend some time reflecting on the ethical application of the research reported in the article. Many journals no longer accept papers about research which has not been approved by an ethics panel.

Step 7

The results/findings of an article:

- Record the key findings to ascertain whether they are understandable.
- Consider the different forms of assessment and measures (or qualitative themes).
- Summarise these findings rather than going into too much depth.
- Are the findings relevant to the previously stated aims of the study?
- You only need to note down the results that are relevant to the aims and hypotheses.

Step 8

What were the interpretations and conclusions?

- The first section of the discussion will usually reiterate the findings in relation to the **hypothesis**/research question. The study findings also need to be related to existing research.
- Then the authors should provide their interpretation of their results/findings. You should understand from this what the implications are for practice.

- The authors should also acknowledge the limitations of the study in this section and maybe provide ideas for future research.
- You should question how well the discussion and conclusion match the hypotheses and the aims and objectives of the study.

Are the conclusions justifiable given the findings?

Step 9

General critical appraisal:

- Do an overall coherent appraisal.
- Do this in your own words.
- Demonstrate your understanding of the paper as a whole.
- Identify the key messages and the key limitations.
- Consider the implications for practice in the field.

When reviewing the literature, you need to ensure that it is either historically important or up-to-date. You need to examine the arguments presented and the interpretations made. You need to think about how and why a piece of research might be limited and how and why that matters in practice. Being critical includes taking note of the positives about the article and the research messages. You should note down the contribution of the research and the value of the article when making your notes.

Reading critically and writing critical notes will help you to write a more effective argument when you come to develop your notes into something more meaningful. Remember though that when you are writing you are providing an integrated discussion and presenting a number of articles to serve as evidence for the point you are making, and therefore the critical notes you have made will need to be modified to make a core point.

Summary

This chapter has provided you with the foundations to begin a project researching children. In this chapter we have outlined many of the main decisions that you need to make before embarking on a project. When you are certain that it is research you are going to do you need to choose a topic and develop a research question/hypothesis. You need to be clear whether you are engaging in quantitative or qualitative work and you need to develop a research proposal. To do this effectively you need to conduct a literature search and critically analyse the relevant articles.

Useful resource

Methods space – www.methodspace.com.

Further reading

Eve, J. (2008) 'Writing a research proposal: planning and communicating your research ideas effectively', *Library and Information Research*, 32 (102): 18–28.

Fink, A. (2005) *Conducting Research Literature Reviews: From the Internet to Paper* (2nd edn). London: Sage.

Freeman, C. and Tyrer, P. (2006) 'Getting started in research', in C. Freeman and P. Tyrer (eds), *Research Methods in Psychiatry* (3rd edn). London: The Royal College of Psychiatrists, pp. 3–15.

Greenhalgh, T. (2001) *How to Read a Paper: The Basics of Evidence Based Medicine* (2nd edn). London: BMJ Books.

Kuyper, B.J. (1991) 'Bringing up scientists in the art of critiquing research', *BioScience*, 41 (4): 248–252.

Punch, K.F. (2000) *Developing Effective Research Proposals.* London: Sage.

Rumsey, N. and Marks, D. (2004) 'Getting started: the practicalities of doing research', in D. Marks and L. Yardley (eds), *Research Methods for Clinical and Health Psychology.* London: Sage, pp. 21–38.

Sandelowski, M. and Barroso, J. (2003) 'Writing the proposal for a qualitative research methodology project', *Qualitative Health Research*, 13 (6): 781–820.

7

Children with Specific Characteristics

Overview

After reading through this chapter you should be able to:

- Identify some of the different groups of children who get involved in research projects
- Differentiate the various issues pertinent to different groups of children
- Modify some of the research techniques to relate to these groups of children
- Plan a research project involving these groups of children
- Communicate with these different groups of children

Key words: bereavement, chronic illness, disabilities, homeless, life-limiting illness, mental health, refugee, vulnerable groups, young offender

Introduction

This chapter is designed to help you think about any special considerations for your research project. It is important that you remember that children are not a homogenous group. They are diverse in many ways, and particular groups of children are not homogenous either. This chapter helps you to think about some of the different groups of children. This should help you to think about some of the special issues for researching these groups and perhaps challenge your views about children with particular characteristics and how you relate to them.

As you read this chapter bear in mind children may belong to several groups at the same time and just because there is a likelihood that children belonging to a particular group will have a particular experience or view, this does not mean it will apply to all members of that group. The principles discussed earlier in the chapter on cultural issues are as relevant here as everywhere else. You might want to start thinking about what constitutes a 'normal' child as a benchmark for the rest of the chapter. See Box 7.1 for some ideas.

Box 7.1   **What is normal?**

If we were to ask you what is normal, it is likely your answer would vary from many other readers. Normal is often conceptualised as really meaning what is normal to us. Normal can be difficult to gauge as the opposite is abnormal and using the latter term can cause offence. 'Normal' in terms of children can mean that they are meeting their developmental milestones (in social, cognitive and other spheres) within expected timescales, that they are meeting academic goals expected of them, and complying with family, social and cultural expectations and so on. So when you are using the term, think about how you are using it and what you are conveying when you use it.

Very young children: neonate–4 years old

Although very young children, especially babies, constitute a particularly vulnerable group of children, it is nonetheless important to gain knowledge about them through research. Over time a number of studies, including developmental, psychological, sociological and medical, have been conducted on children from newborn to 4 years old.

If you intend to research children aged 4 or under you need to be aware that this carries some unique practical and ethical challenges. Children in this age group are unable to consent or possibly even assent. The parents/guardians therefore will be providing consent on their behalf. Because of this it is imperative during your research that you look for signs of distress or indicators that the child may want to withdraw. We would advise you to use your common sense and stay tuned to the child and their parents.

Parents are generally supportive of neonatal research and are able to see the value of it, although some parents have expressed anxiety about enrolling premature babies (Morley et al., 2005). You need to be aware of their anxieties and think about this when you are communicating with them and especially when you take their consent. Parents are generally able to weigh up the risks and benefits of enrolling their baby in research (Morley et al., 2005) but you need to spell them out as there may be risks or benefits that they are unaware of.

Young children: 5–11 years old

There have been, and continue to be, concerns about engaging young children in research because of their perceived vulnerability. Young children are especially vulnerable to coercion, distress and anxiety, so the issue of power is an important consideration when engaging them in your research project.

You need to employ research methods that reflect children's interests, values, experiences and routines (Christensen, 2004) and it will be your responsibility to fit into the child's world rather than expecting the child to understand yours. There are some strategies you can use to reduce the power and equalise the asymmetry. It is useful if you give the child some control in the research, let them fill in the questionnaire without you present, are flexible in the interview, or encourage them to tell stories, either written or verbal. Encourage children to ask you lots of questions, even if they are not entirely relevant to the project (Mauthner, 1997). Box 7.2 contains some helpful hints.

Box 7.2   Helpful hints for researching young children

- Try to familiarise yourself with the child's vocabulary. You may find it useful to spend time in advance of your research in child environments, such as volunteering in a school classroom or at a youth club.
- You need to be able to appreciate the diversity of this group as well as the similarities between them. Try to understand the level of language they have, the tasks they enjoy and dislike and the general way they relate to adults.
- Seek advice from teachers, parents and youth club leaders or other relevant individuals, about children in general from this age group and then gather some specific background information about the children participating in your research.

The usefulness of the data you obtain from young children may relate to their age and developmental abilities so be flexible and encouraging, getting the most out of them. Keep in mind that young children have a tendency to give the answers that adults want to hear, so think carefully about your questions and phrase them in an age-appropriate and non-leading way. For example, when asking 'Would you like to have more friends?' the natural answer of a young child will be 'Yes'. However, if you ask the same child 'Do you think that you have enough friends?' the answer is also likely to be 'Yes' but may be 'No'.

You may be tempted to provide refreshments for the children, as a treat, but be careful with this as you need to be mindful of allergies and parental views. For example, when one author was interviewing children aged 5–11 years old, a decision was made to provide orange squash and marshmallows. Notably, however, each parent was consulted in advance of the interview to ensure that none of the children was allergic to any of the ingredients and that parents were happy with their children having this in the middle of the school day. All parents who consented to the research also consented to the refreshments.

Older children: 12–18 years old

Clearly, researching this age group is going to be different from researching younger children as they have a greater capacity to understand and decide for themselves if they want to engage in research. However, there are also greater demands on their time in terms of physical development, changing social relationships, academic challenges and so on.

Having read the capacity chapter you are in a good position to think about the role that informed consent plays in this type of research. Despite the ostensible competence and good levels of communication, this group are regarded legally as minors, therefore safeguarding remains an important issue and you should consider their welfare and potential ethical issues when planning your project.

You will need to hold the attention of your young participants during your project so you will need to implement measures to keep your research and their involvement interesting. One way of keeping them engaged is through the inclusion of participatory methods. While these may not be helpful for some forms of research such as randomised control trials, they can be helpful for questionnaires and interviews. Remember that children in this age group may find the inclusion of participatory methods patronising, they may find the language or tone you use demeaning but at the same time may struggle with complex terminology. Just because some methods such as drawing and painting may appear patronising to this age group, it does not mean that you should abandon the idea altogether – you just need to be age-appropriate and creative.

It is possible that using media technology, photography or vignettes will facilitate your data collection. One of our PhD students found the use of video (role-played) vignettes especially helpful in engaging young people in her interview research. Most young people today live in a world of social networking, internet usage, computer games and vibrant visual stimulation. You could use this to your advantage when designing your project and think about using these mediums to engage young people in research but remember to think about those that may be less technology savvy. For example, in a study of 412 teenagers with a median age of 15.8, about half of them felt more engaged and preferred to use the internet as a source of health information, in particular when issues enquired about were of a sensitive nature (Borzekowski and Rickert, 2001). More recently, a report on the use of new technology by difficult to reach teenagers stated that web-based resources, in particular social networking sites, as one of the components of a comprehensive outreach plan are very useful to reinforce messages following in-person contact, engage shy and geographically remote youth, present a teen-friendly image and encourage teens to electronically contact staff at their convenience (UCSF, 2008).

The issue of power is still present in research with young people and you need to be conscious of any influence you have in the research context. Try to spend some time getting to know your participants in other contexts, particularly in those settings where they feel comfortable, and build some rapport with them before you start engaging them in the research process.

However, you need to be aware that by building up a relationship in advance of the research, there is a greater risk that you will influence their responses. Try to be clear that a researcher's role is different from a teacher's role and that they have more control over their participation. You could let them have control of the recording device, for example. Try to nurture an atmosphere whereby the young people are positioned as experts and you are trying to learn from them.

As younger children do, some young people may also be anxious about responding to your questions for fear of retribution or feeling stupid. You need to put them at ease by assuring them that the data collected will remain confidential and by taking steps to reduce your social status in the interaction. It may be tempting to treat them like adults, and while this may be appropriate for older teenagers, for younger teenagers this may not be suitable. Try to talk to your participants on their level, but do not pretend that you are their peer. Treat your participants with respect and try to break down any barriers that may exist. Remember that young people are more likely to disclose information if parents, family members or friends are not present and therefore you may have to do some work to negotiate privacy (Mauthner, 1997).

On the other hand, if your participant specifically requests to have someone with them during the research it would be unethical to refuse. This can be their parents or another person who the young person feels comfortable with, such as friends or other workers. Some shy and less adventurous young people take longer to warm up when meeting new people, in particular adults. Your role is to make them feel at ease and work at their pace to build up a rapport if they are to genuinely contribute to your research. As long as you feel you are getting honest answers to your questions, you should not worry about having somebody else in the room. Our experience is that it will be just a matter of time, as once the young person feels comfortable with you and they feel they can trust you they will be more than happy to be on their own.

At this stage, it is worth noting that it is sometimes the parents who find it difficult to let go, and they would like to hear everything their teenage children say, rather than the young people refusing to see you on their own. In these cases, you taking control of the interview and reassuring parents about your duty to disclose information should safeguarding issues arise during your conversation with their children usually does the trick.

Researching specific groups

While doing research with children raises special methodological and ethical issues, there are a number of groups of children who warrant further special attention due to an increased vulnerability. In this chapter, we explore some of the important issues to consider for the following groups: ethnic minorities, refugees and asylum seekers, looked after children, homeless children, young offenders, children with disabilities, children with mental health problems/illnesses, children with life-limiting conditions and children who are bereaved.

As we discussed previously, the ethical aspects of accessing particularly vulnerable populations are complex and commonly perceived as huge obstacles in the research process, which are sometimes discouraging and frustrating. These processes are in place to protect the rights of children and young people physically, mentally, ethically and emotionally; and to ensure they are not exploited. Also, they reassure parents and others concerned with their welfare and safety that research conducted with these particular children is designed to protect the interests of children and young people. On the other hand, the practical aspects of accessing difficult to reach or marginalised populations may prove a challenge and will require imaginative designs and a lot of perseverance. However, it is important to remember that research with these groups of children is essential if research is to socially include and empower these groups, understand their worlds and help them to make improvements to their lives. The broader ethical issues were discussed earlier in the book and you may find it useful to return to that chapter.

So, if you are going to undertake research with a particularly vulnerable group of children then there are specific issues pertinent to that group that you will need to think about. There are, however, a number of general issues that you will need to consider when engaging any of these groups in your research project.

General issues pertinent to all groups

The key to working with any group of children is to be **child-centred** and if you are going to engage children with additional vulnerabilities in your research then you will need to think about what constitutes their life interests, what their limitations are, what their important relationships are and what their key concerns might be. Remember, however, that just because a child falls into one of these groups does not mean they will share the characteristics of all children in that group or that they will have the same needs or views.

You need to think about the consent process for these children. We looked closely at informed consent and capacity earlier in the book and you may want to refer to that as you read this chapter. If you are doing research with children who have additional vulnerabilities you need to think more carefully about the consent process and how you go about explaining the research to them. You need to use simple language, you may want to use a larger font if the children have visual disabilities, you may want to include pictures if the child has learning disabilities and you will certainly want to spend some time talking with the child to supplement any text.

You also need to consider the issue of coercion more considerably. For example, think about how much power you have over the group you are engaging in research. For instance, young people with drug and alcohol conditions may be motivated by financial incentives to take part (see Fry and Dwyer, 2001) and therefore such incentives may not be appropriate.

Ethnic minorities

There are a number of factors which may facilitate or hinder your communication with these groups and these tend to relate to the beliefs and experiences of those families, their social relationships and their empathy with the research team (Holder et al., 1998). Remember that an understanding of culture will be necessary for this kind of research. You will need to seek advice from people who know about the cultural values, the composition of families and the power issues that may operate, but do not take any views at face value; remember that their perspectives may be just their perspectives and are unlikely to be 'representative' of the diversity within any group. You may find it useful to engage with community leaders about the culture and to allow this gatekeeper to help you access the sample. Be mindful, however, that community members helping with recruitment may have a particular religious, ethnic or clan affiliation which may deter certain segments of a refugee group and lead to inadvertent exclusion of other groups (Ellis et al., 2007).

There may be particular methodological issues when researching any potentially small group, as samples may need to be stratified to ensure that there are enough participants from smaller groups to enable the results to be usefully interpreted and applied. Dogra et al. (2012) argued for instance that national surveys are not especially helpful when developing surveys for communities that do not represent the 'national' situation. For example, the ethnic population in the UK is about 10 per cent but in Leicester it is nearly 50 per cent. Local Authority and the Office for National Statistics (ONS, 2011) websites are a good place to look for data of this kind.

Refugees and asylum seekers

Over time there has been an increase in research with refugees and asylum seekers which is inevitably undertaken in complex, sometimes difficult and dangerous situations. Refugee communities are especially vulnerable and marginalised and research therefore places these populations at great risk of exploitative and harmful research practices (Hugman et al., 2011). If you decide you want to do research with refugees or asylum seekers you need to think about where and how you will access the population and what this means for ethics and practice. Are you planning to go to a foreign country to talk to them or will you be conducting your research in your home country?

This decision will affect the types of challenges you face. For example, in some foreign countries you may have to compromise certain stringent ethical procedures. It may simply not be possible to acquire consent from an adult caregiver, which may increase the child's vulnerability (Millum and Emanuel, 2007). This does not mean that such groups should be excluded from research, but places greater responsibility on you to behave in an ethical and thoughtful manner.

Key issues for this group are going to be access, language (many are unlikely to speak English or the language of the host country, and using interpreters may be prohibitively expensive for a small project), participation and interpretation of findings. Refugees and asylum seekers have often faced difficulties or trauma at the hands of 'authority' so may be reluctant to engage with other formal bodies or those perceived to be in authority. Remember that refugees and asylum seekers may be fleeing countries where they experienced or feared persecution or torture and may be suffering from post-traumatic stress (Ellis et al., 2007). They may also have good reason not to be fully open as there may be significant implications for their ongoing safety. For example, we have clinically seen refugee 'children' who it was suspected were actually young adults but had they said their true age various services would have no longer been available. There is also often fear of disclosure because of how that may affect their refugee or asylum seeker status.

Children are likely to have to attend school and may learn English (or the host language) well before their parents, changing some of the family dynamics as they become the spokesperson for the family merely because of their ability to communicate. The trauma experienced by these groups may be especially harrowing and probably out of the realms of what most of us are likely to have heard or experienced. There is a big difference between knowing that rape, for example, is widespread in times of war and hearing someone's personal account of the experience. In planning your research, consider seriously what supports there are for the participants and you as a researcher to address distress. Consider the helpful hints in Box 7.3.

Box 7.3 **Helpful hints**

If the child has language or communication problems then you will need to think about the methods you use. Consult with the parents, teachers or social workers about any existing specialised techniques to help build the child's communication abilities and respect these in the data collection. You may need to use photographs and pictures to communicate or use a computer.

Activity 7.1

Carmen has just gained her Master's degree in psychology and has taken up her first post at the local university as a researcher. The senior consultant there has enlisted her help with his research project and part of that role is to interview 11–16-year-old refugee children who have undergone surgery and lost limbs during war and conflict. Carmen is particularly worried about doing the interviews as she has little research experience, is a white middle-class researcher and has not undertaken research with children before. What advice would you give Carmen?

When you have completed this exercise you might want to go to the back of the book where we provide a list of the types of advice we would provide to Carmen.

Looked after children

There is a lack of literature on 'looked after' children, particularly with methodological quality (Davies and Wright, 2008). Researching children placed in foster care raises special ethical issues, mostly in relation to consent. It is difficult to ascertain whether to seek the consent of social workers, foster parents or biological parents. Seeking the consent of biological parents can be time-consuming and it can be difficult when the child is keen to participate but the biological parent fails to communicate with the researcher (Bogolub and Thomas, 2005). Bogolub and Thomas did find, however, that biological parents appreciate being respected and may become angry if not consulted. On the other hand, one of the reasons why children may be in foster care is because their birth parents do not place their best interests first and therefore may not provide consent (King and Churchill, 2000).

The bottom line is that when researching looked after children you will need do an in-depth exploration of the legal and social status, be sensitive to their life experiences and the traumas they may have encountered and bear in mind the wishes of all responsible adults in their lives as well as those of the child.

An alternative option is the possibility of researching abandoned institutionalised children, again in your country or abroad. In some countries, this may simply be unethical and should not take place, as there is no adult caregiver concerned with the child's welfare, which puts them at greater risk. But of course this would mean excluding this important group from the evidence base which could also be considered unethical (Millum and Emanuel, 2007).

Homeless children

Many of the ethical dilemmas that researchers face when working with homeless young people were covered in the chapter on ethics and thus we focus here on more practical issues of engagement. While wandering the streets at night, where homeless populations become more overt, might seem like an obvious place to start in looking for homeless young people this can pose significant risk to your own safety and may alienate the population you are trying to access. It is better therefore to try to access the population through agencies and charities. Across the UK, for example, there are a number of shelters for young people and if you approach these and build up a relationship with the institutional representatives you may be able to gain access to your sample in a more controlled and safe way for yourself and for them. They may also provide you with a room to conduct your research in and this will help the young person feel more comfortable in an environment that is familiar to them.

To talk to homeless young people you will really need to think through the most appropriate methods for communicating with them so that they do not feel pressured or patronised by you, or so that you do not understand them. While parental consent is usually preferable it may not be feasible. You may actually endanger the young person by actively seeking out their biological parent (Rew et al., 2000). It is important here to get advice from your colleagues, from your supervisor and from the homeless shelter staff. Remember also to consider the legal implications before embarking on your project.

It is also important that you remember that there may be several reasons why the young person is homeless and consider the potential impact of these factors on the individual. The young people you access may have additional issues such as having suffered from abuse, drug or alcohol problems, co-existing or mental health difficulties. You really need to understand your population before you begin the research and get advice from gatekeepers before recruiting.

Example one

Our research[1] with homeless populations (O'Reilly et al., 2009b; Taylor et al., 2007; 2006) required considerable planning and ethical considerations before proceeding. With considerable communication through both written letters and telephone conversations we were able to elicit the support of a range of homeless shelter managers and senior staff. This took a long time and a lot of patience. It was our intention to interview the young people who utilised the homeless shelters about their mental health needs and their understanding of mental health, as well as to evaluate a new mental health service that was being provided to them. We relied heavily on the shelter staff for accessing the young people and helping us to communicate the purpose of the study to them. It is essential that you have good working relationships with those who are close to the population you want to access, otherwise you are likely to find recruitment very difficult.

Young offenders

Little research has been produced on young offenders in the prison context, with little more from a community context. Prisoners are a particularly vulnerable group, open to exploitation and abuse (Moser et al., 2004). It is not unreasonable, however, for policy-makers to want evidence of the effectiveness of services aimed at reducing youth crime but this is not as straightforward as they might want. Simple formulas cannot be applied in an operational way to individual children and young people as they are unique in many ways and trying to apply a single method to all children is not likely to be successful (Whyte, 2004).

These children are often also members of other groups that may increase their vulnerability, for example, they could be looked after children, have mental health problems and/or have a learning difficulty. For some, it is in their interests to participate in research as this may be a way of accessing support or an opportunity to share their experiences, or they may have a misperception that their sentence may be reduced. Others may be dismissive of any research as for them it mirrors other areas of their lives, where they may feel they have little say in decisions about their own lives. Previous life experiences and socio-cultural factors may increase the likelihood of hostility towards research and an unwillingness to participate.

Remember that young offenders may have vested interests in being less than truthful in their responses depending on the nature of the research. You need to be aware that gaining the trust of this group of vulnerable children is likely to be difficult and yet without it your research is likely to be limited.

---

[1]This research was led by Professor Panos Vostanis.

Activity 7.2

Marcus is an anthropology researcher and he is interested in youth crime culture and how young people protect each other through not disclosing information to authorities. What difficulties might Marcus encounter in his aims to explore this type of issue? We provide a brief overview at the back of the book.

Activity 7.3

Before you read the rest of this chapter think about the next group of children we introduce – those with mental health problems or mental illnesses. See if you can define these key terms before proceeding:

Mental health problem
Mental illness
Mental disorder
Learning disability
Learning difficulty
Disability

When someone says the words 'mentally ill' what kind of image do you conjure up? What kind of images do you associate with the term 'disability'?

Defining these terms can be difficult to do and we provide some of our own at the back of the book for you to compare your answers with.

If you think mentally ill resonates with the symptoms of schizophrenia and disability with someone in a wheelchair, then like many others you are simply linking with the stereotypical images of these concepts. If you are going to successfully research a particular group of children then you need to recognise that, first, most of these children are unlikely to conform to the stereotypes and, second, that within each subgroup of children each child will be unique and different. While we classify them in groups for discussion purposes, you really need to think about your preconceptions and how you will manage the individual differences between participants in your research.

Children with mental health problems or mental illnesses

It is important to state at the outset that there is no widely agreed consensus on the meanings of the terms mental health problem/illness/disorder and their use. Many outside the health arena challenge the terms, and mental illness as a concept is widely challenged by the anti-psychiatry and critical psychiatry movements (which do include doctors). However, the reality remains that if an individual experiences difficulties which impact on their emotional and inner worlds, their functioning can be affected. Mental health and mental illness can be viewed as two separate, yet related, issues.

The World Health Organization (WHO) definition of health is: 'A state of complete physical, mental and social well-being, and not merely the absence of disease' (www.who.int/topics/mental_health/en). The WHO adds:

> Mental health is not just the absence of mental disorder. It is defined as a state of well-being in which every individual realizes his or her own potential, can cope with the normal stresses of life, can work productively and fruitfully, and is able to make a contribution to her or his community.

Another way of looking at this is that mental health includes: how people look at themselves, their lives and the other people in their lives; how they feel about these different components, evaluate their challenges and problems; and how they explore choices. This includes handling stress, relating to other people and making decisions. The way that the normal stresses of life are defined will vary from society to society and within subgroups. A useful way of viewing the definition in practice is that someone is considered as having mental health when they manage day-to-day living without too much difficulty in a way that satisfies them and fulfils familial and societal expectations of them without causing them undue stress.

Definitions of mental health relating specifically to children have been provided by several bodies and emphasise the expectations of a healthy child. So, a mentally healthy child is one who can, for example:

- Develop emotionally, creatively, intellectually and spiritually.
- Initiate, develop and sustain mutually satisfying personal relationships.
- Face problems, resolve them and learn from them. (Mental Health Foundation, 1999)

This could also easily apply to adults and in some way is developmentally rather than culturally contextual, as these functions apply in whichever society the young person is living. The term 'mental health problems' is one that encompasses a range of experiences and situations and therefore might usefully be viewed as a continuum of experience, from mental well-being through to a severe and enduring mental illness.

Mental health problems can affect anyone, of any age and background, and can impact on the people around them such as their family, friends and carers. A minority of people may experience mental health problems to such a degree that they may be diagnosed as having a mental illness.

Common mental health problems include anxiety (including phobias), obsessive compulsive disorders, adjustment disorders and milder mood problems.

A mental illness is an illness that causes disturbances in thinking, perception and behaviour beyond those that might be experienced even in an acutely distressed state. They can be severe: seriously interfering with a person's life, significantly impairing a person's ability to cope with life's ordinary demands and routines, and even causing a person to become disabled. The majority of people will not experience mental illness, but will undoubtedly experience mental health problems at different times in their lives. Another common term is mental disorder, and this is often used in the sense that a person who is mentally ill is suffering from a mental disorder.

Children with mental health problems may be more vulnerable due to the nature of their problems. They may be reluctant to engage with research if they feel they will be judged or stigmatised. Seriously mentally ill children may not have the capacity at certain points to consent to participate. Children with mental health problems may have additional anxieties about participating in research and these anxious children and/or parents may worry about the implications of the research. The data collection process itself, particularly methods such as the research interview, may generate too many anxieties.

In research involving children who have mental health problems you may decide that it is more appropriate for the clinician responsible for their care to ask if they wish to participate in the research. Ethics committees often prefer this as they feel that clinicians are best placed to advocate for their patients. This tends towards **paternalism** and can also impinge on the clinical relationship. Parents and children may want to please their clinician and participate without really feeling they have a choice. This is something you need to consider and discuss with the clinical team. You will need to decide whether to approach the children yourself, with the clinician as a gatekeeper, or have the clinician acquire consent for you.

Knowing that the research will take place in a confidential context and setting may influence participation (for example, participating in a school context may be an unattractive option for some as they may feel exposed, despite whatever reassurances can be offered). Remember that some children will not have shared their diagnosis with their peers and may prefer to keep it secret. Be aware that if they have experienced specific life events, this may either increase their desire to participate in research on the issue (for example, they may feel they have a useful contribution to make) or reduce their wish to participate (for fear of evoking fear, hurt or other feelings). Consider the helpful hints in Box 7.4.

Box 7.4   **Helpful hints**

If the child has a learning disability then a wide variety of skills may be affected such as concentration, memory or appropriate behaviour. Try to minimise distractions when engaging the child in your data collection, avoid having too many toys available (particularly noisy toys), plan ahead and learn about the child from parents and teachers, make decisions regarding what is developmentally appropriate and consider the time of day you talk to them (avoid choosing a time when they are tired or hungry) (see Benjamin and MacKinlay, 2010).

If the child has a condition such as Autistic Spectrum Disorder then you will need to think about social communication and social interaction. Autistic children may have poor communication skills and difficulty in social situations. If the child has ADHD, then bear in mind that they may find it difficult to focus their attention and may be over-active. In the context of clinical consultations Benjamin and MacKinlay recommend that it is important to talk to these children in a quiet environment and allow the child to choose where to sit. This is also useful advice for the researcher. Make the child feel welcome and comfortable and try not to become distracted by their behaviour. Using the child's name frequently can help focus their attention.

Seeking advice can be helpful in learning about the child's abilities and helps to establish a rapport with the gatekeeper. It is a good idea to gather as much information as you can about the child and the nature of their problems before starting research with the child. This information will help you to build a relationship with the child and handle them sensitively. Some children with special needs will use alternative communication methods, from voice output devices to multisensory references, and you need to engage with these.

Children with disabilities

Children with disabilities have traditionally been excluded from research and often these children are treated as a homogenous group (Davis et al., 2000) without an understanding that there is huge diversity within these groups. Although accessing these children can be difficult, their views are important and valuable (Garth and Aroni, 2003) and research with children with disabilities is now starting to flourish (see, for example, Garth et al., 2009; Garth and Aroni, 2003; Hall and McGregor, 2000; Hestenes and Carroll, 2000).

Policy-makers want children with disabilities or learning difficulties to be a priority and it is essential that more research with this group of children is undertaken. When communicating with disabled children it is important to use specific techniques but often researchers are given limited training in how to communicate with this group (Benjamin and MacKinlay, 2010). Furthermore you may need to pay special attention to the type of disability. A child in a wheelchair is likely to have different needs in the research context to a child who is deaf or blind.

Some training in relation to the nature of that disability (there are many and you should have a good knowledge base before starting) and in terms of communicating with children with that particular disability may be helpful. Remember that not all communication is verbal. You need to think carefully about how you construct consent forms and information sheets and you may need to produce a larger font and a more simplified language. For children with physical disabilities you may need to think about how long they are able to sit and talk to you, whether they have the physical capability to fill in a questionnaire, whether wheelchair access is required, and be very careful not to patronise or talk down to them. Consider the helpful hints in Box 7.5.

Box 7.5 Helpful hints

Benjamin and MacKinlay (2010) argue that the nature of the disability is relevant to communicating with children and they advise clinical practitioners to consider this in their clinics. This advice can be adapted to the research context and we recommend that if the child has a hearing impairment you might need to think about the need for a communication aid, or an interpreter for sign language. You will need a quiet room with few distractions and you may need to be face-to-face for lip reading. Remember, though, that you may have to pay an interpreter and this can cause issues regarding who you make eye contact with – the deaf child or the interpreter. It is easy to make eye contact with the person who is actually speaking but do not lose focus on the child.

If the child has a visual impairment there may be little in the way of eye contact and this makes it difficult to ascertain whether the child is paying attention. Children with visual impairments may miss non-verbal cues. It is important to think about the type of visual impairment, consider the lighting levels and keep auditory distractions to a minimum. If you are going to do research with children who have visual impairments then you will need a nice quiet environment and you will need to minimise any hazards. Think about where you do your research.

If the child is in a wheelchair or has a physical impairment it will affect their movement. The child may become fatigued during the consultation and so you don't want to take up too much of their time and you may need to consider wheelchair access. You need to choose a building with a ramp for them to get in and think about how the chairs are arranged.

Children with life-limiting conditions

Children with chronic illnesses, sometimes also referred to as life-limiting or life-shortening, are children with a health condition which cannot be cured, and from which the child will die early (ACT for Children, 2012). These children face ongoing visits to healthcare professionals and clinics, and failure to engage children with chronic conditions in their healthcare can have serious ramifications for their health later in life (McPherson, 2010). Problematically there is little guidance related to the best ways to conduct research with families and children with life-limiting conditions. This is particularly evident in research using clinical trials, although this group is now being more actively engaged in epidemiological, biological, genetic and social research (Dixon-Woods et al., 2006).

In relation to clinical trials the issues relate to harm, consent and communicating with families; in other forms of quantitative and qualitative research there is little help about how to communicate with families. Accessing children and families with life-limiting conditions can be difficult and it is likely that access will be negotiated through a clinical team in a hospice or hospital, and you will need the cooperation of clinical teams and clinical mangers to be successful (Stevens et al., 2010).

To collect data from these children you will need to have a series of meetings with clinical teams and you will need to build a rapport with them. Evidence suggests that clinical gatekeepers may be reluctant to allow you access because of concerns about the amount of pressure you may put on families in terms of time, stress and anxiety, and they may have reservations that you will be evaluating their clinical performance (Stevens et al., 2010). Therefore, you will need to spend a lot of time reassuring them about what your research involves, developing strategies to decrease any additional burdens you may impose and convincing them of the ultimate benefits of your study. You need to be especially sensitive to the emotional stress that the family is under and you will need to allow plenty of time during the planning stages for recruitment and data collection.

Evidence suggests that these families are pressured and stressed and so involving them in research has the potential to heighten their vulnerability and increase this stress (Stevens et al., 2010). When you finally gain access to parents you will need to go through that again and you will need to be very sensitive to the trauma these parents are going through. It is likely to be necessary to undertake some additional training in this area. Children and families may find the research burdensome, lacking in personal benefit and in some cases invasive (Gattuso et al., 2005).

Bereaved children

Cole et al. (2003) show that although the numbers of children experiencing the death of a parent are comparatively small, it does lead to elevated levels of mental health and adaptation problems. Furthermore the vast majority will experience the death of a close person before the age of 18 years old, including grandparents, siblings, friends and older relatives (Ribbens McCarthy, 2007). There is some research done with children who are bereaved but many of our lessons about studying bereavement tend to come from adult studies to translate techniques and recommendations for research with children.

Bereaved individuals are especially vulnerable due to the nature of their distress but research can be done safely and ethically. Our understanding of children and young people's experiences of bereavement has mostly centred on cognitive understandings of death but the meanings young people ascribe to bereavement are equally important (Ribbens McCarthy, 2007), with isolation and loneliness being prominent themes, which is particularly important as much of the grief experienced by children and young people goes unrecognised (Holland, 2001).

If you are going to do research with bereaved children you will need to be especially sensitive to their distress. It is recommended that you will need to have some bereavement training and some experience in the field before you attempt research of this nature (Dyregrov, 2004). Children are often sheltered from bereavement and are not afforded opportunities to talk about their grief and distress (Black, 1996). Therefore, research has potential to give them a chance to talk about their feelings. Parents have reported that participating in research interviews can have a therapeutic effect (Hynson et al., 2006) and it is possible that this applies equally to children.

If you are going to undertake a research project with bereaved children, then a number of lessons can be learned from research. Research with bereaved parents indicates that it is best not to approach participants during the first six months of their bereavement and that the initial approach should be in the form of a sensitively written letter (Hynson et al., 2006). In the same way as other types of research, in order to approach the children you will need to address this letter to a guardian/parent in the first instance. Be careful as research could be seen as an unwanted intrusion and may cause additional distress (Holland, 2001).

However, remember that ethics committees are likely to have concerns about the potential intrusiveness of research. It is important that you consider the needs of the participants and what they want, rather than what suits you. There are clear issues of risk in research with children who are bereaved as they experience powerful emotions of grief and their sense of vulnerability is heightened (Ribbens McCarthy, 2007). It is important that you provide your participants with information on further support and inform them that you are not a counsellor (Holland, 2001).

Summary

In this chapter we have shown that children are not a homogenous group, but are unique individuals with unique characteristics. For research purposes you may need to categorise your child group in some way but remember that even when you do this children will not all conform to a particular set of characteristics. In this chapter we have highlighted a number of especially vulnerable groups and provided some practical strategies for beginning a research project with them. You will need to take particular care with especially vulnerable groups of children in terms of the whole design process and the material presented in this section of the book should be useful in thinking about those issues.

Further reading

ACT for Children (2012) 'Terms explained'. www.act.org.uk/page.asp?section=35&sectionTitle=Terms+explained (accessed 07/02/2012).

Benjamin, H. and MacKinlay, D. (2010) 'Communicating challenges: overcoming disability', in S. Redsell and A. Hastings (eds), *Listening to Children and Young People in Healthcare Consultations.* Oxon: Radcliffe Publishing, pp. 151–168.

Borzekowski, D.L. and Rickert, V.I. (2001) 'Adolescent cybersurfing for health information: a new resource that crosses barriers', *Archives of Pediatrics and Adolescent Medicine,* 155 (7): 813–817.

Dixon-Woods, M., Young, B. and Ross, E. (2006) 'Researching chronic childhood illness: the example of childhood cancer', *Chronic Illness,* 2: 165–177.

DuBois, J.M. (2008) *Solving Ethical Problems in Ethics in Mental Health Research.* New York: Oxford University Press.

Ellis, B., Kia-Keating, M., Yusef, S., Lincoln, A. and Nur, A. (2007) 'Ethical research in refugee communities and the use of community participatory methods', *Transcultural Psychiatry,* 44 (3): 459–481.

Heptinstall, E. (2000) 'Gaining access to looked after children for research purposes: lessons learned', *British Journal of Social Work,* 30: 867–872.

Murray, C. (2005) 'Children and young people's participation and non-participation in research', *Adoption and Fostering,* 29 (1): 57–66.

Stevens, M., Lord, B., Proctor, M.T., Nagy, S. and O'Riordan, E. (2010) 'Research with vulnerable families caring for children with life-limiting conditions', *Qualitative Health Research,* 20 (4): 496–505.

UCSF (University of California, San Francisco) (2008) *Use of Web Based Outreach Strategies to Reach Teens: Findings from the Teen SMART Outreach Evaluation.* www.familypact.org/Files/Provider/Research%20Reports/TSO_Web-BasedOutreachStudy_FinalReport_1-16-09.pdf (accessed 05/02/2012).

Vostanis, P. (ed.) (2007) *Mental Health Interventions and Services for Vulnerable Children and Young People.* London: Jessica Kingsley Publishers.

8

Recruiting Children and Families: Communicating with Gatekeepers, Parents and Children

---

| Overview

After reading through this chapter you should be able to:

- Identify some of the broader challenges related to accessing children for research purposes
- Recognise the value of building good relationships with gatekeepers
- Modify your communication techniques with institutional representatives
- Plan for communicating with parents
- Differentiate between different types of gatekeeper
- Discriminate the special challenges with different groups of children
- Relate to children in a more effective way
- Appreciate why people engage in or refuse research participation

Key words: communication, gatekeepers, institutions, recruitment, samples

---

Introduction

This chapter is designed to help you to think about the challenges and difficulties in accessing a sample of children for your research. It highlights the broader issues you need to think about when designing your project in terms of access and communication. The chapter focuses on helpful recruitment strategies and gives guidance on how to communicate with gatekeepers as well as the children themselves. It is written to help you decide how you practically recruit children to research projects and how to communicate with children during the research process.

Involving stakeholders in research

The use of the term 'stakeholder' has gained popularity over the last few decades, meaning a person or organisation that has a legitimate interest in a project or entity, and has mostly been applied in the world of business and economics. Primarily in a progressively market-driven private sector, it involves large business corporations, government agencies and non-profit organisations with an interest, or 'stake', in what the project or entity does or should do. Stakeholders also include vendors, employees and customers, but even members of a community where its offices or factory may affect the local economy or environment.

Post et al. (2002: 19) define stakeholder as 'the individuals and constituencies that contribute, either voluntarily or involuntarily, to its wealth-creating capacity and activities, and that are therefore its potential beneficiaries and/or risk bearers'. In other words, stakeholders are defined as those groups without whose support an organisation has no purpose and would be unable to survive.

Stakeholders in research with children

Stakeholders are also important in research and are those who have interest in the research project and its outcomes. They can help the design and implementation of research. For example, if you are researching children with autism and their experience of psychiatric services, then useful stakeholders might be children who have autism, parents of children with autism, psychiatrists, service managers and autism charity representatives. These are all people who have a perspective about autism and services, and may be able to help direct your research.

The sociology of childhood and the discourse of children's rights (discussed in Chapter 1) have started to change the way children are viewed and the way they are researched. Involving children and families in the research process is now more commonplace and researchers are now taking children's views more seriously. It is, therefore, important that you use a stakeholder group to help with your project. This can be quite difficult in practice and you need to be careful not to just do this in a tokenistic way. You need to ensure you really listen to your stakeholder group, that you give them enough information about your project so that they can actually help with it and that you consider the changes suggested and justify when you do not act on them. As stated previously, in thinking about your stakeholders take a critical and reflective approach, challenging your assumptions.

Locating the sample

Different types of research with specific aims and objectives will require recruitment of various groups of children. It is not simply a case of going out onto the street and finding children who seem suitable for inclusion. You need to plan ahead and think about the best way of accessing the type of children you want for your research. Many studies involving families rely on samples of convenience (Holder et al., 1998) but while convenience sampling can be effective, it may miss broader or more specific populations.

Institutions often provide a useful 'gate' for accessing children. A number of common locations from which to recruit children include but are not restricted to:

- Schools/nurseries
- After school clubs
- Church/religious groups
- Hospitals
- Hospices
- Child and Adolescent Mental Health Services (child psychiatry)
- GP surgeries
- Charity organisations

- Sports groups
- Youth clubs
- Play groups
- Support groups

Schools are common places for researchers to find a particular group of children for their study. Hospitals and other child services are also common sources, often for health related research. While a school or a hospital might seem like the most obvious location for accessing children, they may or may not be the most suitable place to try to recruit. Schools, hospitals and many other institutional settings have a variety of demands placed on them and may have been approached by a multitude of researchers previously to you. They may also not be representative of the samples required for your study, for example, schools in advantaged areas may not be representative of children in the wider locality.

It is important, therefore, that you really think about where you might find the groups of children you are seeking to research. Obviously if you are looking at issues like education and the national curriculum, schools may be ideal. Likewise if you are researching children dying from chronic illnesses, a hospice may be a primary choice although not necessarily your only option. It is important nonetheless not to narrow your thinking at the beginning of the project.

There are many places where parents can be consulted without the need to include an institutional representative. You could also advertise in local papers, use the internet, or use opportunity sampling by asking people you know to identify suitable children for your research. For example, if your research project is relatively broad, such as exploring children's healthy eating patterns, you could put up flyers in a local supermarket or advertise in the local paper. There is of course the possibility that your **response rate**s may be lower than if you have an institutional gatekeeper helping you out and this may create a bias in terms of who responds to your project. The nature of your research may also make a difference. It may be easier to get parents/children to fill in a one-page questionnaire than engage in a 30-minute interview by recruiting in these ways.

Activity 8.1

Write down all of the possible sources where you may be able to access the population of children and families you want to reach. How many possibilities are there? What is the most realistic? Think about how many children you need to access as this may make a difference.

Screening the sample: inclusion and exclusion criteria

When you have decided the most appropriate location for accessing the children you want to include in your research it is important that you screen the sample in relation to the inclusion and exclusion criteria that you put in place. You should have decided which types of children you want to include and which you want to exclude when you were planning your project. For example, it may be as simple as only wanting girls in your research, or you may want to exclude those over a particular age. You may need to consider how a school which has both girls and boys will view excluding boys from the research. However, approaching all-girl institutions may bring its own biases.

While you may have clear inclusion and exclusion criteria for your research you need to remember that if you are accessing children through an institutional gatekeeper you will not have full control over the screening. There are several issues associated with access through a gatekeeper:

1 Gatekeepers may try to be overly helpful and only give you names of children they think will cooperate, thus eliminating potentially interesting cases from your research.
2 Gatekeepers may also screen the sample and not allow you access to children who may be difficult, may cast the institution in a poor light or who are viewed as too vulnerable.
3 It can be quite difficult to convince gatekeepers that you want a range of different children for your project and you will often not have direct access to the full available sample.
4 Access will, however, be facilitated if you build up a good rapport with the gatekeeper. This will be discussed in more depth later in the chapter.

Often studies involving families as participants fail to adequately document the recruitment issues, fail to justify their subject selection sample, fail to specify their sample recruitment success/failure, and don't provide an estimation of effect from inherent biases of partial failures in recruitment of desired samples (Holder et al., 1998). It is important to note down in your research diary any recruitment issues you have as your project unfolds and relate back to these issues during dissemination.

The role of the gatekeeper

For a research project to be successful recruitment of the 'right' number of participants is essential, as problems in recruitment can cause significant delays to the project. Recruiting children to research often relies on a number of gatekeepers to protect them (Emmel et al., 2007; Murray, 2005; Piercy and Hargate, 2004) and is often especially challenging as children are viewed as vulnerable and not fully competent to make their own decisions (Munford and Sanders, 2004). A key aspect of whether children will participate in your study will relate to the role of the gatekeeper and your relationship with that gatekeeper. This means that gatekeepers have the potential to silence and exclude children from research without actually consulting them (Alderson, 2004). You might want to refer back to the previous chapter on children's capacity to make decisions to think about how influential the gatekeeper is.

We demonstrated earlier in the book that views of children and childhood are changing. There are four key components of the new studies of childhood approaches which include: children and young people are competent to choose to participate; children and young people's perspectives are not necessarily the same as the adults responsible for them; power relations between adults and children and young people require that care is exercised in how researchers engage them and the adults responsible for them; and childhood is not a unitary entity (Munford and Sanders, 2004).

To achieve this in research contexts, however, is difficult and you need to think about how you can provide children with some autonomy in your research process without offending, upsetting or patronising the gatekeepers who provide you with access. For example, if a child says that they do not want to take part in your research study, you may find that the parent becomes coercive and tries to persuade the child to take part. The parent might feel that the research is important or may just not like the child contradicting them. You should not allow this child to participate in the research if you are not certain that they want to take part, but you need to handle this sensitively to avoid compromising parental authority.

You need to think about the cultural context of this too. Remember that directly approaching young people in some cultures may be inappropriate and it is important to engage in dialogue with relevant communities so that you can identify appropriate strategies for talking to children and giving them some agency in the research while still respecting cultural precepts (Munford and Sanders, 2004).

While many forms of research will require communication with an institutional gatekeeper, most research with children will also require communication with the primary gatekeepers, i.e. the parents/legal guardians. There are few exceptions to the need to obtain the informed consent of parents/ guardians to access child participants for your research. Parents have primary responsibility to ensure their children's safety and while researchers are trying to promote children's freedom to participate and speak for themselves, there is still a need to respect parental authority and parents' legal position as the child's guardians; you may want to refer back to Chapters 3 and 4 at this point.

Communicating with institutional representatives

To undertake research with children in institutional settings you need to gain permission to access that setting and it is possible that you may encounter some barriers at this point. Institutional gatekeepers may have some concerns regarding the ethics and legal implications of your proposed research and they are likely to have limited time to engage in consultation with you about those issues. It is thus very important that you concisely communicate the key issues in your research in a convincing and clear way. This will be necessary both in correspondence and face-to-face.

You will need to think about how you manage your contact with the institutional gatekeeper. It may be possible that you have an identified key contact through a friend, through your work, through your supervisor or some other means. If, however, you have no contacts in that institution then you are likely to find it more difficult to identify an appropriate point of contact and convince them to talk to you about your project. There are several ways you can do this. Using the internet to identify key personnel in organisations will mean that your contact can be more personal and that you have a better chance of identifying the right person to help you. You will need to write that person a clear and friendly letter outlining who you are and why you are contacting them. In this letter you may want to say that you will follow up the letter with a phone call on a particular date and ask them to contact you if this is not convenient. It is important that you provide them with as many means of contact as possible, include your work landline, your mobile (cell) number and your email address. An example that we have used for one of our projects can be seen in Box 8.1. Note, however, that this letter was sent after telephone contact with the manager and extensive communication with that person.

Box 8.1 Invitation letter

[*Sponsoring organisation logo here*]

[*Researcher's name and address here*]

[*Email address and telephone number here*]

Dear [*you should insert the name of the gatekeeper here to make it personal*]

We are writing to you to invite you to participate in a research study. We work for the University of [*insert name*] and are currently undertaking health research at the [*name place here*].

(Continued)

(Continued)

The research is a study looking at the interactions between families and clinicians at the first appointment with the mental health service. We recognise that the relationship between families and the professionals they see is an important one and we want to look in greater detail at the development of this relationship from the first appointment. It is essential, therefore, that we can record these sessions to analyse at a later date to explore these details.

We hope that our research will lead to improvements in service delivery and the communication in this important setting.

Please find attached the information sheets which will provide greater detail regarding the study. Please also find attached copies of consent forms for family members. If you have any queries please feel free to contact the research team using the above contact details. Members of the research team will also be available on the day to answer any of your questions.

Yours sincerely

[*sign your letter here*]

Be prepared for many rejections as people in organisations are often busy and you and your research will not be their primary concern. Try to put something eye-catching and interesting in the letter to grab their attention and make them remember you. If they decline to participate, ask them if they know of anyone else in that institution or another one that might be interested. That way when you get in touch with them you can say that you were given their details by a specific named individual (snowballing).

When deciding whether to allow you access to the institution it is likely that the gatekeeper will draw upon their personal preferences, experiences and opinions and you need to be respectful of them as you attempt to persuade them of the benefits of allowing you in. Gatekeepers are likely to base their decisions on models of children's competence and developmental age and fears of or confidence in parental reactions (Heath et al., 2004).

There may be several reasons why you are denied access by an institution and you will need to be patient with them and think about possible alternative places for you to recruit your sample. Try not to be too dependent upon a single institution as they may not grant you access. Institutions may also have concerns about the potential institutional inconvenience, perceived inappropriateness of the research topic/methods, or a reluctance to expose quasi-private worlds to public scrutiny (Heath et al., 2004). You may need to change your strategy for recruitment and you may need to think of ways to access your sample without involving institutions (for a case study see Campbell, 2008).

There are various factors you need to remember when communicating with institutional representatives – some of these relate to your style of communicating with people (Box 8.2), some relate to the demands on the gatekeeper (Box 8.3) and some relate to ethical concerns (Box 8.4).

Box 8.2 Your style of communicating with people

- Always be polite.
- Demonstrate that you are aware that they are very busy people and you are yet another demand on their time.
- Follow up discussions in writing to clarify and confirm key objectives or actions. This can be in email form if helpful.
- Try to build a relationship with that key gatekeeper. Show that you can be trusted. Do what you say you will do and within the agreed time frames. Be organised and clear at all times and be professional.
- Avoid patronising language.
- Avoid research jargon.

Be aware that the way in which you communicate with people, the language you use and the nature of the relationship you build is essential for gaining access to the group of children you want to reach.

Box 8.3 Demands on the gatekeeper

- Be patient. Institutions can often take considerable time to respond to you. It is acceptable to chase people up but be careful not to become a nuisance.
- Expect to fit in with their schedules rather than expecting them to fit in with yours (for example, a school we (Dogra) approached to participate in a study said yes simply on the basis that we were respectful of their time. They had also just been approached by other researchers who stipulated their expectations of the school (to the point of stating when they expected questionnaires to be completed) and were surprised to find that the school declined to participate.
- Avoid bothering people at especially busy times (for example, during the exams in schools, or at the times of religious festivals).

If you are dealing with institutions you need to think about the time of year and time of day you are getting in touch and you will need to be patient. You may need to remind them that you need their help but be careful not to be pushy when doing this.

Box 8.4 Ethical concerns

- It is useful to write to the gatekeepers to introduce yourself and the project and then follow this up with a meeting
- Identify a key member of personnel and have all communication with that one person so as to avoid confusion and to ensure that communication is consistent
- Be clear where you have your ethical approval from and show the gatekeeper how you are addressing any key ethical concerns
- Be prepared to answer lots of questions and offer to set up a meeting for all interested parties
- If they say no then do not be pushy. You sometimes just have to accept that you cannot recruit through that institution

---

When you are communicating with gatekeepers it is important to be mindful of the ethical commitments that you have. At this point you may want to refer back to what you agreed with the ethics committee. In practice it can be challenging to be patient and address all of the concerns that gatekeepers may have. This will be facilitated if you forge partnerships with the gatekeepers and actively involve them in the whole process, rather than just at the recruitment phase (O'Reilly et al., 2012b)

Factors to consider when recruiting children from schools

Recruiting children through schools can be especially challenging. Schools are busy places with educational concerns and often a large number of staff. Schools also have layers of personnel with a head teacher usually overseeing the running of the school. It may be necessary to secure the consent of the head teacher to access the teachers before you can gain access to the children. Remember that you may have to gain permission at a number of levels and remember that the primary objective of schools is to educate children, not involve them in research.

It is also useful to think about the type of school you are approaching. Schools with younger children are likely to have a different staff/child ratio, are more likely to have more personal relationships with parents and potentially have fewer children attending, but may have greater concerns about vulnerability and competence. Schools with older children are likely to be busier places, have more exam stress and children are more likely to have lots of different teachers and it may be more difficult to identify key gatekeepers to support you.

When you are trying to gain access to a particular school you should prepare for and understand the specific characteristics of that school, identify the gatekeeper or person with authority and communicate the benefits of your research project to the school (Rice et al., 2007).

Example one

In the new project exploring mental health in Gujurati children (Dogra), children were recruited through schools from London and Leicester. This recruitment happened in three stages. First, because of the target sample, appropriate schools were identified using the internet. Second, school head teachers were contacted by letter and invited to an open discussion in their respective parts of the country. This meant one meeting in Leicester, but more individual meetings with interested schools in London. Third, because of the focus on mental health and evaluation of a particular initiative, child mental health professionals and school representatives, including SENCOs (Special Educational Needs Coordinators) and Pastoral Care Managers were invited to a second meeting to discuss strategies for questionnaire administration, for those schools expressing an interest in participating. Nine schools from the 30 invited participated, with a total of 2,900 children involved in the questionnaire.

You may not require such a large sample of children for your research but the lessons are important. You must identify suitable schools depending on your criteria and research question. It is a good idea to contact head teachers of those schools and invite them to a meeting. If you are only using one school then you should request a meeting with that head teacher to discuss your ideas and then follow this up with additional meetings involving interested parties. Remember to leave them printed documentation of the research with your contact details. You will find it useful to have some knowledge of the administrative structure of the school and bear in mind that ultimately you will need a named representative to help you recruit the children when you get to that stage (Testa and Coleman, 2006).

Factors to consider when recruiting children from clinical settings

It can be especially difficult to recruit children from clinical settings. It is likely to be the case that these children are especially vulnerable because of a physical or mental health problem. Children with chronic illnesses, disabilities, mental health problems, learning difficulties, physical impairments and so forth are considered especially vulnerable and in need of protection by gatekeepers. Clinical professionals, such as doctors, psychiatrists, surgeons, consultants, nurses and so forth are charged with a duty of care for vulnerable children and their families. Bear in mind that if you are recruiting children from clinical settings it is likely to require negotiation with multiple layers of gatekeepers at different stages of the research process (Coyne, 2009). The nature of the child's condition can position the whole family as more vulnerable and the professional will take care to protect all members; their positions may be influenced by a range of factors including assumptions about what young people may or may not want. Health professionals, due to their in-depth knowledge of the child's illness and the family's situation, are well placed to screen and select suitable children for the research and thus protect those who are more vulnerable from the 'burden' of research participation, although problematically this may mean that some children are excluded without a sound rationale because of the gatekeeper's personal beliefs and varying positions on protection (Coyne, 2009).

Example two

Terminally ill children may present specific challenges. In a hospital or hospice setting a range of clinical staff may have been involved in providing care and support for the children and their parents. If asked by those clinicians to participate in the research they may feel coerced and clinicians may be wary of this and not ask some families who may in fact want to participate. The clinical professionals involved in the child's care may feel that the child does not have the physical strength to participate and that the family does not have the emotional strength to engage or that research is not something the family have time for and may refuse you access. It is important to be aware of the complex nature of these relationships.

Example three

General practitioners see children about their general health care needs and this can often be an interesting setting in which to understand children's health. GPs are, however, very busy people, seeing a lot of patients in a day (not all children), and may not have the time to accommodate reading information sheets and providing consent. It can be disruptive of their practice and time-consuming. They will really need to understand the benefits of your research to engage and will need to be motivated to help you recruit. In this case if a GP is not really convinced about the value of your research, they may take the simplest route and decline to participate in any way.

Example four

Children with mental health problems are potentially more likely to attend at a CAMHS to be assessed, although it is important to note that many do not. These children are considered more vulnerable by virtue of their problems and families are often stressed and finding life difficult. You will need the psychiatrist/psychologist or other mental health professional to agree to help you recruit families to your study, and again these are busy professionals with a job to do and bear in mind that their own experiences, both personal and professional, may make a difference.

Difficulties in recruiting children: a case example

Things do not always go as planned when recruiting children and communicating with institutional representatives. You may need to rethink your strategy, change your institution or alter your project.

A PhD student studying with us faced considerable challenges when recruiting 14–16-year-old young people for a study about emotional and behavioural difficulties and mental health. The qualitative study required interviews with approximately 15 young people and 15 teachers. During the planning stage of this project it seemed obvious that the most suitable setting to obtain both samples was school.

Ethical approval was obtained from the University. The student had links with two schools through her occupation so easily identified key gatekeepers in both schools. Accessing the teacher sample was relatively straightforward but it soon became apparent that accessing the young people was going to be more complicated. We outline the main difficulties in Box 8.5. Before you refer to the box, can you think of the potential issues raised?

Box 8.5   Difficulties in gaining access

After a number of letters, phone calls and emails, not a single adolescent had been interviewed. Following some communication between the student and the school three main reasons came to light regarding why access was problematic.

1 Practicality: there was at that time significant pressure on teachers' time which gave way to a general reluctance for teachers to take up the gatekeeper role and thus facilitate access to the necessary population. This is likely to have been because of the additional time demands required to liaise with parents and engage in consent procedures.
2 Reliability of pupil data: the terms behavioural, emotional and social difficulties seemed to be used in a more encompassing way by teachers to describe a large range of different pupils. Problematically this had potential to reduce the reliability of the data, as it was dependent upon the subjective judgement of the teachers. Because teachers had different interpretations regarding the terms emotional and behavioural difficulties, they were recommending access to pupils that would not provide the kind of data desired as related to mental health, and this had potential to compromise the project.
3 Validity of pupil data: gatekeepers seemed especially reluctant to allow access to children with more severe behavioural and emotional difficulties as they feared that this may exacerbate the situation.

After some consideration it was agreed that in this case sampling from school was probably not the most appropriate method. As this project focused on the mental health of children with emotional and behavioural difficulties these young people could also be accessed via a Child and Adolescent Mental Health Service. The student had links with this service and already had good relationships with clinical professionals and service managers. The decision to switch location for the young person data was a difficult one to take and one that is not often taken by researchers, as it can have a negative effect on final outcomes. To make such a major change at this point in a project can feel daunting and like hard work but to maintain the quality of the research it may be necessary. This student appreciated that perhaps the best route for data collection had not been chosen. As the research had not progressed too far it was realistic and sensible to seek out alternative strategies.

As the mental health service was an NHS one, ethical approval was required from NRES. Fortunately contingency time had been built into the project during the planning phase and there was additional time available for this process. This reflects good planning on the part of the student to recognise that research does not always go to plan and thus confining oneself to very tight time frames would not be sensible. By planning ahead this student had sufficient time to change location and undertake the additional work necessary.

What this case example highlights is that even when gatekeepers are willing and cooperative, there may be factors beyond their control and yours as a researcher which delay or hinder your research project. It is important to have contingency plans for recruitment, recognise the complexities and sometimes make radical and brave choices to rescue your research. Misunderstanding, different jargon and different interpretations of phenomena can leave the researcher unmotivated or with very different data which fails to meet the aims of the research or answer the research question. It is important to take steps early on in the project to ensure this does not happen, and not wait until it is too late.

Activity 8.2

What difficulties can you foresee for your own research project? Write down a list of possible settings from which you could access your sample and think about which one is more appropriate. What do you think might be the potential barriers to access? How might you be able to overcome these?

Factors to consider to ensure relevant participation

Communication

There are a number of specific issues that you need to consider which may be relevant to your research question and one of the most important relates to communication.

- Are factors of participant literacy taken into account?
- Are materials translated and are interpreters available if required?
- Does the interview have the flexibility to allow participation of those with disabilities such as hearing impairment or speech difficulties?
- Where and how does recruitment take place?
- Are invitations inclusive or likely to exclude some groups/individuals?
- Are the tools or schedules being used in the research age and context appropriate?

Working with communities where you are not a member

There are potentially advantages and disadvantages of working with communities that one does not personally belong to. Much has been made about the need to employ community link workers or brokers who can mediate for the research team. The individuals who play these roles have as many vested interests as anyone else and how their participation influences the research process needs to be considered. As in health care delivery there are those that are reassured by seeing someone who speaks the same language or superficially looks like them. But there are those who worry about confidentiality within small communities. Again the research question may be the most important factor to consider in how to best engage the community. The Gujarati project run by Dogra (highlighted earlier) involved recruitment through schools and some of the success in recruiting schools was because great care was taken to make sure that assumptions were not made that each school operated in the same way. The researchers were mindful that each school is a community in its own right and the engagement process left it open for the school to communicate how they could best help.

Addressing fears or suspicions about the research

To some extent this may be covered by thinking about the issues discussed in the section on communication above. However, at times one may need to demonstrate awareness of the historical or local contexts that may impact on local communities to participate in research. In the USA the infamous Tuskegee experiments understandably left African American communities suspicious of research supposedly in their interests. Research in sensitive areas may provoke defensiveness and fears in others. A very emotive example is that of the small but real increased risk of child disability linked to children of marriages between first cousins. The acceptability of this practice is limited to particular groups though not banned except in most of the USA. Trying to research in such an area means considering the sensibilities of both sides but ensuring the research is driven by quality information rather than the polar perspectives that tend to be publicised. Those who are supportive of the principle of such marriages argue on the basis that to identify such practices is discriminatory and those that are not in favour argue that the science cannot be argued. Addressing questions of the different ways in which girls and boys are treated can also threaten people in that they may feel they are being identified as being guilty of something.

In practical terms, good community links can help address some of these issues. It is worth noting that the more potentially sensitive an area, the more ground work is generally needed.

Communicating with parents

To access children or young people for your research it is very likely (with only rare exceptions) that you will need to gain the informed consent of their parents/legal guardians (maybe social workers in some cases) first. This means that you need to communicate effectively with these gatekeepers in order to secure their support for your project. This can be done face-to-face by setting up a question–answer meeting or can just be through letters sent out. It is helpful to have the cooperation of gatekeepers who can send out letters on your behalf to parents as you may not have access to addresses and so forth.

Parents play a key role in consultations with children and are important gatekeepers. The more supportive parents are of your research the more likely the child will be to engage in your project and talk to you; alternatively parents may shut down the child's involvement by denying access or limiting their contribution by remaining present and interrupting the child (McPherson, 2010). You will need to handle this sensitively. You need to respect the parent and their contribution and listen to what they have to say but always return your focus back to the child and do your best to allow the child space to express their opinion. This may mean that it takes longer to collect your data than anticipated, but be careful not to rush the child or be rude to the parent.

In some research situations, it will be necessary for you to build up a rapport with the parents and build up a trusting relationship. To facilitate trust you need to be empathic towards the parent and the child and you may need to spend considerable time among the community and with parents to build up and develop relationships (Emmel et al., 2007). You will need to reassure parents that there will be no severe detrimental effects on the child because of their participation. For example, some parents worry that participating in research takes the child away from valuable education time (Rice et al., 2007). You really need to think about when you collect the data. Does it have to be done during class time? Will the child be resentful if you do it at break time? By communicating effectively with both parents and teachers a suitable time for all parties should be agreed.

A useful way to facilitate communication with parents, as with most gatekeepers, is to involve them during the planning stages of the research. This does not necessarily have to be the same parents who are involved later. By having parents involved in the design and planning of your project they are likely to identify issues or problems that you had not thought of. They can also be helpful in thinking up solutions. Furthermore you can show how parents have been involved in the research process when engaging in the recruitment process, which may make parents of potential participants feel more secure. It is also important to talk to parents of whom you are seeking consent in advance of the research, asking them about any concerns or fears they may have and asking them to propose their concerns or ideas about how to talk to their children or gain any information that may be useful to you (Hadley et al., 2008).

Communicating with children

In contemporary research it is now generally accepted that children have the ability to make decisions for themselves and that they are competent to integrate information and beliefs to communicate effectively with professionals (McPherson, 2010), as discussed in Chapter 4. It is good practice in research to actively involve children in decision-making and give them the opportunity to ask questions and express their opinions (Willmott, 2010). When communicating with children through the recruitment and data collection phases of your project you will need to think about their chronological age, their cognitive ability and their communication abilities. You need to consider what it is you are asking the child to do and ensure that it is within the child's capabilities. Identify what you can do to help them. During recruitment this will mean that you need to prepare a child-friendly information sheet, a simple comprehensible consent form.

You need to have some respect for the child and their autonomy. By the time you actually get to see the child you may have had to go through a long and onerous process. You may be tempted to see the child's consent as a simple formality. If the child then declines to participate it can be tempting to try and persuade them, or see them as being obstructive or deliberately obtuse, but it is important to remember that whatever may have gone before, and no matter who has agreed to the child being asked to participate and however much time you have invested in getting access to this child, the child still has to consent to participate.

You need to maintain insight into the power relationship you have with the child. Children can be anxious during the recruitment process. Remember, you may be a stranger to them and either way you are potentially an adult with authority. You need to be mindful of how your status may influence the ways in which the child responds to you. Try to take special care over the way you give instructions, check with them that they understand things and be careful not to use jargon.

It may seem like what we present here is just a list of problems and difficulties you are likely to encounter, but there are a number of solutions and strategies that can facilitate communication and improve your research:

1 Be patient. You need to stay calm and recognise that research of this nature will be time-consuming. You shouldn't be undertaking a project with this group if you don't have sufficient time for the early stages.
2 Be polite and professional. Keep communication channels open. Send email or postal reminders without being pushy. Follow up with phone calls and be friendly.
3 Identify a core person and maintain contact with that person.
4 Be aware of coercion, particularly when communicating with children. Try to be sure that they really are happy to participate and provide them with opportunities to change their mind.
5 Be sensitive to the needs of all parties during recruitment.

Effective communication with children and their parents is essential for the success of your research project, but it may also help you to think about the reasons why these children and their parents might agree to participate in your research. By understanding what motivates participation in research you may be able to address some of the limitations or problems in recruitment.

Activity 8.3

Make a list of all the reasons you can think of regarding why children and their parents might agree to participate in research and then narrow this list down to think about why they might engage in your specific project and why they might not. We provide some general answers to this activity at the back of the book.

Why do children and families get involved in research?

Recruiting children and families to your project might be more difficult than you expected. Asking children and families to engage in research means that they have to give up time, go through the process of filling in forms and trust that you will treat them with respect and protect them from harm. Some types of research, such as medical research, are more demanding than others and the levels of personal gain from participation can vary. To help you think about how you might recruit and persuade children and families to take part in your research with the ethical restrictions in place it is useful to think about why families agree to take part.

Children and family participation

It is considered desirable to include children and families in research, as researching their perspectives can help with policy developments. There are some differences in the literature regarding how parents feel about allowing their children decision-making rights. Some research shows that most parents see their children as lacking the maturity to decide whether to take part in research (Swartling et al., 2009). This is supported by ethics committees who tend to stipulate that you need consent from the child as well as the parents, and if the parent believes that the child cannot make his or her own decision then you need to maintain respect for the parent while still obtaining some form of assent/consent from the child, which can be tricky. Talk to the parents at length: you need to build up a rapport with them and understand why they are engaging with you in your research. Make sure you respect their viewpoints, do not be too pushy and be sensitive to their culture, class and family dynamics.

There is little information about what motivates children and families to cooperate in research or about what factors influence their decision-making (Dixon-Woods and Tarrant, 2009). In quantitative research the researcher relies heavily on successful recruitment of large numbers of volunteers and people can be put off from taking part because of risks or scandals publicised through the media.

There are several reasons why people participate in quantitative research and these tend to be on a personal and social level. On a personal level, motivation for engagement relates to the fulfilment of a personal need to have a voice and on a social level, motivation relates to being altruistic and helping others (Tarpery, 2006). This is consistent with medical research where participants often agree that they view medical research as doing a public good deed (Dixon-Woods and Tarrant, 2009).

Participants are generally prepared to reveal a large amount of personal and sensitive information in a piece of qualitative research (Clark, 2010) and this may reflect the fact that participants commonly hold the view that qualitative research is a harmless activity and is less risky (Peel et al., 2006). Some participants may feel that the interview or focus group is therapeutic or supportive and, coupled with the perception of low risk, may be more willing to engage (Clark, 2010). It is therefore evident that people take part in qualitative research to be altruistic, gain some therapeutic benefit and because they see it as less risky. As a researcher, however, you need to be clear what risks are involved in your qualitative project and be sure that participants have fully understood what is expected of them.

Taking part in medical/clinical research

While parents will need to weigh the risks against the benefits in allowing you access to their children for research in all types, allowing access to children for medical research is more specialised. Medical research carries specific risks to the child and may mean that the child is especially vulnerable. While medical research is essential to advance our understanding of a range of childhood illnesses and conditions, it does rely on the cooperation of parents.

Fisher et al. (2011) reviewed the literature regarding the reasons parents chose to accept or decline an invitation to enrol their children in clinical research. They included 16 qualitative studies, written in the English language, which explored the experiences of parents living in five countries whose children had a range of health conditions of varying severity. The health status of the child appeared to influence parents' reasons for participation. Parents whose children had life-threatening conditions often considered they had no choice but to participate and many welcomed the innovation offered through research participation. It is worth noting that research may also have offered hope in otherwise hopeless situations, so it is perhaps understandable that such parents also viewed the risks of research less negatively than those whose children were healthy or in the stable stage of a chronic condition. They concluded that a tailored approach is needed when discussing research participation with parents of eligible children. For example, while parents of healthy children may be more open to discussions of altruism, those whose children have life-threatening illnesses should be given adequate information about the alternatives to, and risks of, research participation. However, children should also be asked about their participation and this is discussed in more detail later. Research with children and families is therefore important to help us better understand children's perspectives about the issues that affect their lives.

Summary

In this chapter we have drawn your attention to a number of issues related to the challenges of recruiting children and families to your research project. Ostensibly it may seem that children are everywhere and you may have thought that it was relatively straightforward to access children but as this chapter highlights there are actually a number of complexities that you need to think about. You need to be introspective about your skills and ability to communicate with a number of different parties, including children themselves. At this point you may want to readdress your training needs and certainly you should consult colleagues before you begin.

Further reading

Clark, T. (2010) 'On "being researched": why do people engage with qualitative research?' *Qualitative Research*, 10 (4): 399–419.

Dixon-Woods, M. and Tarrant, C. (2009) 'Why do people cooperate with medical research? Findings from three studies', *Social Science and Medicine*, 68: 2215–2222.

Emmel, N., Hughes, K., Greenhalgh, J. and Sales, A. (2007) 'Accessing socially excluded people: trust and the gatekeeper in the researcher–participant relationship', *Sociological Research Online*, 12 (2). www.socresonline.org.uk/12/2/emmel.html (doi: 10.5153/sro.1512) (accessed 23/07/2012).

Gattuso, J., Hinds, P., Tong, X. and Srivastava, K. (2005) 'Monitoring child and parent refusals to enrol in clinical research protocols', *Journal of Advanced Nursing* 53 (3): 319–326.

Hadley, E., Smith, C., Gallo, A., Angst, D. and Knaff, K. (2008) 'Parents' perspectives on having their children interviewed for research', *Research in Nursing and Health*, 31: 4–11.

McPherson, A. (2010) 'Involving children: why it matters', in S. Redsell and A. Hastings (eds), *Listening to Children and Young People in Healthcare Consultations*. Oxon: Radcliffe Publishing, pp.15–30.

Melo-Martin, I. and Ho, A. (2008) 'Beyond informed consent: the therapeutic misconception and trust', *Journal of Medical Ethics*, 34: 202–205.

Peel, E., Parry, O., Douglas, M. and Lawton, J. (2006) '"It's no skin off my nose": why people take part in qualitative research', *Qualitative Health Research*, 16 (10): 1335–1349.

Rice, M., Bunker, K., Kang, D., Howell, C. and Weaver, M. (2007) 'Accessing and recruiting children for research in schools', *Western Journal of Nursing Research*, 29 (4): 501–514.

Willmott, A. (2010) 'Involving children: how to do it', in S. Redsell, and A. Hastings (eds), *Listening to Children and Young People in Healthcare Consultations*. Oxon: Radcliffe Publishing, pp. 45–55.

PART 3

PRACTICAL ISSUES

9

Choosing a Method for Your Research

Learning outcomes

By the end of this chapter you should be able to:

- Describe what is meant by ontology, epistemology and methodology
- Define quantitative research with children
- Define qualitative research with children
- Appraise the usefulness of mixing methods
- Distinguish the quality criteria for different methods
- Identify ways of engaging with stakeholders in your research project
- Conduct a pilot study

Key words: mixed methods, pilot study, qualitative design, quality, quantitative design, stakeholders

Introduction

This chapter is designed to provide you with knowledge to choose an appropriate method for your project with child participants. It is designed to help you decide on your methodology and demonstrate that there are many factors which contribute to those choices. In thinking about these issues you should be able to identify the methodological differences in research projects and the theories that underpin them. The importance of conducting a pilot study before you embark on the main data collection is discussed.

Introducing ontology, epistemology and methodology

Complicated terminology like this can be confusing for researchers and it can be difficult to see how theoretical levels are associated with the practical decision-making in a research project. Before we introduce you to the main methods you need to have some indication of the assumptions that underpin the methods. So we start with definitions:

- **Epistemology** is the theory of knowledge and relates to what we can know about something and how we can know it. Epistemologies ask questions about knowledge.
- **Ontology** relates to the nature of reality and questions whether the real world exists. It asks whether there is an independent reality which can be accessed through research.
- **Methodology** is the theory of methods and refers to the overall principles which define a set of methods which are tools for generating data. The methodology has to be chosen carefully as it is the means of testing reality.

(Guba and Lincoln, 2004).

The belief system of the researcher will have an impact on how the research is shaped. Epistemology means that different research designs have different ideas about the nature of knowledge, the value of knowledge and how knowledge should be generated.

Quantitative research is typically underpinned by **positivism** and views social reality as objective. Although there is a range of perspectives that use quantitative methods, quantitative research believes that human behaviour can be reduced and can be measured as it argues humans have fixed measurable qualities that cause them to behave in particular ways (Guba and Lincoln, 2004). In practice what this means is that they view children as fixed beings with measurable qualities. For example, they believe that children have personalities, intelligence levels and development in stages and that all of these can be measured through research.

Positivism reflects the natural sciences with the idea that objective knowledge can be generated from research and is value free. Among other things quantitative research seeks to establish what causes something to happen and what relationships exist between different factors and to determine frequencies. Research with children underpinned by positivism holds the view that knowledge can uncover the causes of behaviour. For example, with quantitative methods one can explore what observable aggressive behaviour occurs in the classroom, what types of behaviour and even when it occurs. Different theories have been developed regarding what may be causing the aggression (usually making reference to genetic and environmental influences) but these methods are less able to help us understand what might be complicating factors in specific children, especially if particular to a specific child and/or context, or why children are behaving in that manner.

Qualitative research focuses on words and meanings and does not seek to find a single or objective truth. Qualitative research operates from a number of different epistemological positions, including social constructionism, social constructivism, feminism, interpretivism and critical approaches. There are too many perspectives to detail here, but suffice to say that qualitative methodology has considerable diversity in its approaches.

Importantly, the ways in which the researcher views children and childhood will shape methodological choices. The nature of the research question and the position of the researcher will ultimately inform whether a quantitative or qualitative design is appropriate. We now introduce you to the main methods of research with children so that you might choose which method is most appropriate for your project.

Choosing quantitative or qualitative research

It is a good idea to situate which **paradigm** you are operating from before you start refining your topic and questions. The research process is dynamic and you will have to go back and forth through the stages to prepare adequately for your research.

Example one

If you are interested in comparing two groups of children, for example, boys with girls to record behaviour, then you can use a quantitative design. For example, a common quantitative question has been whether boys are more aggressive than girls. The levels of aggression are measured in controlled conditions and compared statistically to decide.

Example two

If you are interested in understanding the world from the child's point of view, appreciating how they experience something or what their opinion on a particular issue is, then you will need to use a qualitative method. In relation to the above topic, if you are interested in how children experience aggressive behaviour against them, for example, how they feel about being bullied, then qualitative methods will be more suitable.

Quantitative research with children

Using quantitative designs in child research is common and 'scientific' approaches to human behaviour have been dominant for decades. Quantitative research aims to isolate cause and effect, measure and quantify phenomena, determine frequencies, look for relationships between factors and use research to generalise findings. So in a quantitative study the child's characteristics or behaviours are coded and quantified and these numbers are analysed statistically.

Quantitative researchers typically use experimental designs, questionnaires and controlled trials to test out hypotheses and we provide more detail on these methods in Chapter 10. To conduct experiments with children effectively there is a need for **objectivity** and control and therefore the laboratory has historically been favoured. The experimental method has been used frequently in child research to explore a number of aspects of children's lives. For example, experiments have been conducted to measure typical levels of cognitive development, to explore children's social relationships and also their levels of intelligence, to name but a few.

Much of the information held about children comes from quantitative research. For example, you may suspect that boys are more aggressive than girls, you may suspect that children with extravert personalities are more likely to be bullies and those with introvert personalities more likely to be victims, you may suspect that older children have stronger cognitive abilities than younger children and so forth. These suspicions are most likely to come from the reading of the literature you have undertaken in any particular area and you will then want to test these ideas out. To do this you will need to develop a formal hypothesis and test it.

Developing a hypothesis

Quantitative research begins with a hypothesis – a prediction. You need to turn your area of interest into something that can be measured. Hypotheses make statements about the relationship between variables and differences between groups and the researcher tests that relationship. In research an experimental and a null hypothesis are developed.

An experimental hypothesis predicts that there will be a relationship between two variables:

- In children aged 5–11 years, are boys more aggressive than girls?

A null hypothesis predicts that no relationship will be found between the two variables and that there will be no difference between aggression in girls and boys, that is:

- Boys and girls display similar levels of aggression.

This means that a hypothesis predicts the relationship between two or more variables. In other words we believe that there will be a relationship between two or more variables (the experimental hypothesis). On some occasions, however, one has to accept that there may be no relationship between these variables and in this case accept the null hypothesis which predicts that any difference found is due to chance not an actual difference.

By testing a hypothesis using quantitative methods of data collection you will analyse the results using statistics to see if your hypothesis is supported or whether you accept the null hypothesis. From this you gather quantitative evidence to support your predictions.

Benefits and limitations of quantitative designs

There are several advantages to using a quantitative design in your research. Quantitative research designs are often favoured because the research problem is set out in very precise terms. What this means is that you are clear about which element of children's social world or developmental stage you are researching. You have a clear hypothesis to test and an objective measure. Typically conclusions about children may be considered more objective and may be judged to have been more scientifically reached. High levels of reliability are achieved which means that the experiment/observation can be repeated to test the results. This means that you can be more confident about your findings and about the robustness of your design.

Particularly advantageous in quantitative designs is that they minimise the influence of the researcher's attitudes and beliefs about children on the research. Be warned, however, that although quantitative design has procedures to minimise researcher bias, your attitudes, opinions and experiences of children may still influence the research.

Quantitative designs allow the researcher to analyse and measure the data to make predictions about particular groups of children. As quantitative research involves large numbers of children you are better placed to make claims about how other children may behave or act in similar situations to the conditions laid out in your research project. For example, if your research illustrates that boys are more aggressive than girls, you can make predictions about how boys and girls will play in the playground at school. This means that the results are generalisable to larger groups of children, assuming the inclusion criteria are not too restrictive.

One of the reasons therefore why quantitative research is popular is because data can be effectively communicated by the use of effective visually appealing and easily understood charts and graphs so that stakeholders and potentially the children themselves can access the findings. It is useful to feed back your findings to the children and the parents, as well as to wider academic audiences, and quantitative designs allow you to simplify your findings in layman's terms through visual means. Most children by a certain age will have seen a graph or a pie chart.

While it is clear that there are advantages to using a quantitative design for your project you do need to be aware that there are some limitations to using a quantitative design. Unfortunately, it may not always be possible to take context into account when designing the study. Using a quantitative design does not always provide the depth of information required about children's lives; this means that one may know that there is a difference between two groups of children but one will not know why. Going back to our earlier example, one may know that boys are more aggressive than girls and predict that they will play more aggressively in the playground, but from this data one will not know the reasons for the gender difference. Remember also that the answers may not actually reflect how children really feel about something. Just because a child provides a certain answer in response to a question does not mean it is accurate or true. The child may be providing you with socially desirable answers or may think it is funny to provide a certain response.

Quantitative research has been heavily criticised because statistics can be misrepresentative or misleading. Statistics can be manipulated to convey a certain message. Politically there are advantages in convincing the general public that unemployment figures are lower than they might be seen to be by leaving out certain groups of the population or changing the criteria for educational tests so that it looks like children are achieving higher standards. Have a think about all the statistics you see in everyday life and consider how they may be misleading you. How are children represented through statistics and why and how might these figures appear misleading?

If you are going to undertake a quantitative design with children then you will need to pay attention to your data collection technique. Data collection may be more difficult as younger children are likely to need extra help for some methods such as completing questionnaires. Remember that the cognitive ability of the child will influence whether they are able to answer the questions. This means that parents or teachers may be helping the child fill in the responses and the answers may reflect their attitudes or fears more than those of the child.

From this discussion you should now have some ideas regarding the benefits and limitations of using a quantitative design with children for your project. While there are some clear advantages to using this method there are some problems which may need your attention during the planning stages. An alternative design is qualitative research and you may choose to engage in a project using qualitative methods instead.

Qualitative research with children

In qualitative work there is more focus on meaning and qualitative researchers generally do not use numbers or statistics. Qualitative methods are typically used for exploratory work and generating understanding of phenomena. These methods access personal accounts and capture how individuals talk about their life experiences.

Due to the flexibility of qualitative methods they are well suited to understanding the meanings and experiences of children. Children tend to respond well to qualitative methods as they are the focus of attention and work is typically conducted one-to-one or in small groups of peers. Qualitative methods appreciate diversity and uniqueness and look at children in a very different way to more traditional quantitative techniques. By using a qualitative method you are able to explore rich and detailed accounts of children's lives.

It is important for you to appreciate that the term 'qualitative method' is a general term for a heterogeneous group of different methods. If you decide to undertake a qualitative approach you will need to understand that within this paradigm there are several different methods for doing research and these reflect different theoretical positions. These will be discussed in Chapter 11 in more depth so it is advisable to look at these before making your final decision.

Developing a research question

Qualitative research begins with a research question (*not* a hypothesis), and potentially related sub-questions. This means that in qualitative research you are not exploring cause and effect, and you are not making a prediction about children. This is because you are researching with a different set of assumptions about children, a different epistemology (as outlined earlier). Instead you have a question that you want to answer. You need to turn your area of interest into something specific that can be explored in depth. Methods chosen should therefore reflect the types of questions being asked (Bryman, 2007). The research question relates to what it is about children's lives that you want to find out and should relate closely to your aims and objectives. There are many different types of qualitative research question. See Box 9.1.

Box 9.1   Qualitative research questions

Questions can relate to knowledge:

- How do children describe people who have mental health problems?

Questions can relate to opinions and attitudes:

- How do children with cancer view their relationship with their doctor?

Questions can relate to experiences:

- How do children experience bullying?
- How do children experience poverty?

Questions can relate to feelings:

- How do children feel when taken away from their parents and put in foster care?
- Why do children feel unsettled during transitions from one school to another?

Questions can be more descriptive:

- What do children fear about school trips?

The best way to develop a research question is to do so systematically. The most rational approach is to write down every question that arises in one's head, regardless of how sensible (or not), that links to your topic. Some of these questions will help to inform your focus groups or interview questions if they are the methods chosen. You then need to categorise all your questions so that there are several questions under one category which fall under one rubric. Delete/dismiss any less prudent questions as there may be a few of these, and then write a single question which encapsulates all questions in that category. This should narrow down approximately 50 short questions to about eight or nine. It is at this point that you really need to think about what the main aims and objectives of your research are and consider how your research questions are going to enable you to meet those aims. When you have the main list of questions narrowed down, these can then be refined and reduced further collaboratively with supervisors or colleagues. You should also use the literature to help you do this, as your research should be original and build on existing evidence.

Benefits and limitations of qualitative methods

As with quantitative research design there are several benefits to designing your project using qualitative methods. This is because the researcher has more freedom to allow the design to unfold naturally. In other words, because qualitative research does not predefine all of the conditions, you will be able to explore interesting phenomena that the children introduce during the project. For example, if you are interviewing children and one child raises something interesting and novel that you had not thought of, you can add it into your interview schedule.

A particular advantage of qualitative work is that richer and fuller detail is provided. This means you can explore the reasons why participants think what they do. So returning to our earlier example, 'boys are more aggressive than girls' might reveal that in reality girls are also very aggressive in their play. You might find that they manipulate situations and verbally abuse their peers and you can investigate the reasons why they do this. This means that you can explore interesting things about children's lives during data collection that may not have been thought about at the planning stage. Furthermore context and social meaning are accounted for because qualitative research is less restrictive.

Using qualitative methods means that the researcher can directly interact with the children and build a rapport with them. This can encourage them to open up more. In qualitative research it is more typical for you to spend some time getting to know the child and their teachers/parents. You are likely to spend some time with them in advance of the research which means you will be less of a stranger to the child when the research is carried out. This means that you get the child's version of his or her life which is more authentic than the one that you hold and you can use your research to develop new theories about children and childhood.

This discussion should demonstrate that there are some advantages to using a qualitative research design with children. You do need to be aware, however, that like its quantitative counterpart there are also some limitations to using a qualitative design. The researcher is heavily involved in the process and may influence the research findings. Although qualitative research encourages you to reflect on your role in the process it is possible that your feelings, thoughts, ideas, opinions, attitudes and so forth can unduly influence the research process. You will need to be aware of how you interact with children, how you influence their answers to questions and how you treat them during the research process to minimise your influence.

There are some issues of quality with qualitative work as it is more difficult to determine validity and reliability of the findings. Qualitative research has slightly different quality criteria (discussed in Chapter 11) and so the study is less easily replicated. Furthermore you may find that a large amount of data is generated and you may only analyse a small amount of it or find it difficult to make sense of. You are likely to be constrained by word limits, however, for journals and theses and so only a small proportion of that data will actually be written up.

As with quantitative research it is important that you are aware of the limitations of qualitative research when planning and conducting your project. While you may not be able to ameliorate all of the disadvantages to a particular method, being constantly aware of them can help to minimise them or their impact on your research. Remember, there is no such thing as the perfect research project.

Activity 9.1

What is it about children and families you want to explore in your project? Have a go at developing your ideas and write down some key questions. Turn this into a research question or hypothesis.

Key differences between quantitative and qualitative research

Broadly speaking, you have the choice between researching children quantitatively or qualitatively. You should not be guided by your preference, however. The research question and the type of knowledge you are aiming to generate should determine the choice of method. Your aims and objectives and overall research question should determine whether you need to develop a hypothesis or qualitative research question, as discussed previously.

It should be clear from the discussion so far that a hypothesis and a qualitative research question are very different. This stems mostly from the theories that underpin the methods. As we noted earlier in the chapter quantitative research is interested in measuring things, in relationships and cause and effect. Because of this quantitative researchers have research questions which inquire about the relationships between things and they develop hypotheses which make predictions and then measure the effects. By testing out their prediction (hypothesis) they can then make generalisations about that group of people – this means that the hypothesis must be testable. Qualitative research questions are different as they do not make predictions, but instead explicate an issue for exploration. This central research question should be specific to the mode of inquiry.

If you are frightened of undertaking complicated statistics you may lean towards qualitative methods, but be warned that undertaking qualitative analysis is not necessarily the simple option. Whichever approach you choose, you will need expert support and some training in that method. You cannot expect to be an expert overnight. By this point you should have some appreciation of what quantitative and qualitative approaches are and Box 9.2 puts these into context by directly comparing the two.

Box 9.2 Comparing quantitative and qualitative approaches

Quantitative	Qualitative
• Tests a hypothesis	• Explores a research question
• Is considered objective measurement	• Is more subjective
• Aims to eliminate researcher bias	• Embraces the influence and role of the researcher
• Makes generalisations to the wider population (infers that the rest of the population linked to that study will also behave in a similar way)	• Has **transferability** of findings (means the degree to which the findings can be transferred to other settings and the extent to which you can relate those findings)
• Uses statistics to analyse data	• Uses a range of methods to analyse data
• Uses controlled settings (often laboratory)	• Uses more naturalistic settings
• Is concerned with cause and effect and measuring human behaviour	• Is concerned with understanding people and their experiences
• Is outcome-oriented	• Is process-oriented
• Is underpinned by positivism	• Is underpinned by a range of theoretical positions

---

Whichever design you choose for your research it is important to appreciate the meaning of the method. The theoretical underpinning, the epistemology and ontology, of any method is an important influence on the type of research conducted and the type of knowledge produced, and it is therefore important to appreciate this aspect of research.

Activity 9.2

Write down three main reasons why you have chosen quantitative/qualitative methods. Be truly honest with yourself. Are your preferences interfering with your choices? Are you anxious about learning the new jargon and style of qualitative methods or just plain afraid of number crunching? Lots of people feel like this but you need to make connections between your research aims and objectives, your theoretical position and your methodological choices and you should be able to provide a clear rationale and links between them. Try writing this down now and discuss your ideas with your colleagues or academic supervisor.

Mixing methods in child research

Ostensibly you might think that the most sensible solution is to combine some quantitative research with qualitative methods. For example, you might send out questionnaires to 500 parents and then select some of them to interview. By combining the data you would be able to provide an overview of the broad issues about a topic and then cover them in more depth. You might send out a questionnaire to see what parents consider important in education and then interview some of them to explore why they think that. Mixing methods in this way is not, however, straightforward, as research needs to be academically rigorous and must meet quality criteria. Notably, therefore, the literature is littered with debates about mixing methods and this is known colloquially as the 'paradigm wars'.

Over time integrating methods has become more popular and acceptable, reflecting an increased understanding of the strengths and weaknesses of individual methods. It is arguable then that the strengths of quantitative research and the strengths of qualitative research can be combined to give a more holistic and valuable method of research. The differences between quantitative and qualitative methods are considered to transcend the mere presence and absence of numbers and the central argument in favour of mixing methods is to provide a fuller and richer picture of any phenomenon (O'Cathain and Thomas, 2006).

It is important to bear in mind when making your decision that there are two key arguments in the mixing methods debate – those that are in favour of pragmatism and those who advocate the influence and importance of philosophy. Pragmatism appeals to more practical and common–sense approaches to research design decisions and seeks a middle ground between the two paradigms, whereas others argue that the competing epistemologies and ontological positions underpinning methodological choices make combining quantitative and qualitative impossible (O'Cathain and Thomas, 2006). In practice this means that some researchers argue that it is practical to combine more than one method as this allows the two paradigms to complement one another and give a stronger picture of children's behaviours. Alternatively, others oppose this saying that because there is conflict at the epistemological level, any findings are flawed.

You need to be aware that just because mixing methods seems appealing this approach is not necessarily superior to a single method design and there has been a tendency to use mixed methods because they are fashionable or to please funding bodies (Bryman, 2006). You need to think about what your research questions are asking. If a mixed methods design is appropriate, you need to decide whether they will be afforded equal status (50–50) or whether a qualitative design will support a quantitative project, or a quantitative design will support a qualitative one.

Bear in mind that the qualitative paradigm is especially diverse and has a range of methods with different perspectives and epistemologies and therefore the combining of more than one qualitative method is subject to similar problems as combining paradigms (see Barbour, 1998).

Example one

You want to explore what kinds of food parents give to their children at weekends and whether this is balanced with their children's level of activity. You therefore send out a questionnaire to a large number of families to answer this question. You include lots of questions about food and exercise. When you have your data you find that there are some interesting differences. You find that children do less exercise and eat more processed and high fat foods at the weekends than during the week. You are unlikely to understand why this is the case or what effect it has. To help answer this question you have a small qualitative element. This is a few open-ended questions at the end of the questionnaire, or some semi-structured interviews with parents. In this way your qualitative data is supporting your quantitative findings.

Example two

To explore the experiences families have had when taking their children into hospital you set up some interviews with parents and children. Your interview data reveals that many children felt that they waited a long time to see the doctor and were anxious while doing so. From this you want to see exactly how long children wait by undertaking an analysis of actual waiting times. This helps understand whether children perceive it as a long time or whether it really is. In this way the quantitative data supports the qualitative.

In Box 9.3 we provide you with a checklist to help you make your decisions regarding research methods.

Box 9.3   **Research methods checklist**

- Is the research method being used because it is the best way of answering the research question or is it being used for less clear reasons?
- Sample selection – is it biased towards particular groups that are not required to answer the research question?
- Are certain groups excluded and others over-included?
- Are the right groups included to answer the research question?
- What efforts are made to ensure appropriate representation of the population that the findings will be applied to?
- Is the sample a convenience sample and is this acceptable to answer the research question?
- Are the instruments appropriately validated for the sample being researched?
- Validating instruments can be a particular problem when researching different cultural groups as translations do not always allow the intended meaning to be conveyed.
- Sometimes research design bias is unavoidable and the researcher needs to show that they have attempted to minimise the impact of this. It is important that limitations are recognised at all times including when the research is disseminated so that findings are not given inappropriate or undue weight or attention.

Quality in research

If you are going to successfully conduct research with children, then you need to be aware of the quality criteria. Both quantitative and qualitative work is measured against a set of criteria to ascertain its quality. Notably there are limited quality criteria as yet for mixed methods (O'Cathain et al., 2007). These are discussed in detail in Chapters 10 and 11.

Activity 9.3

Sarah is required to undertake an undergraduate research project. She is very interested in cyber bullying and has been funded to explore how children experience cyber bullying during adolescence. She defines adolescence as being aged between 13 and 16 years and has statistics to show that there are quite high rates of cyber bullying in this age group. Sarah decides she wants to interview young people about how it affects them, who they are supported by and what they do about it. She is not sure of her exact research question and does have a preference for a qualitative perspective. She decides she will formulate a proper research question after she has done some interviews. Sarah is not sure how to access children of this age so decides to get in touch with some local schools. She discusses the idea with some teachers and gives a talk to several, leaving her email address and asking young people to get in touch.

Sarah wants to start with her data collection as quickly as possible as she has received no funding. She sends a brief overview of the project to her supervisor and sets up two interviews with different children. She is quite upset when the supervisor sends back a long list of problems with the project and tasks that Sarah needs to complete before she can start her data collection.

1 What do you think is in the supervisor's list of tasks?
2 What advice would you give Sarah?
3 How might this influence the supervisory relationship?

When you have developed your answers to these questions turn to the back of the book where we provide a long list of ideas and suggestions. Compare your answers to the ones we provide and see if you managed to identify everything.

Would you allow Sarah to undertake this research for her undergraduate degree? Why? Why not?

Conducting a pilot study

When you have decided on your methodology you need to try it out. In any research, including that which involves children, there are many potential practical and theoretical challenges. A pilot study identifies these early on and enables you to modify your project to successfully achieve the objectives.

A lack of preparation can reduce the quality of the research and the dissemination (Sampson, 2004). A pilot enables you to see how children will react to the research process, the questions asked of them and their competence and ability to undertake what is required of them (Singh and Keenan, 2010).

Sampson (2004) argues that there are five main benefits to conducting a pilot study. Sampson argues that pilot studies:

1 Provide useful information allowing you to judge the feasibility of your project.
2 Allow you to test your methodological tools and make changes.
3 Help you to identify children and gatekeepers who may like continued involvement in your research.
4 Allow you to learn things you may not have anticipated.
5 Result in data that is analysable in its own right.

To help you think more about these five points we provide you with a case example in Box 9.4 to highlight some of the practical benefits of conducting a pilot study.

Box 9.4　**Case example**

A student is undertaking a PhD involving qualitative semi-structured interviews with young children for whom English is a second language. He has recently undertaken a small pilot study with three children of the correct age group to 'test' his research agenda, interview questions, consent forms and information sheets, and interviewing style. This was an important pilot study as, although he had some interview experience, he had limited interview experience with children who are asylum seekers or refugees. Before looking at the different issues that the pilot study identified, we advise you to return to Chapter 7 on particular groups of children and review the special issues related to doing research with asylum seekers and refugees and consider what issues might be raised from the student's project.

Issues identified from a pilot study

We provide several issues here for you to consider. We base these on the real case in Box 9.4 but exaggerate them to illustrate our points.

Ethical issues

- The children signed the consent forms without looking at the information sheets. Action – the student realised that he would have to spend some time going through the main features of the information sheets with the children to check their understanding.
- Not all three of the children could read. Action – it was agreed that a clear audio version of the information sheet should be produced and that the student should spend some time going through the key points of the study with the children regardless.
- For one child's interview there were two interruptions as the interviews took place in a community hall. Action – a large sign was created for the door to ask people not to enter.
- In one child's interview the child found the topic distressing (the study is on a sensitive topic area) and became upset. The student was unprepared and unsure of how to respond. He panicked and upset the child further. The interview was terminated. Action – the student identified a need to develop strategies to manage distress including: stopping recording while the child recomposes themselves, offering the opportunity to withdraw, reassuring the child and calming them down whether they choose to continue or not. Time, space and patience are the key here. Ideally this should have been pre-empted with effective planning.

Issues relating to interviewing technique

- The children had difficulty understanding some of the words used in the questions. Action – the student consulted the children in the pilot and between them they came up with better words to use.

- The children had some difficulty understanding the meaning of some of the questions. Action – the children helped the student formulate questions which were clearer for their age group.
- The interviews were supposed to last 45 minutes but the student found that they were finished in 25 minutes. Action – reflection with the audio files and the supervisor revealed that the student was rushing through the interview because of his anxiety. It was agreed that more pilot interviews were needed and that the student should find ways of relaxing, use more prompts to encourage the children to continue and not be afraid of silences.
- The children seemed to have some difficulty understanding the accent of the student and this embarrassed them. Action – the student slowed down his speech and articulated more clearly. Again, anticipating this possibility may have reduced any problems.

Issues relating to rapport

- The student reported that he had some difficulty relating to the children. Action – it was agreed that the student had not received enough specialised training in interviewing children and provision was made for further training.
- Some younger children reported that they became bored during the interview. Action – being aware of the possibility enables effective preparation by including some participatory action methods and potentially having a short break in the interview.
- The student provided some refreshments during the interview but the noise created reduced the quality of the recording. Additionally, one child had allergies. Action – refreshments were to be given during a break and the student liaised with parents about potential problems.

Issues relating to technology

- The recording device did not pick up all of the speech during the interview and the sound quality was poor for transcription. Action – an external microphone was purchased for the recording device.

Although some of the issues encountered by the student are exaggerated here for illustrative purposes, the pilot study identified several shortcomings in the interview, in the written information and in the student's style of interviewing. Remedial action was taken to rectify the issues and a second pilot was then undertaken to test the new style and materials. Imagine how difficult the real interviews would have been if that student had not taken the time to test things out first.

Summary

This chapter has provided you with the information to make practical decisions about your research design. You should now be able to assess whether a quantitative, qualitative or mixed methods design is most appropriate to address your research question. You should be able to see that choices are tied to epistemology and ontology. You need to be clear about why and how the design is appropriate for what you are doing and consider the quality criteria to assess the stringency of your work. It may also help you to think about why children and families might agree or decline to participate in your project and think clearly about the recruitment issues you face.

Further reading

Bryman, A. (2007) 'The research question in social research: what is its role?', *International Journal of Social Research Methodology*, 10 (1): 5–20.

Greenstein, T. (2006) *Methods of Family Research*. London: Sage.

Grodin, M.A. and Glantz, L.H. (eds) (1994) *Children as Research Subjects: Science, Ethics, and Law*. Oxford and New York: Oxford University Press.

Guba, E.G. and Lincoln, Y.S. (2004) 'Competing paradigms in qualitative research: theories and issues', in S.N. Hesse-Biber and P. Leavy (eds), *Approaches to Qualitative Research: A Reader on Theory and Practice*. Oxford: Oxford University Press, pp. 17–38.

Mauthner, M. (1997) 'Methodological aspects of collecting data from children: lessons from three research projects', *Children and Society*, 11: 16–28.

O'Cathain, A. and Thomas, K. (2006) 'Combining qualitative and quantitative methods', in C. Pope and N. Mays (eds), *Qualitative Research in Health Care* (3rd edn). Oxford: Blackwell Publishing/BMJ Books, pp. 102–111.

Sampson, H. (2004) 'Navigating the waves: the usefulness of a pilot in qualitative research', *Qualitative Research*, 4 (3): 383–402.

Silverman, D. (2005) *Doing Qualitative Research: A Practical Handbook* (2nd edn). London: Sage.

10

Quantitative Methods of Data Collection and Analysis

| Overview |

After reading through this chapter you should be able to:

- Identify the different types of quantitative data and how to group them into variables
- Understand the main data collection tools and the differences between them
- Plan and design a qualitative data collection tool
- Discriminate the special challenges with different groups of children at the time of collecting your data
- Identify the basic descriptive statistics
- Recognise the different inferential statistics
- Identify the relevant computer programs for performing statistics

Key words: observations, quantitative, questionnaires, SPSS, statistics

Introduction

This chapter builds on previous chapters to provide more detailed information about quantitative methods and associated concepts. It begins by introducing some basic statistical concepts you need to consider as you design your project. This should help decide how you can collect data from children using the different quantitative methods available, and give you a general understanding of statistical analysis. An overview of statistical procedures only is provided here and it is recommended that you consult more specialist texts (suggested at the end of the chapter) if you are going to perform statistical tests on your data.

Quantitative data

The term quantitative data refers to a type of information that can be counted and expressed in numerical form. This means that the methods of data collection need to be designed in a way whereby the data can be numerically coded and then statistically analysed. It is vital that you are clear about the type of data you are using from theoretical and practical perspectives because, as we will discuss further in this chapter, the statistical test that you decide to run will vary depending on the type of data you have available.

Overall, quantitative data can be grouped into two main categories:

- **Discrete/categorical data** – this is data that can only take certain values, for example, number of siblings or number of pets.
- **Continuous data** – when data can take any value, such as height (i.e. 125 centimetres) or weight (i.e. 23.2 kilograms).

In addition, categories of data can also be considered as discrete, hence counted, be given a value and be associated with a quantitative scale of measurement. For example:

- **Nominal (or categorical) data** – when there is not a natural ordering of the categories but they do not relate to one another in a particular way, such as that one is not better than the other. This is data which is named rather than numerical. Nominal level scales could measure, for example, gender (allocating some labels or values to the categories, i.e. male = 1, female = 2). Race and religion are also examples of this type of data. When there are only two possible options, such as in gender, these scales are called binary scales.
- **Ordinal data** – when the categories may have an intrinsic order, but, again, the distance between them is not something that can be measured. For example, 'small, medium, large' is an ordinal scale, as is 'strongly disagree, disagree, neutral, agree, strongly agree' (called a **Likert**-type scale). The latter is a very popular approach used in questionnaires.
- **Interval data** – also includes items that have an intrinsic order, but in this case they represent quantitative values. Interval data is continuous data where there are differences but no natural '0'. This means that the numbers have meaning, and are in order and the differences between the numbers are measurable.

Variables

By obtaining any type of data (either discrete or continuous), one observes certain characteristics of the population one is studying. For this chapter we will consistently refer to the following example:

Example: *Do girls aged 11–16 years old eat healthier food than boys of the same age group?*

From this example, we may observe that a child is female, aged 11, and strongly agrees with what you asked her, 'Do you eat sufficient portions of fruit and vegetables per day?', with possible options presented in a Likert-type scale. Characteristics like these describe your population and give them attributes, which will vary from one respondent to another.

Therefore a logical collection of attributes is called a variable; in this instance, the variables would be, first, gender (composed of the attributes male and female); second, age (in this case we suggested a continuous way of presenting the variable age but this can also be described as in categories, given by age groups, i.e. 11–12, 13–14, 15–16 and so forth); and finally, level of agreement to a statement (for example, composed of the traditional five items of Likert scales: strongly disagree, disagree, neutral, agree, strongly agree).

It is generally conventional to refer to the variables one is especially interested in as primary (or response) variables. For example, based on the above, if you wanted to know whether children's level of agreement with regards to your statement 'Do you eat sufficient portions of fruit and vegetables per day?' changes with their age, then children's age and level of agreement with your statement would be your primary variables. However, one usually also collects information on other variables, hoping to better understand other elements around your primary variables, which are referred to as secondary (or supplementary) variables. Inclusion and exclusion of variables should be preceded by a literature search, and should be evidence based, not arbitrarily selected on the basis of personal preference.

In quantitative research there are two important types of variable: the **independent variable** (IV) and the **dependent variable** (DV). The independent variable is the variable which you change to see if it has an effect. The dependent variable is the variable you are measuring. With reference to our example, if you want to know if girls eat healthier food than boys, then the variable which is changing is gender (IV) and the variable you are measuring is the quantity of healthy and unhealthy food consumed (DV).

Sampling for quantitative research

The extent to which your results can be generalised depends on how representative the sample is of the population from which it was drawn. To determine the size of the sample needed for quantitative research it will be necessary to conduct a **power calculation** and we suggest you seek expert statistical advice from your institution to do this effectively. Power is the probability that your study will detect a difference and there is a statistical formula to work it out.

For quantitative research you will need a comparison/control group to maximise the similarities of life experiences and circumstances so that the difference between them is the item under investigation. So, for example, you may be interested in whether having a longer lunch break helps children concentrate better during lessons. Your experimental group will be given the additional 15 minutes at lunch but you need to be able to compare it to a control group who have the usual lunch time.

Remember that to have statistical power and to make generalisations you will need access to a large number of children for your study. If you look at some quantitative papers with child populations you will see that response rates vary considerably. It may be useful to just have a look at some articles now to see what kind of sample sizes have been used for quantitative work. We include three articles for you to look at in the further reading section of this chapter. You will see from looking at these that sample sizes vary greatly. Turkheimer et al. (2003) used a national survey and included 48,197 mothers and 59,397 children in their study of IQ and socio-economic status. In a study of obesity and television watching, Gortmaker et al. (1996) included a much smaller (but still significant) 746 adolescents aged 10–15 years old but in a study of children with cystic fibrosis (CF) and eating disorders 58 adolescent patients (aged 13–20) were included, along with a control group of 43 healthy individuals (Raymond et al., 2000). Notably it is much more difficult to access those with CF and eating disorders, than a general population of young people who watch television and may be classified as obese. You need to remember that your sample size is likely to be affected by what you are studying and the availability of the population.

Often what happens is that when particular samples are small, they are merged and statements are made about the combined sample without realising potential pitfalls. An example of this comes from our own experience of trying to make some sense of the data collected on the prevalence rate of mental health problems and service need and use in the under-16 population of the UK Office of National Statistics (Green et al., 2005) survey to attempt to identify prevalence rates in minority groups. However, it soon became apparent that, since the survey had not employed oversampling techniques to increase data from ethnic minority groups, any detailed analysis of ethnic data would lack power and reliability. Therefore, the data did not enable a meaningful statistical analysis, as the number of minority groups represented in total was less than 10 per cent of the whole sample, making it difficult to draw any conclusions about prevalence.

Quality in quantitative design

Assessing quality in quantitative research is fairly straightforward: quality is ascertained mainly by validity, reliability and **generalisability**.

The concept of reliability refers to the stability, consistency and the not self-contradictory data collection or measurement. The main types of reliability are:

- Internal consistency: it ensures that all items of the test to be used assess the same construct.
- Inter-rater reliability: it examines the degree of agreement between raters that use the same test.
- Test–retest reliability: used to assess the consistency of a measure from one time to another.

Validity refers to whether one is measuring the concept intended to be measured, approximating the truthfulness of the results. Three main types can be identified:

- Face validity: this is the least scientific method of validity. It refers to whether it seems like one measures what one claims to. Here one looks at how valid a measure appears on the surface and makes subjective judgements based on that.

- Content validity: this is also subjective and refers to whether the content of a test covers the full domain of what one wants to know (i.e. the content validity of a test to measure depression should ensure that all the elements of depression are measured by the test).
- Construct validity: this represents a test that provides evidence of a theoretical concept, in other words, it shows that the theory actually corresponds with reality.

It is especially important that your research is reliable, in the sense that your study could be replicated by someone else, and is valid, in the sense that you are measuring what you set out to measure and not something else. We will address the concept of generalisability later in the chapter.

Collection tools

There are a number of different types of data collection tools that are considered to be quantitative and this chapter focuses on the following:

- Questionnaires
- Structured interviews
- Observations

Questionnaires

You have in all likelihood completed many questionnaires and received even more requests to do so. You will have been inclined to fill in some more than others and you may want to think about the reason why. Maybe the topic interested you, maybe you wanted your opinion to be heard or maybe there was a financial incentive? If you are going to ask children to complete your questionnaire, you need to review how they are approached and how the questionnaire is designed. You need to consider how you are going to convince the parents that it is worth their time and is not just 'another questionnaire'.

The point of a questionnaire is to ask participants questions in a structured and systematic way. You need to decide how you are going to administer your questionnaire, as there are different ways of doing so (see Box 10.1).

Box 10.1 **Ways of administering questionnaires**

- Self-administered
  - By post
  - By internet

- Researcher administered
  - Face-to-face
  - By telephone
- Administered by parents/teachers or other gatekeepers (this may be dependent on the child's age and the complexity of the issue under investigation)

In this section of the chapter we focus mostly on those questionnaires that are self-administered by post or by internet. We return more specifically to the structured interview (researcher administered) in the next section of the chapter.

The benefits of questionnaires

There are several advantages to using a questionnaire for your research and they are widely used in child research. Questionnaires can be quite short in length and therefore children are less likely to get bored, which may not be the case with other methods. The useful thing about a questionnaire is that you can obtain quite a lot of information in just a couple of pages. Remember that it is going to be difficult to persuade a young child to sit and fill in several pages of a questionnaire, particularly if you are relying on parents to take the time to help them fill it in.

Providing the design is easy to follow, it is unlikely that the child will fail to answer a particular question. Unanswered questions on a questionnaire can affect your results and in some cases mean that you can't include the questionnaire in the sample. Questionnaires are typically cheap to administer, and those delivered over the internet can be especially economical and also save having to enter the data separately.

By using a questionnaire delivered by post or internet there is also the benefit that researcher effects are eliminated or certainly reduced. If you are present when the child is answering the questions you may have an effect on the types of responses you get or you may put the child under pressure to give socially desirable answers. By allowing the child to complete the questionnaire at home with the parent and posting it back, there is less risk of this.

How to design questionnaires

When designing your questionnaire for child populations it is important that you address various issues. When you get started on your design it is useful to start with a brainstorming exercise. This should be informed by a good literature search on the topic and the method. Write down all the questions that come into your head regardless of what they are, as this will reveal interesting ideas for the final draft.

Activity 10.1

Returning to our earlier example, consider the research topic of children's attitudes towards dieting and healthy eating. You hypothesise that girls are more
actively concerned about their weight and their diet than boys and that their
behaviour will match this attitude. Brainstorm ten questions you might include on
a questionnaire designed for children aged 11–16 years old. Refer to Box 10.2 to
help you assess what constitutes a good question for children. When you have
done this, reflect on these questions and see if you can develop five good questions for a questionnaire. When you have completed this activity you might want
to refer to our suggestions at the back of the book.

Box 10.2 Attributes of a good question

A good question for children should be:

- Short
- Written in child-accessible language
- Clear
- A single question with one point
- Focused on the topic
- Related to the aims of the project
- Able to allow for a precise answer

When you have got a feel for the types of questions you might want to ask it
is important to go back to the literature and contextualise your ideas within
the broader evidence base. Writing a questionnaire is more than just coming
up with a number of good questions and there are a number of issues you
need to think about. We highlight these below.

- Writing an introduction section on the questionnaire

A questionnaire needs an opening introduction which reminds the reader
about the overall topic. When writing this section, you really need to think
about who the questionnaire is aimed at, the age group of the child and
whether you have written the questionnaire to be filled in by the parent or
the child. Use child-friendly language and you may even want to include
some pictures to make it look more attractive. Keep the introduction short
and clear. Reassure the participant regarding confidentiality and any ethical
points.

- Writing the instructions for the child

You cannot assume that the reader will automatically know what to do with your questionnaire and therefore you may want to provide a bullet point list of some simple instructions, just underneath your short introduction. You may also find it useful to consult with children, parents and teachers when designing and planning the questionnaire. Many questionnaires illustrate a worked example of how to complete the questionnaire.

- Using open or closed questions

Closed questions are designed to limit the responses offered by the child. Children are required to choose from pre-existing answers, such as yes/no, agree/disagree or true/false. Closed questions are advantageous, as they are simply coded (i.e. the **quantification** of the data and converting into numbers) and analysed statistically and are therefore favoured in quantitative designs. They are particularly useful with child participants because they are more specific and require the child to provide a clear and focused answer.

Open-ended questions do not give the child a range of options, but require the child to articulate an answer in their own words. **Open questions** can be useful but these allow a longer more free response which some children may struggle with, depending on their literacy ability and how much help they have. Furthermore these have to be analysed either qualitatively or converted to numbers for statistical analysis.

Generally use closed questions so children find them easier to answer. Remember that if you ask young children long complicated questions, they will find them even more difficult to answer. If the questions are complex then you might find it useful to have some stories, or examples, or some children's characters to use to help them understand what you mean. If you are not going to be there when the questions are answered, then you may need to provide some guidance for the parents.

- Deciding on the number of questions

As mentioned, it is always best to have a questionnaire that is as short as possible, but the length will ultimately depend on the research question and the age of the children. With internet questionnaires it is useful to have information about how much they have left to go to encourage them to keep going to the end. For child-specific questionnaires, you may want to include animation features or pictures. There is not a set amount of questions and you need enough to address the hypothesis, but try not to have too many or the questionnaire becomes a laborious task. There is also evidence that longer questionnaires are likely to have lower response rates (Roszkowski and Bean, 1990), so it is probably best to try to have two printed pages. Remember, however, that you do need to include questions which may contradict previous ones to check that the child is not simply ticking random boxes.

- Deciding what types of questions to ask

You need to ensure that your questions provide you with the data you need to address the hypothesis. Consider what your main research question is, what you need to know and how you would answer the question. Do not use long words or jargon in your questions and avoid phrasing questions in a negative way. Consult with people who work with children, and children directly, to ask their opinion of your questions. You need to avoid using ambiguous terms and very long or double-barrelled questions. More importantly, do not use leading questions where you direct the child to provide the answer you are looking for to confirm your hypothesis.

Once you have devised some questions, you need to consider how you want them answered and the order you will present them in. Consider whether you want to make a set of statements and just ask if the child agrees or disagrees with them. In this case, you may be better off using a Likert scale as this is both effective and efficient. For some research questions, multiple choice questions with true or false options may be sufficient. It can be helpful to have an option for 'other' as for future work that may provide useful information on revising questionnaires. Remember that the choices you make and the type of data you work with (nominal, ordinal, interval – discussed earlier in the chapter) will have an effect on the robustness of your analysis and the types of statistical tests you are able to perform.

- Piloting the questionnaire

If you are using a self-designed questionnaire or even only modifying a pre-existing questionnaire, it is essential to pilot it before you use it for your main study. You need to identify people who match the criteria of your target audience and ask them to pilot your questionnaire. Once they have done so, you need to find out how they found the exercise, what problems they encountered, whether any of the questions need clarification or rewording. You can then use their feedback to revise your questionnaire.

Limitations of questionnaires and techniques for resolution

The most obvious limitation to the questionnaire method relates to response rates. Postal or internet questionnaires have the advantage of being cheaper to administer and make it easier to reach broader geographical locations and thus you may think that you will increase your recruitment using this method. However, response rates may be hard to calculate, as knowing how many people received the questionnaire can be hard to confirm. There is the risk that children will not complete them, that your response rates will be low or that parents will forget about helping the child. There is also an assumption that everyone has access to the technology required and this may not be the case, for example, if you are researching the effect of poverty on development, then there is the possibility that the families you are targeting will not have a computer or internet access. There are, however, various strategies to increase your response rates:

- You should design your questionnaire with a particular group in mind and tailor it to their preferences. Keep it as short as feasible and make it visually attractive.
- If possible notify your participants in advance of sending out the questionnaire, so that they are aware that it is coming, and make sure that your questions are sensitive to the target group.
- If you can, provide an incentive, but be careful about offering financial incentives to children as this may be considered coercive. A prize draw for toys may be a good idea, or educational book tokens. You may offer a donation to a charity, which may appeal to parents.
- It is useful to understand your demographic when making decisions so do some information gathering beforehand. Asking audiences to complete questionnaires in certain contexts may increase response rates, for example in the classroom.
- You may need to send out reminders, but you do need to be careful not to be coercive. Remember that ethically you cannot put pressure on the children or their parents to participate. On the other hand, with time distractions and other priorities, parents may simply forget about your questionnaire so it is worth gently reminding them about it.

While response rates are particularly important in questionnaires, there are other limitations to be aware of:

- There is little opportunity for correction once you have distributed out to your respondents, a questionnaire that is heavily dependent on the design. A badly designed questionnaire will be an ineffective method of collecting data. One way of overcoming this limitation is to do a pilot run.
- There is often a requirement that the questionnaires be validated. This means that they are shown to be accurately asking what they purport to. Validating a questionnaire is considerably time-consuming, but the value of a questionnaire that has not been validated is questionable. There are, however, many questionnaires which have been validated and are widely available (although this may incur a fee).
- If the child is having trouble answering the questions or interpreting the questions, you are not there to help explain what is meant unless you do a face-to-face delivery. It can be quite useful for the researcher to help the child to answer the questions (although you do have to be careful not to influence their answers).
- The child may not have the competence or educational level to be able to complete the questionnaire. If you think back to earlier chapters, we considered some of the special groups of children and some issues relating to capacity. Not all children can read or have the necessary literacy skills to fill in a questionnaire and what you may end up with is a reflection of the parents' views and not the child's. Again, part of the solution to this is to do a face-to-face delivery of the questionnaire so that you can help the child yourself.

- There is a tendency for some people to generally agree or disagree with a set of questions (Bryman, 2008). Children may simply get used to circling the 'agree' option and therefore may not really read the questions properly. It is a good idea to put contradictory questions in and mix up the positive and negative questions in your questionnaire so that you can identify if that is the case. Furthermore children may give socially desirable answers.

Activity 10.2

Think about the following questions on a questionnaire designed to find out what children aged between 6 and 11 years old like to do for after-school activities. Consider which are good questions and which are not well-designed questions and write a rationale for your response.

1 Which of these activities do you enjoy doing?
  a Equestrian activities
  b Angling
  c Sculpting
  d Genealogy
  e Scuba diving
  f Fossil hunting
2 Which of these activities do you enjoy doing?
  g Football
  h Basketball
  i Cricket
  j Art and design
  k Dancing
  l Reading
3 Would you like to stay at school to do extra football or dancing?
4 Would you be prepared to stay in the school environment for an additional half hour on one of the days of the week to do an after-school club activity such as football or drama with one of the teachers in the main hall, so that your parents could pick you up slightly later than is usual for you?

We provide some answers to this activity at the back of the book.

Structured interviews/researcher-administered questionnaires

In the previous section we dealt with some of the issues for questionnaires by post or by internet. In this section we explore the structured interview, which has some similarities with the questionnaire design and some similar advantages and disadvantages.

The structured interview is also known as the standardised interview and the researcher-administered questionnaire. This is when the researcher goes through a sequence of questions, either face-to-face or over the telephone, with the participant and ticks the responses for them. In this way, each respondent is asked exactly the same questions, in exactly the same way and in exactly the same order as a questionnaire. Questions are typically specific and usually closed.

Benefits of structured interviewing

Using this form of interview with children has the advantage of engaging the child in the research, which is more difficult when sending out a questionnaire through the post or over the internet. Misunderstood questions can be explained and additional field notes can be made. You will need to decide, however, whether to conduct your structured interview over the telephone or face-to-face.

Telephone interviewing has the advantage of being cheaper as there are reduced travel costs, but children may not be completely comfortable talking to you over the telephone and may be easily distracted by other things around them. If you spend some time on the telephone with the child you may be able to build a rapport which can facilitate answers. Face-to-face has the visible advantage of encouraging the child and building a relationship, but you may intimidate the child and they may become uncomfortable. Again you will need to factor in time to address the child's needs.

By engaging the child directly, you can explain any terms or questions that the child does not understand. Even with good planning it is still possible that some children will not understand all of your questions. If you are engaging with them directly, you can explain what words mean or give illustrative examples to help them answer the question. Furthermore you can reassure the child about confidentiality and the right to withdraw. Although a written questionnaire will contain information about these important ethical principles in the introduction, when engaging the child more actively in an interview it gives you an opportunity to explain this more clearly to the child and to the parents during the interview and again at the end of it. This will leave you feeling more confident that the child's participation really was voluntary.

With this kind of data collection method you are likely to get a better response rate. To perform a structured interview you will need to agree a time slot with the parents and because they have made a commitment to meet with you or to answer a telephone call, they are more likely to proceed. This is not a guarantee and parents may cancel your appointment or may forget about it and therefore you need to be flexible and may need to send them reminders.

How to design and conduct structured interviews

If you are going to perform a structured interview with children then you need to make sure you know your interview schedule very well. In quantitative interviewing, it is important that the questions are asked in the same way and in the same order. Therefore, you need to familiarise yourself with the questions in advance of recruiting participants.

Talking to children face-to-face may be preferable despite the costs. In the adult methods literature it is generally agreed that there is little difference between telephone and face-to-face interviews in terms of content, style and results when interviewing adults (Shuy, 2001; Sturges and Hanrahan, 2004), but the ways in which children interact with adults are different to adult-to-adult interactions and therefore it is likely to be more difficult to conduct an interview with a child over the telephone.

When designing your interview schedule you need to use similar techniques to those of questionnaires and therefore we would encourage you to go back to this section for advice, rather than repeating it here. You may also want to have a look at the section on qualitative interviewing, later in the book, to help you think about the issues of interviewing children more generally.

Activity 10.3

Do you think that telephone interviewing is an appropriate method for interviewing children? Why do you think this?

When you have written down some of your reasons you may want to refer to the back of the book for some additional thoughts.

Limitations of structured interviews and techniques for resolution

There are some limitations of using a structured interview with children and you might want to consider some of these problems in advance of carrying out your research.

- Children can be eager to please you and may think there is a right or wrong answer (social desirability bias). This is true of factual questionnaires and attitudinal questionnaires. This may mean that the answers given to you in the interview do not reflect the child's true opinions, but reflect what they think you want to hear.
- Face-to-face interviews can become expensive if you have to travel. Remember that the design is quantitative and you still need large sample sizes that are representative.
- There is the problem of power between you and the child. We have talked about the power issue in relation to ethical considerations. Remember that this is an ongoing issue that you will need to address, and can be potentially problematic in structured interviews.

Observations

A structured observation is when the researcher follows formulated rules for observing children and recording their behaviours in a particular context. Observers will have a specific checklist of behaviours they are looking for and will tick boxes on a predesigned sheet.

There are several different observation types that you can use with child populations but some fall more under the rubric of qualitative research. Qualitatively, there are two main types of observation (see Box 10.3).

Box 10.3 **Types of observation**

More common quantitative forms of observation are:

- Non-participant observation – the researcher observes but does not participate in the child's environment and usually follows a structured format.
- Non-structured observation – there is no schedule of behaviours to look for but the researcher records as much detail as possible and remains a non-participant.

In quantitative observations it is essential that you think about your observation schedule and coding scheme (Bryman, 2008). In advance of your observation you need to be clear about the categories of children's behaviour that you are keen to observe and why, as this will inform the observation schedule you develop.

There are several benefits to using an observation with children. If your observation schedule has a clear focus, it will be comprehensible exactly what is to be observed. You will need to decide how many children you are observing and how many actions, events, verbal displays and so forth you are looking for. The more children you are observing and the more factors you are looking for the harder it will be. It may be useful to have a second observer, or use of a video camera to check for accuracy. Remember, though, that you may have observer disagreements if you use more than one observer.

The observation method allows you to observe children in their natural environments, which may be better than using the laboratory. This can make the method more natural as the children are free to behave in the manner that they normally do. Remember, however, that because of ethics, it is probable that they will be aware that they are being watched so you may want to wait a while for the novelty of your presence to wear off. If you have time, you may want to undertake several observations of that group of children before you start the 'real' observation, so that they become accustomed to your presence.

An advantage to the observation method is that several children can be observed at once, which may give you additional insight. You do need to think about the possibility of inaccuracies as you observe their behaviour though. The observation method allows you to observe children in groups and this means that you can investigate their social skills, their play and their interactions. You can reduce the effect of the researcher on what happens during the observation. You may choose to stay on the side-lines so that you can reduce the effect you have on the interactions. You may, however, choose to be an active participant and therefore you will need to be aware of how you influence the behaviour of the children and account for that.

Remember that even those children who may not have the cognitive skills to participate in research can be included here. Observation methods are a useful technique for children from special groups, as you can observe them in their natural environments, and their levels of competence, language ability and so forth become less relevant.

However, there are some limitations to using this method. Observers need to be trained so that they do not become confused when faced with a number of options. You may find it useful to enrol on a short course within your institution on carrying out observations. Furthermore observations are in part dependent upon the interpretations of the observer and this can be complex. It is difficult to access the intention of behaviour, simply by observing it. For example, if Johnny kicks Katie, then the observer may record the kick and interpret it as aggressive behaviour; but will not know why Johnny has kicked Katie, or if it actually was an aggressive act and not playful.

If you are conducting an observation remain aware of the context and setting. You need to be careful not to become so focused on the individual behaviours that you detach them from the context in which those behaviours occur. Remember that observations are time-consuming to conduct and may require more than one observer. If you are observing lots of children over a period of time then you are going to need to make room in your weekly schedule to do this effectively. Behaviours may be missed if obscured by other children, or large objects and so forth. You will need to visit the location before you start your research and identify any potential barriers to your observation in advance and take steps to remove them.

Access to the setting may require considerable negotiation. Observations can take place in many settings, but some parents may be uncomfortable about you watching their children and so you are going to have to provide information for the gatekeepers and build relationships with them.

Quantitative analysis

Until now we have discussed how quantitative research collects data which can be translated into numerical values. It then requires the use of statistical processes in order to make sense of the data and to answer your specific questions. This may feel a little daunting, especially if you are new to research and have little or no experience of statistics. In this book we only briefly consider analytic methods as analysis is not child-specific and is relevant to all types of quantitative data. We recommend some statistics texts that may be useful in helping you work through what is required. It is also a good idea to enlist the help of an expert statistician if one is available.

At a glance, statistics are used in a variety of ways to support your research, and there are two main types:

- **Descriptive statistics** are numbers used to describe a group of items (or data).
- **Inferential statistics** are computed from a sample drawn from a larger population with the intention of making generalisations from the sample about the whole population. The accuracy of inferences drawn from a sample is critically affected by the sampling procedures used.

Descriptive statistics

Descriptive statistics are those that describe your data set and give you some indication as to the frequency of how often things occur, for example, how often a specific symptom or event occurred for a young person.

Measures of central tendency

The type of measure you choose to use to analyse your data will depend on the type of scale you obtained. The most common form of descriptive statistics is measures of central tendency which give you some indication as to the typical score. There are three main measures of central tendency and they are the mean, median and mode.

- **The mean** – This is also known as the average score and is calculated by adding all of the scores together and dividing by the number of scores.
- **The median** – This is the value that lies in the middle of the sample and therefore will have the same number of scores above and below it. To calculate the median effectively you need to rank your scores and identify the middle score.
- **The mode** – It is the value that appears most frequently in your sample. You need to look through your scores and identify the one that is most commonly occurring.

The choice of which measure of central tendency to use will be influenced by the type of scale you have chosen to express your data. For instance, the mean can be used for both interval and ratio data; the median is used for ordinal and interval data; and the mode is used only for categorical data.

Data distribution

With all the above measures, you now should be able to describe the distribution of your data. This is important because it will influence the type of inferential statistics you will need to use to analyse your data further.

- **Normal distribution** – If the data you collected is normally distributed, often called the bell-shaped curve (Figure 10.1), most of the scores in this graph accumulate around the middle; the mean, median and mode are all equal. For example, a curve representing the results of an intelligence test would have the most number of people in the middle or around the 'average' intelligence range, while the number of people decreases as the scores get farther away on either side of the average value.

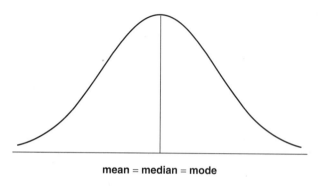

mean = median = mode

Figure 10.1   Normally distributed sample

- **Skewed distribution** – This is a measure of the asymmetry of the distribution. The skewness can be positive or negative (Figure 10.2). A negative skew indicates that the *tail* on the left side of the probability density function is *longer* than the right side and the bulk of the values (possibly including the median) lie to the right of the mean. A positive skew indicates that the *tail* on the right side is longer than the left side and the bulk of the values lie to the left of the mean.

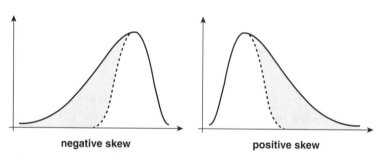

negative skew   positive skew

Figure 10.2   Skewed distribution

Measure of dispersion

However, without knowing something about how the data is spread across a range dispersed, the mean, median and mode have little value. For that reason, it is important to consider some of the measures of dispersion, which will give you a clearer picture about your data:

- **Range** – This is calculated by taking the difference between the maximum and minimum value in the data set.
- **Standard deviation** – This shows how much dispersion exists from the average value. A low standard deviation indicates that the data points tend to be very close to the mean; whereas a high standard deviation indicates that the data is spread out over a large range of values.
- **Interquartile range** – Like the standard deviation, the interquartile range (IQR) is used to summarise the extent of the spread of your data and represents the distance between the 1st quartile (25th percentile) and 3rd quartile (75th percentile).

Inferential statistics

So, while descriptive statistics will provide basic information about your sample, they will not tell you about how the variables you collected relate to each other. This is what inferential statistics will help you obtain, as well as generalise your findings by extrapolating them to the general population (providing that your initial sample was representative of the population in the first place; see Figure 10.3). Therefore, the tests of inferential statistics will allow you to know whether your variables are related or associated, including the strength of such association; and to conclude about differences or similarities between your sample and the general population.

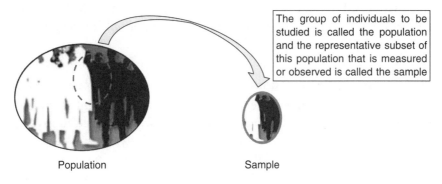

The group of individuals to be studied is called the population and the representative subset of this population that is measured or observed is called the sample

Population   Sample

Figure 10.3   From population to sample

Inferential statistical tests

Any statistical inference will require some assumptions. In order to choose the most appropriate test of inference, statisticians will distinguish between

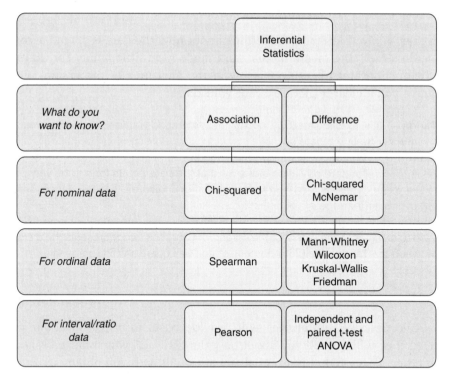

Figure 10.4   Main inferential statistical tests

parametric data, which has an underlying normal distribution, and anything else, described as non-parametric.

The type of test to be used in inferential statistics, as well as the information you will obtain from it, will depend on the type of data you have collected, and you will need to refer to specialist books regarding statistical analysis. As a brief summary, we present some of the most important inferential tests in Figure 10.4.

Statistical assumptions: hypothesis, P value and confidence interval

As we previously mentioned, one of the main ideas of inferential statistics is that you want to extrapolate from the data you have collected to make general conclusions. In order to do that, statistical analyses will assume that there is a large population of data out there from which you randomly sampled your participants; but also, that each subject you selected was sampled independently of the rest (this is called the assumptions of independence).

Now, for example, consider that you want to measure the effect of sugar consumption on children's concentration. You will randomly select a group of healthy volunteers and proceed to give them a certain amount of sugar per day, measuring their concentration levels. At the end of your experiment, you notice that there have been several changes in concentration. But you want to know whether those changes are related to the sugar your participants had or whether they happened by chance. Therefore, you come up with two opposing hypotheses:

- Sugar will decrease children's concentration.
- Sugar in diet will not decrease children's concentration, and the changes you have seen in concentration levels are chance occurrences.

The latter assumption, that the changes have nothing to do with your intervention (rather, they happened by chance), is called the null hypothesis (H_0) and it is the one that statistical tests, through something called the P value, will try to disprove. On the contrary, the presumption that an increase in sugar is really responsible for lower concentration is known as the alternative hypothesis (Ha).

In simple terms, the P value is a probability, with a value ranging from zero to one which will answer your question. If the P values you obtained from your statistical tests are lower than 5 per cent (or 0.05), then you can reject the null hypothesis. In the example above, you can conclude that it is probably false that the decrease in children's concentration following high sugar intake is due to chance; in other words, it is likely that your alternative hypothesis is true.

The concept of the P value and its role in supporting or disproving the null hypothesis tends to create a lot of confusion among novices to statistics. What it basically allows you to do is to establish an association between what you think and what you saw in your study. In other words, in the example mentioned above, if the P value you obtained is 3 per cent (or 0.03), then you can assume that by repeating the experiment over and over again, in only 3 per cent of the cases will high sugar in the diet decrease concentration. In this case, the opposite will also apply, which is that in 97 per cent of the repeated experiments sugar will be responsible, and not chance.

Now, imagine that every time you repeat your experiment, you write down the different P values. At the end of several repetitions, you will have many P values which you can describe as ranging from the lower P value to the higher P value (for example from 2.8 per cent to 5.1 per cent). This is what is known as confidence interval, and it expresses the level of confidence (commonly set at 95 per cent) in which you could extrapolate your results from your sample, to an unknown population (generally described as the general population). Therefore, you could say that you are 95 per cent confident that based on your study, the association of sugar and low concentration in the general population will fall within 2.8 per cent and 5.1 per cent, also known as generalisability. Hence, generalisability describes the extent to which research findings can be applied to settings other than that in which they were originally tested.

Please note that during your data analysis, you will be able to obtain a *P value* for every test you run. We have only discussed *P values* in this section, but the additional specific values that you will obtain from each inferential test are very important to understand and describe your results. However, the latter are beyond the scope of this book and you will need to follow this up with some further specialised reading.

Statistical software

Many students panic about their mathematical ability when faced with complex statistical tests and formulae, but there is no need to panic as you do not have to work out your results by hand. There are many types of software to help you perform statistical analysis, such as SPSS, Stata or STATISTICA, which come with good guides to show you how to input your data, how to assign variables and how to perform different tests. The computer programs will also create graphs and charts, which you can copy into your report and print out.

Although the software does all the complex calculations for you, you need to know whether the tests you have selected for the software to run are appropriate for the type of data you have gathered, you need to be able to understand how it achieved those findings, be able to interpret the final numbers produced and apply the numbers to give meaning to your research hypothesis.

Summary

In this chapter, we first introduced you to some basic statistical concepts regarding qualitative data to help you gain knowledge about the different types of data, which you will group into variables to underpin your research hypothesis.

Second, we discussed the main types of quantitative data collection tools, with a particular focus on the most common ones, such as questionnaires, structured interviews and observations. We introduced you to questionnaire design and provided you with some important things to think about when administering and piloting your questionnaire. In addition, we discussed the use of structured interviews to elicit useful information about children and issues in observing children.

Finally, we described ways in which you could use descriptive and inferential statistics to make sense of the data you have gathered, to infer from the sample data what the population as a whole might look like, or to make judgements of the probability that an observed difference might have happened by chance. We then highlighted some of the most important statistical packages that will aid you in statistical analysis.

Further reading

Bell, A. (2007) 'Designing and testing questionnaires for children', *Journal of Research in Nursing*, 12 (5): 461–469.

Coolican, H. (2009) *Research Methods and Statistics in Psychology* (5th edn). London: Hodder Arnold.

Cornish, K. (1998) *An Introduction to Using Statistics in Research*. Nottingham: Trent Focus Group.

Field, A. (2009) *Discovering Statistics using SPSS*. London: Sage.

Fontana, A. and Frey, J.H. (2003) 'The interview: from structured questions to negotiated text', in N. Denzin and Y. Lincoln (eds), *Collecting and Interpreting Qualitative Materials* (2nd edn). London: Sage, pp. 61–106.

Gaskell, G. (2000) 'Individual and group interviewing', in M. Bauer and G. Gaskell (eds), *Qualitative Researching with Text, Image and Sound*. London: Sage, pp. 38–56.

Gortmaker, S., Must, A., Sobol, A., Peterson, K., Colditz, G. and Dietz, W. (1996) 'Television viewing as a cause of increasing obesity among children in the United States, 1986–1990', *Archives of Pediatric Adolescent Medicine*, 150: 356–362.

Petrie, A. and Sabin, C. (2009) *Medical Statistics at a Glance* (3rd edn). London: Blackwell.

Raymond, N., Chang, P.N., Crow, S., Mitchell, J., Dieperink, B., Beck, M., Crosby, R., Clawson, C.C. and Warwick, W. (2000) 'Eating disorders in patients with cystic fibrosis', *Journal of Adolescence*, 23: 359–363.

Shuy, R. (2001) 'In-person versus telephone interviewing', in J.F. Gubrium and J.A. Holstein (eds), *Handbook of Interview Research: Context and Method*. London: Sage, pp. 537–556.

Sturges, J. and Hanrahan, K.J. (2004) 'Comparing telephone and face-to-face qualitative interviewing: a research note', *Qualitative Research*, 4 (1): 107–118.

Turkheimer, E., Haley, A., Waldron, M., D'Onofrio, B. and Gottesman, I. (2003) 'Socioeconomic status modifies heritability of IQ in young children', *Psychological Science*, 14: 623–628.

11

Qualitative Methods of Data Collection and Analysis

Overview

After reading through this chapter you should be able to:

- Identify the different qualitative methods of data collection
- Compare and contrast the differences between various data collection techniques
- Plan an appropriate methodological strategy
- Compare and contrast the advantages and disadvantages of each method
- Identify the more common methods of qualitative analysis

Key words: focus groups, interviews, qualitative, recordings, thematic analysis, transcription

---

Introduction

This chapter is designed to help you to think about the different methods of qualitative data collection available, highlighting the broader issues you need to think about when choosing an appropriate method of data collection for your project. This will be relevant for how you practically collect data from children and the different methods available within the framework you have adopted. Additionally, you are introduced to qualitative analysis. As with the previous chapter on quantitative methods, qualitative analytic techniques are not specific to child participants and therefore the chapter only provides a brief introduction to analysis, recommending that more specialised texts are consulted.

Data collected using qualitative techniques generally deal with talk and text, that is with words rather than numbers. This means that the methods of data collection need to be designed in a way whereby the data is open-ended and participant led or at least participant influenced. There are a number of different types of qualitative data collection methods with some of the most common being:

- Semi-structured and unstructured interviews
- Focus groups
- Ethnography and participant observation
- Naturally occurring data
- Documents

These more common methods of qualitative analysis require modification before they can be suitably used with children.

Sampling for qualitative data

Qualitative sampling is different from quantitative sampling techniques and the amount of children you will need access to varies depending on the nature of the research, the perspective you are operating from and the aims and objectives. In qualitative work, the general consensus is that **saturation** is an appropriate marker for sample size and we discuss this in more detail later in the chapter. Thematic saturation tends to mean that nothing new is emerging during data collection: no new ideas or themes are coming out and so doing more interviews or focus groups is pointless. Notably, however, the original, theoretical saturation concept is tied to the method of grounded theory and has a different meaning. Not all qualitative approaches rely on saturation as a marker for sample size quality and therefore it is not always an appropriate measure of sample size adequacy (O'Reilly and Parker, 2012). Smaller sample sizes are expected in qualitative work and it is expected that recruitment of children will cease when no new patterns or themes are emerging from the data.

Quality in qualitative design

Quality assessments are less straightforward in qualitative research with a number of different frameworks and ideas emerging. The concepts of reliability, validity and generalisability are not applicable to qualitative research in the same way. There are a number of different quality criteria for qualitative work (see Tracy, 2010; Tong et al., 2007; Spencer et al., 2003). While there are differences between these you need to think about how you assess the quality of your qualitative research design. Some authors argue that you cannot have universal criteria for such a diverse set of methods, while others argue that overarching principles are not only possible but desirable. In the real world of research, your qualitative study will be judged and so you need to think about the **transparency** of your work and the transferability of your findings and be reflexive in your approach.

Qualitative data has only become more widely accepted, especially in the health arena, over the last 25 years (Sandelowski, 2004; Elliott et al., 1999). One of the difficulties is that for many people numbers (irrespective of how they may have been generated) provide a certainty (albeit false) and are 'scientific'. Qualitative researchers have had to work hard to ensure that when they present their results, they are aware of their own biases and can demonstrate that most people doing the analysis would have come up with similar themes or outcomes. Transparency can be helped by being explicit about how the analysis was undertaken and being reflexive about one's own perspective as discussed in the chapter on cross-cultural issues.

Semi-structured and unstructured interviews

Interviewing is probably the most common form of qualitative data collection and generally researchers choose between conducting a semi-structured or an unstructured interview. A semi-structured interview is one whereby you have a general schedule of questions but build in flexibility according to the answers provided by the child. An unstructured interview is more like a general conversation but do not make the mistake of assuming it is just that. There should be a few broad areas you want to cover but no particular agenda or questions to lead the interview. We recommend that you familiarise yourself with the general method of interviewing through a general text and then consider how that may need to be adapted with child participants by reading this section. Remember that the goal of interviewing children is to invite them to provide their own perspectives, so you need to allow the children the space and opportunity to do so (Danby et al., 2011). You may also want to return to Chapter 10 to think about whether you are going to conduct your interview face-to-face or over the telephone. We discussed some of the broader issues of doing this in Chapter 10, but with qualitative interviews they tend to be longer than structured and have more depth of conversation so you may feel that face-to-face is more appropriate.

Any interview needs careful planning and especially those with children. You need to think about the purpose of the interview, the general background of each child participant and obtain some relevant personal details of each child such as age, competence and other details specific to your study. You also need to consider the chronological, developmental and mental age of the children you are interviewing. As it can take considerable time to develop rapport with children as children tend to be wary of unknown adults (Irwin and Johnson, 2005), you need to allow enough time to have a general conversation with the child in advance of the research interview itself. You need to adapt your technique for individual children. Make sure that you tailor your interview to suit their needs and you may want to use participatory methods to facilitate the interview. Some of these decisions will relate to the age of the child and their level of maturity. There are creative methods designed to engage the child. Look at Box 11.1 to consider which participatory methods you might want to use.

Box 11.1   Different participatory methods

- Drawings
  - Glitter pens
  - Crayons and felt tip pens
  - Painting

- Cameras and photographs
- Emoticon faces (☺ ☹ and so forth) to represent happy, sad, angry, etc.
- Vignettes
- Diagrams
- Worksheets
- Puppet shows

Although there are several participatory techniques, you should not take using additional methods for granted. It is very easy to think that all children need to have additional activities in the interview and automatically include them but this may not be the case. It is important that you engage in critical reflection of these methods and think about how they actually work in practice (Punch, 2002). No activities can replace good engagement and rapport skills such as identifying when a child might need reassurance or encouragement. Emanating warmth and interest in the child cannot be replaced with props.

There are four main methodological issues of participatory research with children:

1 You need to consider the setting in which the data collection is taking place. Think about the balance of power, the voluntary nature of consent and your own skills and abilities to interview children.
2 You should ensure that you value each child that you interview and make sure that they are equal in the research partnership.
3 Participatory methods can be used in different ways but need to be age appropriate. You will need to be flexible about what is appropriate for each of the children you interview and not use the same technique for all of the children in your sample.
4 It is important that the child can express their opinions and you need to plan for this. Talk to the child's parents/guardians and don't make assumptions that all children enjoy drawing and so forth. Find out what the child enjoys doing and use this knowledge to help engage the child in the interview. Give the child some options to choose what they prefer.

(*Source:* Horstman et al., 2008).

It is also important to take cues from the child, for example, if a child is wearing a T shirt that has a cartoon character or football team colours on it, that may be a great place to start and make the child feel comfortable and immediately indicates you are interested in them and what is of interest to them.

Activity 11.1

We recommend that at this point you conduct a literature search on participatory methods with children to familiarise yourself with all of the available choices and how they work in interview practice.

```
┌──────────┐ Activity 11.2 ┌──────────
│          Make a list of what you think are the main advantages and disadvantages of
│          using participatory methods in an interview with children.
└─────────────────────────────────────────────────────────────────────
```

Activity 11.2

Make a list of what you think are the main advantages and disadvantages of using participatory methods in an interview with children.

There are several advantages to using a qualitative interview for your research and you may want to consider the following:

- They provide a flexible method for data collection. This is because unlike structured quantitative interviews you can vary the order in which you ask the questions and you can add in questions or change the wording to suit different participants. For example, you might have a broad age range of children that you want to interview and therefore while the basis of the question may remain the same, the way you word it and deliver it may change according to particular needs.
- They allow you to engage the child. In the previous chapter we discussed how the structured interview allows you to engage the child more and check their understanding, but with qualitative interviews there is the flexibility to follow interesting issues that the child raises. This means that you can pursue issues that arise but have not been previously considered.
- They allow you to obtain data with depth. In other words when children tell you something interesting you can explore this and ask additional probing questions allowing them to expand on their answers and giving you the reasons behind their answers.
- They allow you to explore sensitive issues.

Having considered the advantages to using a qualitative interview for your child-focused project, we will now review the limitations of using this method. You might want to consider the following.

- It may not be the method of choice for children who find articulating their views difficult. You may want to refer back at this point and think about the different groups of children and really think about whether interviewing is an appropriate method for collecting data from some of them. For children who are asylum seekers you may need an interpreter to be able to interview, for deaf children you will need someone who can perform sign language and for children who have no linguistic ability (for example, some autistic children) you may need to find alternative means of communicating.
- The interview context may appear formal and quite frightening to some children, particularly young children, and therefore you will need to take measures to ensure that the child can relax. For example, you can sit on the floor on cushions with the child so that you are on the same level, have a bowl of sweets available (if parents permit it) and allow the child to eat them during the interview, put up some child-friendly pictures on the walls and make sure that the room is warm, well lit and private.
- Your data may not access the child's real experiences and data may simply reflect the interview. This means that the child may provide you with socially desirable answers as they fear retribution from you and therefore you will need to try to reduce any power imbalances and reassure the child of confidentiality.

- You will need to practise your interviewing skills as it is not necessarily easy to interview children. Think about the last time you had a conversation with a child from the age group you want to interview. You want to make the interview as conversational as possible and as natural as you can. It can be useful to practise talking to children in other contexts before you start interviewing. Practise with children you already know or do some volunteer work in a school or youth club. It is easy to slip into using adult-centred language and not be child-friendly, particularly if you rarely communicate with children, highlighting again the importance of practice.
- The child may say very little and therefore data collection will be limited. You need to be prepared for this possibility. You can do your best to help them relax and use lots of prompts to help open up the conversation but unfortunately sometimes a child will just not engage. You will then have to make the decision as to whether to include that data in your corpus or not.

Because of the number of disadvantages of the interviewing technique when conducting qualitative interviews with children there are several things you need to think about. You need to do some planning and we provide some useful hints about planning in Box 11.2.

Box 11.2   Planning the interview

- Go on some training in terms of communicating with and interviewing children; you may also want to do some general qualitative interview training first if you are new to this type of research.
- Pilot your interview schedule on at least two children outside of your study to practise your interviewing technique and the usefulness of your questions.
- Consult the literature carefully and extensively for advice and pitfalls.
- Be knowledgeable of the child before you start your interview; it is useful to get some information from parents/teachers/doctors.
- Try to build up a rapport with the child before you start. It may be a good idea to visit the children you plan to interview in advance, and spend some time with them at home or in the classroom (whatever is appropriate).
- Make active decisions about participatory techniques and do not use them blindly with all the children.

Interviewing children can be a complex activity and there are a number of decisions you will need to make. Think about the following issues when you are planning your study.

Choosing the number of interviews to conduct

The number of children you interview will depend on the topic being investigated and the resources you have available. You will need to be practical and flexible in your approach to sampling and your sample size should be sufficient to address your research question. A particular quality marker in qualitative research is that of data/thematic saturation, a concept adopted from the method of grounded theory, which is now often understood to mean that nothing new is emerging as more interviews are conducted.

To ensure that you reach saturation it is useful to follow the four-phase model proposed by Francis et al. (2010). They note that the first phase is to use your intuition as you are interviewing as you should get a sense as you go along whether anything new is emerging in relation to your research question. The second phase is to begin coding the data to explore the issues that are emerging from your interviews. Continue interviewing until you are certain of your 'stopping criterion'. The third phase is to code the data properly, using two or more coders where possible. This ensures inter-rater reliability and indicates quality in your research (Armstrong et al., 1997). The final phase is to disseminate your work.

It is generally agreed that to reach this saturation point in a single category of children will require 10 interviews (Francis et al., 2010). This means that by 10 interviews it is likely that nothing new will be emerging but you should conduct three additional interviews to be certain. If you have more than one category then you should try to have even numbers of each group represented and it is likely that to saturate each group will require a minimum of ten participants per category. This will of course depend on the similarities and the extent of the differences between categories. Only you as the researcher can see when you are getting considerable repetition from each group.

Be warned, however, that the marker of saturation is not appropriate to all methods and all types of interview as some qualitative methods analyse a single case and it is questionable whether it can ever truly be achieved with unstructured interviews (O'Reilly and Parker, 2012). If you do use saturation as a quality marker for sample size then it is essential that you are transparent about it in your dissemination practice. For a good discussion on sample sizes for interviews you might want to refer to the ESRC paper, edited by Baker and Edwards (2012) and listed at the end of this chapter, as it provides a range of different points of view on the issue.

Choosing an appropriate place to conduct the interviews

This will largely depend on where you are obtaining your sample from and what resources are available to you. You may conduct interviews in the school environment, a hospital, a youth club or the child's own home. Each of these contexts has its own unique advantages and disadvantages so think these through before deciding on a location. Most commonly children are interviewed in their own homes or in school.

If you interview in school then you may need to pay additional attention to coercion and power as this is potentially viewed as an authoritarian environment. You will also need to consider whether you interrupt a child's break time and whether this is long enough, in which case the child may become restless to go out and play; whether interviews take place after school, in which case the child may simply want to go home; or whether they take place during lesson time, in which case they may be missing valuable education time (parents may not allow participation if this is the case). If interviewing in the home then the child and parents may be more comfortable but you may need to think more about your own safety, as highlighted earlier in the book. Furthermore this may create a number of difficulties for you such as interruptions, noisy pets, unexpected visitors and other pressures (MacDonald, 2008).

Deciding whether to allow the parent to be present

This will depend on the child's age and the issues under investigation. Generally it would be acceptable and often desirable to have a parent present. If the child or the parent expresses a wish that they be present then ethically you have an obligation to allow the parent to stay in the room while the interview is conducted. While ostensibly this may feel like it is a limitation in your design, the reality is that this can add richness to your analysis. If parents contribute in places to the interview then this may give you a deeper understanding of the issues and the child's experiences. This is because using a qualitative framework allows you flexibility and variability in design without compromising the quality of the analysis.

It may be inappropriate for the parent to be present if the child wishes to be alone or the integrity of the interview is likely to be compromised as the parent's presence may influence the truthfulness of the responses, for example, about sexual activity or substance misuse. This will need careful negotiation. Adequate preparation should anticipate these problems so such interviews probably should not be planned to take place in the home.

Managing the issue of power

If you are engaging children in research then you should be aware of the asymmetry that exists between you. You can take steps to ameliorate some of the power issues but you must remain aware and reflexive throughout the interview process. You need to think about your professional role and think about whether you have more than one role that may influence the child's responses. For example, if you are a teacher in the child's school this may influence the type of responses you obtain. It is important that you prepare the child for the interview, debrief the child at the end and engage them in active decisions throughout the process.

When you have planned your interview effectively and you have made all of the relevant decisions, you will actually need to carry out your interviews and in Box 11.3 we provide some advice regarding what you need to think about at the interview phase of your project.

Box 11.3   Being proactive in the interview

- Be sensitive to the needs of the child.
- Have a range of participatory techniques available and tailor them to the child.
- Do not adhere rigidly to your schedule – allow the child to lead you to interesting topics and experiences.
- Do not interrupt the child – allow them space to reflect and think about their answers.
- Be prepared to rephrase your questions.
- Be patient with the child, as they may find the interview difficult.
- Maintain your focus and remember your research question.
- Think about where you sit, try not to sit higher than the child, and take your cues from the child.
- Be age appropriate. If you are interviewing teenagers you will need to behave differently from if you are interviewing nursery children.

Focus groups

Interviewing children in groups has some advantages over one-to-one interviewing as it can help reveal consensus views and can generate richer responses. The focus group method is basically a group interview where you as a researcher facilitate the discussion to keep it on track with the research agenda. The focus group thus allows a range of opinions and experiences to emerge and allows a space for different ideas to be challenged by others. Focus groups with children can provide you with access to the children's own language and can encourage elaboration of issues and concerns (Singh and Keenan, 2010).

In the focus group you will need to encourage children to open up about the issue and be careful not to allow particular children to dominate the conversation. Remember that groups can feel inhibiting for some children and therefore there may be some members who contribute less than they might in an individual interview. Children also need to be reminded about the information they share in terms of who will hear their comments and may need to be reminded to think about what they say before they say it. There will need to be a list of group rules made up for the children to follow as this will help them follow your research agenda and treat each other respectfully. Facilitating focus groups takes skill so attending specific training may be helpful.

There are several benefits to using a focus group for your research with children and they are able to produce rich in-depth data. They provide a holistic picture of children's culture and language. Because you are able to see how children interact with each other you can get some sense of the culture that exists within that group of children and the different ways of interacting. You can explore the different types of language they use to communicate with each other and you can explore the hierarchical positions they occupy.

Focus groups are useful for allowing children to bounce ideas off each other. The 'two heads are better than one' principle applies here. In the focus group children are able to freely explore the ideas that arise naturally from the group and it is likely to lead to a broader investigation of the issues. This means that the group context allows for a variety of voices to be present. In the focus group you can obtain multiple perspectives from one interview. You can test out different ideas in the group situation and see how different children respond to it.

A significant advantage of using focus groups with children is that they allow you to develop an issue and explore themes. For example, you can explore solutions to specific problems such as dealing with bullying in the school environment.

While there are several advantages to using a focus group for your child-focused project, as ever there are also limitations. For example, it can be difficult to coordinate a mutually convenient time and venue that suits the parents, children and yourself. It is likely that it will be the responsibility of the parents to bring their children to your focus group and so you need to consider where they go while you are with the children.

As with adult focus groups you may find that some children are likely to dominate the conversation. Quieter, shyer children are less likely to contribute and yet their contribution may be very important for your research question. There is the possibility of group effects such as conformity and so forth. Children's relationships are complex and there could be outside issues between the children that you are not aware of such as disputes, conflict or bullying. These may or may not become apparent during the focus group but you may find that some children lead the discussion and others follow. As a facilitator you need to be aware of these dynamics and while they may be interesting as interaction issues in their own right, you may want to take steps to engage quieter children in the discussion. When you bring a group of children together you may find that they have little to say on the issue and contribute very little or that they disagree with each other and become disruptive or conflict with one another. You will need to balance an adult authority with a reassurance that they have equal status in the group and that their perspectives are important. Using appropriate humour can be a useful way of engaging children.

Sensitive topics will require additional handling skills. You will need to be careful not to allow discussions to become distressful during the conversation and when sensitive topics are raised you will have to take responsibility for ensuring an understanding among the group. This also raises additional ethical sensitivities such as issues of confidentiality. As there are many members of the focus group the children in the group may gossip about particular members of the group outside of it.

Particularly disadvantageous is that recordings are more time-consuming to transcribe because of the multi-party interaction and do have potential to alter the behaviour of the children, although this is debatable (see O'Reilly et al., 2011; Speer and Hutchby, 2003).

Activity 11.3

James is a teacher at a small primary school and is conducting a small-scale piece of research on children's fears about moving up to comprehensive/high school. He wants to do three focus groups with 10–11-year-olds about their feelings related to moving schools. What advice would you give James?

We provide a list of possible advice at the back of the book. Compare this to your own list and see how many of the issues you managed to address.

Interviewing children in groups can be a complex activity and there are a number of decisions you will need to make. Think about the following issues when you are planning your interview study.

Choosing the number of focus groups to conduct

If you look at the literature you will find that there is considerable variation in the number of focus groups conducted in any one particular study and there is limited guidance on how many constitute an adequate sample size. We recommend you follow a similar rule as for one-to-one interviews and think about data saturation (O'Reilly and Parker, 2012). Conduct focus groups until nothing new emerges from them. This will depend upon how many children you have in each focus group and the nature of the schedule.

Focus groups may be difficult to set up and you may not reach a saturation point before practical reasons force you to stop collecting data. As with individual interviews you will need to be transparent about your sampling strategies during dissemination and you will have to make informed judgements regarding when saturation has been reached. If you cannot reach it, it does not mean your data is invalid. You can still reach useful conclusions and represent the data well. You need to think about the types of children represented in your focus groups and whether this is adequate to address your research question. Do you need children from different age groups, from different ethnic or social backgrounds, from different genders and so on? The more a variety of demographics matter to your study the more focus groups you are likely to need to conduct, although some of this will also depend on the research question.

Considering the number of children to include in each focus group

Again the literature has a variety of examples of different group sizes for focus groups and there does not seem to be any rule of thumb for the best number of children to include. Typically a focus group is made up of approximately eight to ten children (Morgan, 1998) but you could have as few as three or four children present. When deciding how many children to include in each focus group you might want to think about their age, their levels of competence, their social skills, the topic being discussed (you might want smaller groups for more sensitive topics) and the length of the focus group in terms of time.

Deciding how long the focus groups last

This will depend on two main things – the age of the children and the research agenda. Younger children are less likely to sit still for as long as older children and you may need to include participatory methods during the focus group so that conversation is centred around a task. Remember that the children may grow bored with the discussion and start talking about other things or express a desire to change rooms or activities. Try to get to the research point as quickly as you can but not at the expense of rapport.

Considering the depth of involvement of the facilitator

The point of qualitative research is the participant perspective and the focus groups should ideally be participant led. Your presence in the focus group should not be intrusive or structured and you should allow the children to talk as freely as possible regarding the topic. Children are likely to need some leadership to keep on topic so it may be necessary to interject with contributions, guidance or additional questions to get them talking.

Planning the opening and closing of the focus group

Ideally you should start the focus group with an introduction. Remind the children who you are and why you are there, of the key ethical concerns, and show that you value their contributions. Outline the goals of the research in a child-centred manner and remind them of the presence of the recording device. It is useful to get the children to write their names on sticky labels to attach to their clothing so you can remember who they are – this could be turned into a fun starter activity while you build rapport. At the end of the focus group, make sure that you thank the children for participating and explain to them what happens to the data next.

Ethnography and participant observation

Ethnography literally means to write about people and much ethnographic work involving children is concerned with explaining their everyday social lives (James, 2001). The purpose of ethnography is to gain an understanding about a specific group of people and this method has provided us with a wealth of information about children's lives. When the research starts the researcher is a stranger to the child and their family and the ethnographer has to go to considerable lengths to build a rapport with the child and encourage openness and engagement (Christensen, 2004). Ethnography has been an important methodological development for research with children – it has enabled children to be recognised as people to be studied in their own right as it permits the view of the child as a competent interpreter of the social world (James, 2001). Ethnography is a particularly important research method because it ensures that the cultural place is incorporated in our understanding of a child's development (Weisner, 1996).

Doing ethnography encompasses a range of different qualitative techniques, commonly unstructured interviews and observations (James, 2001). While you may record this type of data depending on consent and so forth, it is likely that you will write extensive field notes and reflexive journals and potentially use visual materials such as photographs. It is important to note the time commitment, training requirements and specialised skills needed to be an ethnographer. Remember that ethnographers are engaged with their participants, rather than assessing or evaluating them (Weisner, 1996).

Ethnographers generally employ observation as the main technique of data collection as this is seen as having the most potential to engage children in research (James, 2001). If you decide to engage in ethnography you will need to think about the type of observer you become (there are a number of different types outlined in Box 11.4).

Box 11.4 Different types of observer

- Complete participant – this is where you are a fully functioning member of that social setting and your true identity is unknown to the participants. Your true identity will probably need to be known to the parents though in order to obtain consent to observe their children, but if justified some deception may be necessary for the children. This type of study happens infrequently, and needs a rationale which can be justified ethically, as consent from children is favoured and debriefing may be necessary. For example, you may go into a school classroom and work with the children to observe their behaviours, but you may not want them to know you are doing research until afterwards.
- Participant-as-observer – this is where you are a fully functioning member of the social setting but participants are aware they are being researched. This is where both the parents and the children know who you are and why you are there.
- Observer-as-participant – here you are mostly an interviewer but there is some observation with little participation.
- Complete observer – this is when you do not interact with people and you observe in an unobtrusive way, for example, if you stand in a shop and observe a child's buying habits.

(*Source:* Bryman, 2008)

There are several advantages to using ethnography for your research:

- You are able to observe the child in their natural environment. You can go into school or the family home and watch the child. In ethnography you are expected to be an active participant in the child's life so you are likely to spend lots of time with the child in the family home or whichever environment you are studying.
- Because you are fully involved in the child's culture, lifestyle and general day-to-day activities you can become fully immersed in the field of study and really learn about that child's life.
- Some children have limited competence or speech and therefore it may be more appropriate to observe them than try to interview them.
- Ethnography does well at reflecting the perspectives of the children themselves and in promoting a view of children as competent with rights.

There are also limitations in using this method:

- Gaining access to the social setting is difficult because of the level of involvement required by the researcher. You can gain access to public settings such as parks, football matches and so forth and be a covert observer (although you will have to comply with ethical considerations) or you can actively become a member of the setting and get to know all relevant parties.

- Good ethnography is time-consuming and will require the researcher to commit large chunks of time to the process.

Naturally occurring data

For some research, you may prefer to collect naturally occurring data. Some qualitative perspectives advocate only using naturally occurring data (such as conversation analysis). Some schools of thought go so far as to say that interview data is contrived and reflects nothing but the interview itself (Potter and Hepburn, 2005).

If you decide to utilise naturally occurring child data then the simple rule of thumb is the 'dead researcher test' (Potter, 2002). This means that if the researcher were to die on route to collecting the data would the event still go ahead? So for a research interview the answer is no. Your interview would be cancelled and the child would go back to daily life. If you were going to record a lesson in a classroom then yes, the lesson would still go ahead without you, thus it is naturally occurring. Notwithstanding issues such as ethics and the possibility of altered behaviour, naturally occurring data is that which has limited researcher interference.

You may thus decide that you want to collect data from children that is as natural as possible. For example, you may want to record them having therapy, record them in their lessons, record them at the dinner table or look at how they are represented on television.

Using naturally occurring data in child-based research is particularly useful as it has limited researcher interference. This is because you are not heavily involved during the data collection phase. You can be quite discreet. Although you will have to have ethical approval for the presence of the video camera for some forms of research, children do get used to the presence of the camera quite quickly. Some forms of naturally occurring data do not even require this much from you as they can be television programmes or newspaper reports and thus you have no influence on how the data is presented.

Research that uses naturally occurring data studies people in the real world rather than the abstract one. Naturally occurring data has the benefit of seeing the child in their natural environment. For example, the way children are presented in a magazine is a reflection of the way that magazine sees children, regardless of whether you agree with that representation. Thus it is mindful of the context in which the data is collected. Because you are not taking the child out of their context to study them you can see how they really are within the context. So rather than asking the child what they think of family therapy, you can see how they interact in family therapy. In this way the data is thought to truly represent reality.

However, there are limitations to using naturally occurring data. If you are using real children in your research (rather than publically available texts) it can be difficult to secure ethically. The average UK classroom has 30 children present. To be able to record it for research purposes you will need the consent of 30 sets of parents, 30 children, the teacher and any other teaching staff in that room, along with and the head teacher. If just one of these parties declines it is unlikely that you can go ahead with recording.

It is obvious then that some forms of naturally occurring data collection will require considerable planning. Furthermore, as we have mentioned previously in this chapter, it is arguable whether the presence of the recording device alters behaviour or influences participants in any way. Some people maintain that the presence of the recording device alters the behaviour and thus the behaviour is no longer naturally occurring. Quite often, however, children are used to the presence of video cameras in their worlds as society becomes more and more technologically advanced and they typically forget about the presence of the camera (see again O'Reilly et al., 2011; Speer and Hutchby, 2003).

If you are going to use naturally occurring data for your research project then you will need to question your role in the process. It is questionable whether the analyst can really remove themselves from the process of data collection. Just because you may not have had any influence on the magazine article, or minimal influence on the recording of the family therapy/classroom and so forth does not mean that you are fully removed from the process.

Activity 11.4

What do you think is better – naturally occurring data or interview/focus group data? Why? You may want to return to Potter and Hepburn's (2005) critique of interviewing to help you address this question. We provide some answers at the back of this book for your reference.

Documents

The use of documents for qualitative research is becoming increasingly popular. Written and visual documents are being used more in research (Bryman, 2008). One way of engaging children in research is to ask them to produce diaries, letters or drawings and analyse them for research purposes. Photographs can also be data in their own right and you can ask children to take pictures and then interview them about the activity. Alternatively you can use documents produced about children more naturally and analyse them. For example, you might want to look at a series of special needs statements from educational psychologists, magazine articles about children, doctors' referral letters and so forth.

Official documents can also be used as data. You can look at how children are represented in official documents such as the Children Act 2004 (HM Government, 2004b) or child policies such as 'Every Child Matters' (HM Government, 2004a) and consider what this means for our understanding of children and childhood.

Mass media outputs are also being more commonly used to research children. Newspapers, magazines, television programmes and the internet are all useful sources of data for analysis. Typically you can search for themes in the sources and consider how children are represented in the press.

Interpreting documents can be difficult. The most prevalent approach to analysing documents is thematic analysis and qualitative content analysis which search out patterns and themes in the documents. **Semiotics** is an approach that analyses the symbols in everyday life and looks at signs, codes and hidden meanings (Bryman, 2008). **Hermeneutics** is a more interpretive approach to documents. This pays attention to the social and historical context in which the text was produced as this is seen as influential for analysis.

There are several approaches to using documents for your research project. They are easy to access and often readily available. Notably, some documents are easier to access than others. Naturally occurring documents such as magazine/newspaper articles, policy documents and so forth can typically be found on the internet. If, however, you want children to produce letters or diaries and so forth then you will need to consult the practical advice in relation to interviewing to help you do this effectively. You may also want to think about the literacy ability of the children during the planning stages.

Collecting documents as data is typically cost-effective and often they are free or very cheap. Again in relation to internet-accessible documents you can usually download them free of charge and then explore the common themes and issues. There may be more of a cost incurred for collecting children's diaries, stories and letters and so forth, although this is unlikely to be expensive.

Importantly, collecting documents, particularly public documents, has fewer ethical concerns if not directly involving children. While diaries and letters written by children will carry many of the same ethical issues as other forms of data collection from children, those more naturally occurring documents require very little in the way of ethical planning.

As well as the advantages to using documents for your child-focused project discussed above, there are invariably some limitations with this method.

When faced with several different documents it is not always easy to interpret meaning. You will need to be careful with your interpretations as there may not be an option to obtain clarification from the writer. Some documents may present a bias or political view. This is particularly true if you are analysing newspaper or magazine representations of an issue.

If you decide to use documents as your source of data then you need to be mindful that the quality of the data depends on the writer. As we mentioned before not all children can write well, or convey their meanings well in the written form. You will need to decide whether you will obtain richer data from children in the form of interviews or through allowing them to express themselves more creatively in the form of a diary or letter. You may find that more visual methods such as photography work better for that particular child or group. You will need to consult the teachers, parents or other carers before making this decision. It would also be useful to spend some time with child stakeholders when planning the research.

Practical issues in qualitative data collection

When you are collecting your data there will be various practical issues you need to consider including the types of recording you wish to do, how you go about transcribing your data and how you manage any distress that the children might display.

Dealing with distress

Depending upon the topic you are talking about and the sensitivity of the issues under discussion there may be a likelihood of the child or children becoming distressed during data collection. Talking about difficult issues can cause distress but it may also have a cathartic effect and help the child move forward. Avoid stepping in to reduce distress immediately as that may prevent the child from utilising their own resources. You need to remember, however, that some children may require support after the data has been collected and therefore you need to take some responsibility for identifying support options and access to these for your participants

As we mentioned earlier in the chapter it may be useful to allow the parent to remain present during data collection as they will be able to help you if the child becomes distressed. Distress is not always predictable but if it is likely then it is a good idea to have the parent available and close by. Have a box of tissues with you so you can pass one to the child in the event of crying and stop the tape for a few minutes to give them time to gather their thoughts. Make sure you give them an opportunity to stop if they need to.

Recording issues

With many forms of qualitative data collection it is a good idea to video-tape or audio-tape as this provides a record of the interaction and allows the researcher to evaluate their techniques. You cannot be expected to remember everything that went on in the interview or focus group and if you take too many notes during the data collection the child may become distracted or feel devalued and you may also miss key information or cues. You need to decide whether you are going to use video-taping or audio-taping and think about the ethical sensitivities these entail (O'Reilly et al., 2011).

Whichever type of recording device you choose to adopt you need to think about several factors that are outlined in Box 11.5.

Box 11.5   Factors in recording equipment

- Consider the cost of equipment and tapes. In some locations they are already set up for recording and may have a two-way mirror which is less intrusive, but more often you may need to purchase a digital recorder and these can be expensive.
- Try to choose somewhere quiet to enhance the recording and reduce the level of background noise.
- Test and familiarise yourself with the equipment before you use it.
- Make sure the microphone is near the participant. This can be more difficult if there are lots of participants being recorded at the same time.
- Allow children time to become accustomed to the presence of the recording device.

Transcription issues

If you are undertaking qualitative research then it is highly likely that you will have to transcribe your data. While you may pay a professional transcriptionist to transcribe your data verbatim, you must not underestimate how much additional work you as the researcher need to put in to tidy up the transcript. You need to think about which qualitative perspective you are utilising in your research, as for some perspectives there is a step-by-step process to transcription whereby you collect all of your data and then transcribe it, whereas for other methods you do data collection, transcription and analysis in parallel.

Remember that transcription is an active process and the level of detail required will depend upon the choices you make and the perspective you use. Too often researchers brush over the issue of transcription and fail to be transparent about their choices, but there are different ways of transcribing that draw out different features and may affect the reading and analysis of the data (Lapadat and Lindsay, 1999). What this means is that you have to make active choices about your transcription methods in terms of style and content. You need to think about the level of detail that is needed in the transcript and whether you want to include paralinguistic features such as nodding, sneezing, coughing and so forth. This is not just a pragmatic issue relating to resources but can have actual impact at the analysis stage. This will be influenced by the research question.

Bear in mind that there are high costs in terms of time and potentially money in the transcription process and transcribing for long and sustained periods can be very tiring. It is suggested that a 35-minute interview can take anything from two to five hours to transcribe (Lucas, 2010). It is useful therefore to consider whether full verbatim transcripts are really necessary for your work, and do not underestimate the importance of making field notes even if you are recording your data (Halcomb and Davidson, 2006). Note, however, that some form of transcript is usually needed for analysis and dissemination and it is rare to rely solely on field notes and the tapes for this purpose.

Analysis

There are many forms of qualitative analysis that you can choose from. It is necessary to note that most of these forms require you to choose which method of analysis you will undertake during the planning stages. This is so that your data collection and analysis are epistemologically congruent. Many of the different forms of qualitative analysis, such as grounded theory, interpretative phenomenological analysis, narrative analysis and discourse analysis are specialised and will require you to undertake formal training before you can use them.

For the purpose of this book we introduce you to qualitative analysis by looking at the more generic and more common qualitative methods of analysis only, to give you a flavour of what qualitative analysis of child data involves. We focus therefore on content analysis, template analysis and thematic analysis only.

Content analysis

Although content analysis is predominantly a quantitative form of analysis we discuss it here as it can be both quantitative and qualitative. Furthermore it has often been used alongside other methods of qualitative analysis as a way of reporting more accurate frequencies.

Typically (although not exclusively) content analysis is used to analyse documents and texts. It is not in itself a research method but an approach to analysis. When you do content analysis you will need to establish categories for coding and then count the number of instances in which they are used in the text or image (Joffe and Yardley, 2004). This means that you have to make decisions about what should be counted. Remember that these decisions ought to be guided by your research question and the aims of your project.

In order to do this effectively you will need to develop a coding frame. The coding frame has two central features – the coding schedule and the coding manual (Bryman, 2008). The coding schedule is the form onto which you will enter your data relating to a particular pre-identified code; this consists of a table with columns and rows. The column heading depicts the dimension to be coded and the rows contain the numbers. You also need to develop a coding manual to ensure inter-coder reliability. This means that you develop a manual of instructions for other coders which includes all of the possible categories for any given dimension (Bryman, 2008), and so other members of the research team can also code the data.

There are a number of benefits to using content analysis for analysing your data as it is a flexible method which can be applied to a number of different types of information and it allows for both quantitative and qualitative interpretation. Content analysis is a transparent research method as the coding schemes and methods are set out clearly, allowing for replication and for information to be generated about social groups. Importantly this form of analysis is useful for longitudinal analysis and allows several researchers to work together. Of significant advantage is the fact that it is fairly unobtrusive as the participants are less likely to take the researcher into account.

Content analysis is a useful step-by-step method which is easier for novice researchers to apply, allowing them to analyse a large volume of text through a systematic method of analysis. It is especially useful for providing cultural insights over a period of time.

There are some limitations to using content analysis. As with many other forms of analysis there will always be a level of interpretation required on the part of the researcher and coding large volumes of data can be time-consuming and laborious. When using content analysis it can be difficult to analyse the information in depth, thus potentially having a superficial level of analysis worsened by the potential to lose the context and meaning of the text through the coding process. Typically content analyses lack a theoretical base and remember that the quality of your analysis will depend on the quality of the document you are coding.

Although content analysis is typically a quantitative method it has been used as a qualitative method. Qualitative content analysis attempts to preserve the advantages of quantitative content analysis and often utilises the frequencies generated from quantitative coding and builds upon this to report a more holistic picture of the data. For qualitative content analysis to be successful you will need to develop the rules of analysis, carefully define the categories and ensure there are criteria for validity and reliability (Mayring, 2000). This can be integrated with the quantitative content analysis performed.

Thematic analysis

Thematic analysis is one of the few methods of analysis that is epistemologically free and is thus compatible with a range of theories and paradigms. Thematic analysis is a method used to identify, analyse and report patterns within a data set, allowing the organisation of data in a way that describes it in detail (Braun and Clarke, 2006). Thematic analysis therefore allows you to make simple interpretations about your data by describing what is going on within it (Boyatzis, 1998). You should note, however, that thematic analysis is more than just themes emerging from the data as this suggests that the analyst is passive in the process; thematic analysis is actually an active process (Braun and Clarke, 2006).

Typically thematic analysis is performed on interview data but it can be applied to focus group data, open-ended questions from questionnaires, documents and video-taped materials (Joffe and Yardley, 2004). To do thematic analysis properly you need to go through your data repeatedly and really familiarise yourself with both the tapes and the transcripts. You will need to code your data first and then analyse it by breaking up the data into themes. A theme is something that captures something important about the data and thus relates to the research question in a patterned way (Braun and Clarke, 2006). As this is the most popular qualitative method, particularly for those new to qualitative approaches, we provide further focus on this analytic technique and provide you with core information regarding the 11 main steps to undertaking a thematic analysis.

Step-by-step guide to doing thematic analysis

There are some things you need to think about when you start your thematic analysis. Have a look at Box 11.6 to help you get started. (We also recommend that you read Braun and Clarke (2006) if you are going to undertake thematic analysis.)

Box 11.6   Getting started

Step one: you need to consult your research question. Your thematic analysis should answer the research question so you need to be really clear what that is before you start

Step two: listen to your data. Listen to the interviews, focus groups or re-read the documents you are analysing

(Continued)

(Continued)

Step three: have a full transcript of your data. Transcription is an active process so your transcripts should reflect active decisions. Read through your transcripts and look for interesting things as you go through them

When you have done all of this you will be ready to start coding your data corpus. There are a number of steps involved in coding so consult Box 11.7 to help you do this.

Box 11.7 Coding

Step four: start coding. Boyatzis (1998) argues that there are three levels of coding: first order, second order and third order coding

Step five: first order coding – this is the first level of basic coding that you do. You need to organise and categorise your data to give it some meaning. This level of coding is descriptive and will require going through your transcript several times as you may need to revise or change your codes as you go. In this level of coding you go through each transcript sentence by sentence and assign codes to it. Each sentence may have more than one code and you should end up with a very large number of first order codes at the end of your coding

Step six: second order coding – at this point you need to start interpreting the meaning of the text and thinking about how your first order codes address your research question. You need to capture larger segments of text at this stage and note that some of your previous codes may not be relevant. Then you need to reorganise your first order codes into more meaningful categories and group many of them together to create a shorter list of categories

Step seven: third order coding – this is where you organise the categories from second order coding into themes. This means that you identify large patterns in the data and bring them together to tell a story which answers the research question

Once you have coded your data set you will need to start making some sense of it and actually start managing the themes that have emerged from it. Look at Box 11.8 for the next steps regarding managing themes.

Box 11.8   **Managing themes**

Step eight: you need to scale down your analysis into manageable topics to draw out the themes which best represent your data and the research objectives for dissemination. You are likely to have too many themes from step seven so you need to think about which ones you are actually going to use

Step nine: identify any subthemes. Some of your larger overall themes may need to be broken down into subthemes to best tell the story you want to tell

---

Once you have identified your themes and subthemes you need to start thinking about how you represent that data in a more meaningful way for your audiences. Box 11.9 will help you to do this.

Box 11.9   **Representing the data**

Step ten: you need to identify quotations from the data that best represent each theme and subtheme for inclusion in the final write-up. Remember that you are providing a narrative that is backed up with the literature so you will need to have done some considerable reading in the area and think about how your quotations link in with that

Step eleven: be reflexive as you write. Don't forget to note down the process in your research diary and make notes regarding how you feel and how you made your choices

---

Thematic analysis is a commonly applied method of analysis in qualitative research due to the number of benefits. Thematic analysis is a flexible method free from theory which gives it a broad applicability. It does, however, allow you to be active in the process of analysis and means that you can give all items in your data your equal attention. This means that it is a useful way to organise large amounts of data, allowing you to develop a convincing story from your findings and describe your data in a way which is accessible to a range of different audiences. (You may want to refer back to this point after you have read Chapter 12 on dissemination.)

Thematic analysis is particularly useful for highlighting similarities and differences across a data corpus and has potential to highlight unexpected issues of importance in the data. This may help to inform policy development or practice in the field. Because thematic analysis requires that you use direct quotations from your participants it contains important messages from the children themselves.

The limitations of thematic analysis include the difficulty in deciding what to focus on, given the potentially large volumes of data. If you have carried out a number of interviews with children then you are likely to have obtained a large volume of rich and exciting data and this can be overwhelming when it produces a large number of themes.

Remember that thematic analysis is a largely descriptive method and thus cannot go beyond description. You need to be careful about making any interpretations and unless the data is clearly described there is potential for the messages to reflect researcher bias rather than the data and the children's voices. This is furthered by the tendency to focus on what resonates with the researcher, thus reflecting what you are interested in rather than what the children were really saying. Remember that what is not said may be as important as what has been said.

Template analysis

Template analysis is not a clearly defined single method as it actually refers to a group of techniques which thematically organise textual data, typically from interviews or focus groups, but also from diary extracts, internet blogs or open-ended questionnaires. Template analysis is a particular method for thematically analysing qualitative data. Unlike thematic analysis, template analysis advocates the requirement of a clear philosophical position. Template analysis can be employed to analyse any form of textual data and from most of the epistemological positions (King, 2004).

When undertaking template analysis the analysis involves the development of a coding 'template' which summarises these and organises them in a meaningful way (King, 2012). Notably analysis usually starts with some a priori codes, those themes strongly expected to be relevant to analysis, although you may refine and change these as analysis develops. The templates created from template analysis will form the basis for interpretation and the identification of relationships between themes (King, 2004).

To do template analysis effectively you will need ultimately to create an initial template for which you need to identify codes in the data, which consist of labels attached to a section of the data that you deem important based on your interpretations (King, 2012). This is a key stage in template analysis, and be careful not to produce your initial template too early. When developing your initial template you need to take into account your methodological position. If the approach you are taking encourages you to be open and avoid presuppositions then you should take longer in the development of the initial template. If, however, the approach you are taking requires an answer to a specific question then you may need to produce the initial template earlier. King (2004) notes that a useful marker is when things are getting repetitious, you can develop the initial template.

When you have identified the codes in the data you will then need to organise these codes hierarchically which may require clustering groups of codes together. It is recommended that after you have coded the first transcript/ document in your data set you attempt to create your first draft template (King, 2004). When this is done you can systematically work through your other transcripts/documents and build upon the draft template until you have a final version you are satisfied with.

The benefits of using template analysis for your research are not too dissimilar to those of thematic analysis. Like thematic analysis it allows you to work with large data sets and to make sense of large chunks of data. Template analysis allows you to remain active in the process and means that you can work with several other researchers to create the template.

Template analysis goes beyond description to allow you to make some interpretations based on the template you have created. These interpretations are important for the narrative you disseminate and the ways in which you include the children's voices through quotations in your final dissemination. It is particularly useful for highlighting important policy issues.

The disadvantages of template analysis include that it can be particularly difficult to choose which codes to look for in the data and sometimes this can be difficult to ascertain from the literature and research agenda. Furthermore because you are going beyond describing the data the interpretations you make may be subject to criticism from others.

Differences between content, thematic and template analysis

Ostensibly there may seem to be few differences between content, thematic and template analyses and you could be forgiven for thinking that it is difficult to decide which of these three types of analysis to perform. We provide some of the key differences below to help you decide which method best suits your research:

- In content and template analysis the categories are predetermined by the agenda of the researcher; in thematic they tend to be more data driven and emerge from the data (although their emergence may be guided by the interview schedule).
- In content analysis it tends to be textual data – documents – related to mass media and communications; in thematic and template analysis it tends to be analysis of interviews or focus groups run by the researcher (although qualitative content analysis analyses text produced from verbal communication).

- In content analysis there tends to be frequency coding, where frequencies are determined from the categories – this is generally not done with thematic or template analysis.
- In content and template analysis a predetermined coding schedule and coding manual are designed; this is not the case for thematic analysis, where the codes are derived from the data.
- Content analysis tends to require larger amounts of text, either in the size of documents or the number of them, whereas thematic or template analysis can be done on small sample sizes. There is little point in counting the frequencies of data on one small document. Notably, however, thematic analysis can be done on one interview or document whereas this is more difficult for template analysis which tends to need a few cases.
- Thematic analysis is epistemology free and not tied to a particular perspective. This means that it can be conducted with a generic piece of qualitative research. Although content analysis and template analysis do not have tied perspectives they do advocate being clear about the epistemology driving the research in advance of doing it.

Using NVivo

Some forms of qualitative analysis lend themselves to the use of computer software to aid coding. With advancements in technology more researchers use computer-assisted qualitative analysis software such as NVivo to help them manage large amounts of data. NVivo does not do the analysis for you but it can facilitate the coding process to make analysis easier (Bryman, 2008).

What you need to decide is whether it is worth using NVivo. If you only have a small data set and a short time frame to complete your project then the answer is likely to be no. To use NVivo effectively it is probable that you will need to go on a specialised training course and learn the basics. While there are some useful books out there to help you (and we name a couple of these at the end of the chapter), you may want to think about an introductory course to learn the terminology and the general instructions for use. It can feel quite daunting the first time you encounter the software.

NVivo as a program allows you to organise your data in a manageable way. By importing the transcripts into the program you can go through each transcript sentence by sentence and organise the quotations into labelled folders, which you create as you code (these are called nodes in NVivo). This is suitable for many of the qualitative forms of analysis that require you to code your data as part of the analytic process. You can then print out the quotations from that particular folder, giving you exclusive access to everything coded under that label. You can also create subfolders for each main code which is useful for methods such as thematic analysis.

So, for example, you might be interested in children's experiences of being in hospital. You may have interviewed a number of children about their experiences and transcribed the data. So you pull transcript one into NVivo and start coding. In the first sentence you notice that there are two codes, blank walls and friendly nurses, so you create two folders to represent these codes.

As you go on you find that there is a desire for pretty pictures and colourful stickers and you decide these are also codes. You decide that these are subcodes of blank walls and create a new folder to accommodate it and so forth.

What you eventually end up with is a hierarchy 'tree' of folders containing all of the codes (nodes) you have assigned to them. These 'trees' are built up as you code and allow you to simply open up the material related to one code (node) when required. This also gives you an overview of all the different issues related to your data in a way that may be difficult to achieve with highlighter pens and paper.

Summary

In this chapter we have introduced you to the most common forms of qualitative data collection. We have considered any additional techniques you might need to think about when applying these methods to research with children and have considered the advantages and disadvantages of each method. This chapter was designed to help you think about the appropriate ways of obtaining data from children and make active decisions regarding your own project. Furthermore we have considered the more common and less specialised forms of qualitative analysis to help you think about the most appropriate ways to analyse your data. As we advised you in the chapter on planning, this decision should have been made prior to data collection.

Further reading

Baker, S. and Edwards, R. (eds) (2012) *How Many Qualitative Interviews Is Enough? Expert Voices and Early Career Reflections on Sampling and Cases in Qualitative Research.* London: National Centre for Research Methods, Economic and Social Research Council.

Bazeley, P. (2007) *Qualitative Data Analysis with NVivo.* London: Sage.

Boyatzis, R. (1998) *Transforming Qualitative Information: Thematic Analysis and Code Development.* London: Sage.

Braun, V. and Clarke, V. (2006) 'Using thematic analysis in psychology', *Qualitative Research in Psychology*, 3: 77–101.

Danby, S., Ewing, L. and Thorpe, K. (2011) 'The novice researcher: interviewing young children', *Qualitative Inquiry*, 17 (1): 74–84.

Eder, D. and Fingerson, L. (2001) 'Interviewing children and adolescents', in J.F. Gubrium and J.A. Holstein (eds), *Handbook of Interview Research: Context and Method.* London: Sage, pp. 181–201.

Gibbs, G. (2002) *Qualitative Data Analysis: Explorations with NVivo*. Buckingham: Open University Press.

Horstman, M., Aldiss, S., Richardson, A. and Gibson, F. (2008) 'Methodological issues when using the draw and write technique with children aged 6–12 years', *Qualitative Health Research*, 18 (7): 1001–1011.

Joffe, H. and Yardley, L. (2004) 'Content and thematic analysis', in D. Marks and L. Yardley (eds), *Research Methods for Clinical and Health Psychology*. London: Sage, pp. 56–68.

MacDonald, K. (2008) 'Dealing with chaos and complexity: the reality of interviewing children and families in their own homes', *Journal of Clinical Nursing*, 17 (23): 3123–3130.

O'Reilly, M., Parker, N. and Hutchby, I. (2011) 'Ongoing processes of managing consent: the empirical ethics of using video-recording in clinical practice and research', *Clinical Ethics*, 6: 179–185.

Potter, J. and Hepburn, A. (2005) 'Qualitative interviews in psychology: problems and possibilities', *Qualitative Research in Psychology*, 2: 1–27.

Silverman, D. (2005) *Doing Qualitative Research: A Practical Handbook* (2nd edn). London: Sage.

Silverman, D. (2006) *Interpreting Qualitative Data* (3rd edn). London: Sage.

12

Writing up and Dissemination

Introduction

This chapter describes what dissemination is and the different options for disseminating your research. It provides you with advice about choosing an effective method for presenting your findings. We outline how to write an effective report, how to choose an appropriate journal and the process of peer review, how to write a thesis and presenting at conferences. We provide tips and strategies for thinking about the different forms of writing up and dissemination at different levels and for different purposes. We also address some of the child-specific dissemination issues and how dissemination aimed at children may need to be modified. In thinking about dissemination, it is important to bear in mind the cultural issues discussed in Chapter 2.

Dissemination is an often forgotten but important part of research. The process of disseminating research is not as straightforward as often assumed and involves several choices. As with all aspects of the research process effective planning ensures more effective outcomes. Often it is necessary to provide a separate report for your participants and in this chapter we will provide a section on writing a report for participants and the issues of allowing parents to access reports and so forth.

Activity 12.1

Before we start, perhaps it might be helpful to consider how you define dissemination. What methods of dissemination are you aware of and which of these do you find helpful?

What is dissemination?

There are a variety of definitions of dissemination. The following illustrates the key points:

Box 12.1   Defining dissemination

Dissemination is the process through which target groups are made aware of, receive, accept, and use information and other interventions. (National Cancer Institute et al., 2002)

Dissemination goes well beyond simply making research available through the traditional vehicles of journal publication and academic conference presentations. It involves a process of extracting the main messages or key implications derived from research results and communicating them to targeted groups of decision-makers and other stakeholders in a way that encourages them to factor the research implications into their work. Face-to-face communication is encouraged whenever possible.

Why disseminate?

The answer to this might seem obvious but it is likely that the outcomes of many projects are not effectively disseminated. One of the frequent complaints of communities is that project teams seem to forget about them once the data has been collected, and they are rarely told about the project findings or the impact of the project and how it might benefit the community, and yet feedback from a project is generally viewed as positive by research participants (Dixon-Woods et al., 2011). You might want to refer back to our earlier discussion regarding involving stakeholders in your research design and implementation. Dissemination serves several important functions – we shall discuss each in turn (some of the functions on this list were generated from 'Different ways to disseminate project 2011' at http://piper.ntua.gr/reports/infodis/doc0007.htm, accessed 14/05/2011) and they are summarised in Box 12.2.

Box 12.2   Reasons to disseminate

- Responsibility
- Increased knowledge
- Influence on policy and practice

(Continued)

(Continued)

- Raised awareness
- Feedback
- Improved collaboration
- Quality assurance and transparency
- Sustainability
- Personal gain

Responsibility

It is arguable that given the resources used to carry out research, researchers have a responsibility to disseminate as a matter of accountability. There is also the matter of moral and ethical responsibility to share the outcomes so that others might learn from the project. This is just as important if negative findings are discovered, or findings contrary to the aims and objectives of the research. Participants often give their time freely to research so it is important that researchers respect their contribution and utilise it effectively. There may also be a public or legislated duty to disseminate, for example, when large surveys are carried out such as those done by the Office of National Statistics (2011) (this is a government department responsible for collecting and publishing official statistics about the UK's society and economy, which also carries out the ten-yearly census for England and Wales). For such organisations publication of data demonstrates their role and justifies their existence.

Increasing knowledge

Information is often disseminated in the hope that individuals and organisations improve their knowledge base and subsequently make better judgements in future situations. In the health arena, this might be knowledge about patient experience of services and treatments, about how illnesses are caused and so on. In education it may be to help teachers formulate stronger educational plans and support children in the classroom. In social sciences it may be to inform global changes in relation to poverty, or better understand cultural differences in the structure of the family.

Much has been made about the fact that despite all the research undertaken, findings often struggle to find their way into policy or practice. Knowledge translation and management are fields devoted to this very topic. Dissemination should also prevent unnecessary duplication of projects as researchers will not repeat a project that they know has been undertaken. However, they can only be aware of previous research if it has been disseminated.

Influencing policy and practice

Increasing knowledge in health fields is a part of hopefully improving services and clinical care through, for example, better understanding of what causes certain illnesses or of how patients experience a particular care pathway. In other fields, the knowledge will serve similar functions. For example, increasing our knowledge of how children learn has informed important changes in the ways in which children are taught. One would also hope that good research can effect changes in policy so this is another sound reason for dissemination.

Awareness

Information is often disseminated in order to educate, explain or promote a concept, process or principle. Raising awareness is often difficult as a large research project may need to be reduced to a few lines and deciding what is important can be hard, especially the closer you are to the project.

Response

Sometimes information is disseminated solely in the hope that it will cause some interest and generate feedback that might require further information to be produced or used to validate something. Examples include advertising, questionnaires, market surveys, frequently asked question lists, testimonials and so forth.

Collaboration

Information is often disseminated in order for a group of individuals to share knowledge and routes of communication. Examples include workflow systems to support the flow of information between system entities in order to achieve a common purpose.

Quality assurance of research and transparency

Dissemination ensures that the researchers describe their project and the outcomes generated. As well as accountability as discussed above, this also helps make the methods public and to an extent ensures that the research is of an acceptable standard. This should also enable development and promotion of standardised methodologies. For academic institutions and individuals it can also provide a measure of their performance and how they compare with peers.

The dissemination process requires researchers to reflect and state any potential conflict of interest. This ensures that any research findings can be interpreted in the context of these potential conflicts. For example, large drug companies may have a vested interest in showing that their drugs help with health and illness and they may have a vested interest in concealing any negative effects.

Sustainability

Dissemination informs the community about what you have developed and the benefits of using pilots, from which others can take their lead. The change comes when people take up project outputs and learning and build on them. Dissemination is essential for take-up, and take-up is crucial to the success of the programme and sustainability of outputs in the long term.

Personal reasons

It is also important not to disregard the notion that dissemination and especially publications can help your career as they are excellent methods of getting yourself and your work known in your field. It is also very rewarding after having worked on a project to see how through sharing the experience (both of doing it and the findings), other things happen and you are part of that.

Ethics of dissemination

As we have already discussed, we consider it unethical to undertake research and fail to disseminate. However, there are also other ethical issues to consider such as confidentiality. If the research was carried out on the basis that participant responses would be confidential, it is vital to ensure that this is not compromised in the dissemination process. In writing up research, you have to be sure that identities are not exposed through disclosing other identifying information. It is often stated that should a response reveal a participant's identity then the researcher has to review how to use that information. The chapter on ethics and that on children's capacity covered many of the main ethical issues of research with children but it is important to remember that ethics is a process and continues even at the dissemination stage.

Traditionally participants are promised anonymity in efforts to gain true unguarded responses to the area under investigation. However, there is now an argument that this might be a rather paternalistic approach and that perhaps participants should have a choice about whether to own their comments. This is not quite as simple as it sounds as we discovered when we asked non-vulnerable research participants about their views on anonymity. Most felt that they could only really make the decision at the point of dissemination and even then some vulnerable individuals might regret the decision, which once made is impossible to retract (O'Reilly et al., 2012a).

Dissemination strategy

A dissemination strategy is an evolving plan begun in advance of a research programme that aims to:

- Extract clear, simple and active main messages or key implications from research results.
- Identify credible 'carriers' of the message.
- Pinpoint key decision-maker audiences for the messages.
- Develop ways to deliver the messages that are appropriate to the audiences being targeted and that encourage them to factor the research implications into their work.

(Canadian Health Services Research Foundation, 2007)

In developing your dissemination strategy it is important to consider what your message is, who your audience is and what the most effective way of communicating with them is. This may depend on pragmatic and practical issues as well as the message you are trying to convey. Challenging established practice may require a more personal approach and charismatic presentations to 'win over' a potentially sceptical audience. It is important to tailor the message for the audience as that is more likely to engage them than if they are given a 'standard' response.

It is also important to consider when you will disseminate the findings and also how frequently. If your research has been funded by an external organisation or funding body it will be necessary to discuss the strategy with them. There can be potential conflicts of interest as the funding body may not want to disseminate findings that are inconsistent with their vision or public image, or findings that contradict their position. Some of these issues are potentially defused if discussed at the outset of the project. A dissemination strategy should ensure that the message is consistent although it may be differently framed to meet the needs of the audience. It can also help that as a research group, there is agreement on the use of language. It is recommended that non-sexist and non-racist language should be used and the British Sociological Association (2011) has produced a range of useful guidelines available on their website under the Equality section.

It is also important to be aware that any form of dissemination is likely to require several drafts. Within your work context, it is incredibly useful for a team member to prepare a draft and circulate it to the team for comments, sending it back and forth to achieve a more polished finish. Disseminating as a team can be fun but needs effective planning and clarity of roles and accountability. It can help to have someone not involved in the project to proofread the final version as they may be more objective in their perspective.

Box 12.3   **Potential audiences for your research dissemination**

- Practitioners
- Patients, clients or participants
- Children
- Managers
- Commissioners
- Other researchers
- Educational examiners/supervisors
- Policy-makers (local, regional, national or international) addressed in greater detail earlier in the book
- General public
- Community groups
- Media
- Private sector

Box 12.4   **Types of dissemination**

Written	Oral	Other
Project report	Conference	Media – TV, radio and press
Paper for journal	Local meetings	
Web	Regional meetings	
Thesis/dissertation	Specific or general forums	
Press release		
Leaflet/newsletter		
Poster		

Written dissemination

Writing a report

In producing a written report, a clear structure is vital to effectively communicate your message. It is also important to think ahead of the audience and write a report with them in mind. A more academic report with a more detailed methods and analysis section may be required for an academic audience whereas something less formal and technical may be required for a lay audience. Before you look at Box 12.5, which contains a suggested structure for a report, consider what you think are essential components of a report. The structure presented is widely used but it is worth remembering to ask what the purpose of your report is and who the intended audience is, as that may change the titles of the sections although the contents will remain the same.

Box 12.5   Structure of written presentation

Title
Abstract/summary
Introduction/background
Aims and objectives
Method
Results/findings
Discussion
Conclusion
Implications for the field
References

Depending on the audience and project, it can be useful to translate some of the findings and have a section on 'implications for practice' or 'implications for policy'.

Title

Choose a title that clearly says what your project is about but keep it simple and short if possible. Sometimes witty titles may limit whether your project comes up in searches, especially if the title does not contain relevant key words.

Abstract/summary

This is generally a 200–250-word summary of your project. It does not need to be structured, although journals tend to ask for structured abstracts, and it should not have any references. It is useful to see it as an advertisement for the rest of your report as many readers will glance at the abstract first and then decide if the rest of the paper warrants their time and attention.

Introduction/background

The main purpose of this section is to introduce the reader to what is already known in the area of the report. It is important that any key papers in the field are included. Sometimes, it is useful to include papers of eminent people even if not that useful (especially for journals) as doing so may garner support for your work or at least ensure it is read. The introduction should guide the reader to the justification for your project and finish by identifying the research aims and specific objectives. If a project has several objectives and the report is only going to address some of them then you need to be clear about this.

Aims and objectives

At the end of your introduction section you should make it clear what the main aims and objectives of your research are. Some people prefer to have a separate subheading for this and others prefer it to simply finish off the introduction. Either way it is necessary to show what you aimed to achieve from the research and what your core objectives were. Remember that the aims of your project set out what you aimed to achieve and your objectives illustrate what the purpose of the project was. Do not be mistaken into thinking that aims and objectives mean the same thing. Remember that an objective is an objective measurable or observable thing.

Method

This part will need to cover the sections already discussed in previous chapters on methods and planning so they will not be repeated here, except to say you should ensure that you justify the method used and include the sample, how it was selected and how the research was carried out. It is helpful to be clear and concise. When writing the methods section, it is worth considering whether the reader will be able to replicate your research and if not, where they might get stuck. If you are writing for a lay audience, it might be better to title this section as 'What we did'.

Results/findings

It can be difficult to present results in an attractive and reader-friendly way. Too many tables and too many themes for a journal submission suggest that you might be trying to cover too much in one paper. With mixed methods projects it can be useful to present the findings separately to help the reader. Note that statistics will be presented very differently to qualitative data.

- What is the difference between presenting qualitative and quantitative data?

As you will have learnt already these types of research produce words and numbers respectively, so presenting them poses different challenges. For both, think about what the key findings are that need to be highlighted. A detailed project report may need inclusion of all the findings, but most other forms need you to identify what the really important ones are that will entice people to find out about the project. Presenting qualitative data and adhering to word limits can prove challenging but that is often because quotes are not pruned for the purpose required. For most health research contexts quotes should be succinct and are generally 'tidied up' in that the utterance of speech can be deleted and grammar corrected (as long it does not change the meaning of what was said). Tables are useful for both qualitative and quantitative research. Do not be afraid to use charts and diagrams if indicated as they can be appealing and may be easier to process. You may find it useful to refer back to Chapters 10 and 11 to help you with this.

Discussion

This section relates your findings to other research and also, as it suggests, discusses the implications of your research. You should start this section by reiterating your key findings and then contextualising them in relation to the existing evidence base. Try to show what contribution you have added to the field and acknowledge any limitation in design. Consider the broader implications and applications of your research and discuss your findings in relation to any important practical issues such as policy or resources. The discussion also needs to identify the limitations of the research such as sample size, context and so on. There is no point in trying to hide the limitations as they will be raised by someone somewhere so just be up front as that makes for better discussions about what you did find.

Conclusion

It is self-evident that this section concludes the report. This part should not contain any new information. It can be tempting to overstate the findings so be careful that you only conclude what you can from the data.

Implications for the field

This is an optional part but it can be incredibly useful as it can help you translate an academic piece of work into something that is usable and meaningful in a practice or policy context. It can also indicate the future direction of work that your field needs to undertake.

References

It is important to reference work so that others can be credited for their contributions. Reports look much more professional when accepted reference formats are used and the same format is used throughout the report. There are two main accepted formats for referencing, Harvard and Vancouver, and many variations based on these styles. In this book we are using the Harvard system. Essentially the Harvard system (the reason for the name is unclear) is one in which the author's surname and the year of publication are cited in the text in brackets, and the references are then collated in the reference section and placed in alphabetical order. In the Vancouver system (so called because it was agreed at a meeting in Vancouver that led to the agreement about referencing between medical journals), references are numbered consecutively in the text and then collated at the end and appear in the order cited. (The US National Library of Medicine (2011) has the definitive guide to the Vancouver style.) Consult journal or publisher guidelines for papers and university guidelines for theses. Medical and biological journals tend to use the Vancouver system and social sciences the Harvard system. There are now a number of programs (such as EndNote, Web's Cite, While You Write and Refworks) that help you include references as you write. They can help simplify the process of formatting for journals but need to be used regularly to be effective in terms of time spent learning to use them.

Journal publications

This is often the most important and prestigious dissemination format but not necessarily the most effective at helping change happen. Submitting your work to journals is typically challenging early on but practice makes better if not perfect. Your chances of success are improved if you have planned your research well and made sure it is methodologically sound. The method and data collection cannot be changed so if they were not appropriate for your project, successful publication is unlikely. The following sections consider some useful issues to help you decide what to do with respect to journal publications. Highly ranking journals are those whose publications are most cited by others in their work. The increased number of citations leads to a higher impact factor. This does not necessarily reflect how widely read the article is as many clinicians may read a practice paper but do not then write about it or cite it.

Choosing the right journal

This might sound obvious, but you may be surprised at the number of papers that are submitted without evidence that the authors have thought about whether or not the journal is the right one for their work. Check the aims and scope of the journal and look through some past issues. Some journals make a point of wanting at least one reference from their own journal.

Read the author guidelines carefully. Some editors are happy to receive inquiries and others prefer not to. There may be scope to send out an email to the editorial team, there may be a frequently asked questions page and on rare occasions they may invite telephone enquiries. If you do consult the journal in advance of submitting your manuscript, then be specific in your questions as being vague may simply irritate them.

Make sure you get the basics right, such as formatting, as required by the journal. Journals are frustratingly inconsistent in their requirements and each journal has its own formatting style which you just have to adhere to. This is especially evident in the referencing where different journals will be very specific about how they want the references presented with some limiting the number of references you can cite.

It is useful to consider which journals most of your literature has come from as it is likely that they may be appropriate vehicles for you. Aim high but stay realistic. It is unlikely that a high-ranking journal will accept a paper resulting from a small study. It may be better to consider writing something short rather than a full research report. Whatever journal you go for be prepared for rejections at first. Believe us, it does get better as you become more experienced at writing and choosing the right journals as vehicles for your work. Most senior colleagues will have experienced rejections. Do not take it personally, as it really does happen to most of us! Also, do not let ego get in the way. A publication in a less prestigious journal that is widely read by your intended audience is better than a rejected paper lying unpublished in a drawer because of wounded pride. Sometimes a practice-focused journal (though lower ranking) may be a better vehicle for conveying your message anyway.

The peer-reviewed process

Most (if not all) journals have a review system and the first decision made is often whether the paper will be sent out to review or rejected by the editorial team. If sent out to review, there are usually a minimum of two reviewers but finding reviewers who are timely with their responses can be difficult so sometimes journals may work on the basis of one review (especially if it is very clear). Some journals have open peer reviews where the identity of the reviewer is disclosed. This is felt to be beneficial as it supposedly increases transparency. As editorial members of journals that operate this policy, our view is that this makes it harder to find reviewers, which is understandable especially in small fields. We also think it is harder to be honest, especially when the paper is poor. This is despite the fact that there is an option to make comments to the editor in confidence.

Some journals operate a policy in which the reviewer gets the paper without the author details and this is a blind review (in that the reviewer is blind to the authors). The idea behind this is hopefully to have greater objectivity. In small fields it can, however, be easy to guess the authorship.

As a wide range of people review, reviews can be highly variable. Some are of little use but most reviewers genuinely try and help the authors (which is easier to do if as a reviewer you feel the authors have thought about their submission; it can be obvious at times that an author has just submitted an assignment and made no effort to adapt it for a journal!). Once you have processed what may be a rejection of your paper, go back to the reviews and see how they can help you improve your paper so that you can resubmit to the same or another journal (depending on what the editor has said). Again, try not to take the comments personally and don't let even bad reviews dishearten you. Learn from them if you can. Box 12.6 gives modified examples of reviews we have given or received. Example A was a positive review and very few changes were required; Example B was a critical review but constructive and enabled the authors to respond; and Example C was critical but not constructive and we could do little with it.

Box 12.6   Examples of reviewer comments

Example A:

I think this discussion paper is almost ready for acceptance. There is little to fault in it. Only minor points: pg 4 | 3, a couple of typos. I also wonder whether the paper would be improved by including reference X as that helps provide some additional context.

In response to this review comment the authors can make the simple changes as these are very specific and help the overall presentation. It is also pointless to argue about minor issues unless they change the paper in any substantial way.

Example B:

This is an interesting paper but unfortunately it lacks a clear structure and does not adhere to the format requested by the journal. The introduction covers the relevant literature but is lengthy and unfocused. The authors might benefit from considering what aspects of the literature covered are most useful for inclusion.

Such a review may feel painful to receive but what is clear here is that the reviewer is trying to help by saying what is wrong (from their point of view) and how it might be improved.

Example C:

The paper makes no theoretical contribution and the review of literature is basic.

These rather generic criticisms are not especially helpful when trying to reconstruct a paper. By saying that the literature review is basic implies that there is important literature missed from the paper. We have had reviewers note this on previous papers, but often reviewers will make suggestions in terms of useful additional reading. We did rewrite this paper and it was accepted for publication. In another context, what the reviewer wanted us to do was cite their work which they felt was crucial and including this led to a more favourable review, especially as the reviewer was generally happy with the rest of the paper.

Limitations of journal publications

Peer-reviewed publications do have flaws as they are human controlled. Members of the editorial board may be treated more 'kindly' in the review process and academic worlds can be fairly small so some editors may find it difficult to reject 'big names'. Editors and reviewers may also be unaware of their biases.

Journals may have a long time lag between the paper being accepted and the paper being published (bear in mind papers are often generated anything from a few months to a few years after the research is complete). This means that by the time of publication the findings may already be out of date or irrelevant as new research has taken place. The time lag issue has been mitigated by some journals that have electronic publication some time ahead of the journal being published as a hard copy.

Unfortunately the most prestigious journals may not be the ones that most influence practitioners. Thus there is a need to really think about which journal you send your work to and how you present your findings.

As a new author you should be wary of journals which require payment for the publication of articles, especially those that are not peer reviewed. This is sometimes called vanity publication. Increasingly though, even some reputable journals seek a fee for publication.

Writing a thesis/dissertation

You may be writing your thesis as part of an undergraduate degree, a Master's degree, PhD or other educational qualification such as a clinical doctorate or diploma. These can vary in length according to discipline and the specifics of the qualification, with a PhD being as high as 80,000 words.

Undertaking a thesis at any level is a big task and you need to be prepared to put in many hours of work if you want it to be successful. This is likely to mean that you have to put in some time at weekends and evenings and this will be exacerbated if you have a job at the same time as you are studying. Finding that work–study–life balance is not always easy when you have a thesis to produce. It is often more productive to set aside large chunks of time to write rather than an hour or two here and there. The latter option may mean that on each occasion you spend time recapping your position and starting over again. This can make the process even more drawn out than it has to be.

Writing a thesis or dissertation for educational purposes is not that different in structure and content to a journal article or report. It is, however, significantly longer and contains much more detail and information. You will also need to justify more the stances you take as the awarding body will need to be assured that you meet the educational standards to deserve the award to be made. Remember that the educational institution you are producing the thesis for will have clear guidelines that they will expect you to follow and typically these are published and updated on their web pages. You should consult these carefully and ask your supervisor for assistance if you have any problems.

In practice there are several things you should think about when writing your thesis.

Making a plan

The amount of time you have to complete your thesis will depend upon the qualification you are undertaking and can range from six months to six years, depending on whether you are studying at undergraduate or postgraduate level and whether you are studying full-time or part-time. This can feel quite daunting, especially if you are taking a broad overview of the project as a whole and writing up can feel like an overwhelming task. It is quite important that you develop a clear plan of action in advance. Producing a list of activities for the writing up of your thesis can allow you to tick off successfully completed tasks which will help to keep you motivated. Your list of plans should include small tasks such as 'write draft of abstract' or 'find two more papers on the problems with interviews as the rationale is not yet strong enough'. The list will also include larger-scale tasks such as 'draft methods chapter' and 'find more literature on ethics and children'. You might find it useful to break up these larger tasks with more achievable subtasks such as 'write the rationale for using interviews' or 'read downloaded paper on X'. This will help you to perform the tasks successfully without becoming overwhelmed by the volume of work. It is helpful to show your plan to your supervisor as they have a lot of experience in this area and will be able to help you identify anything that is missing from the plan. Furthermore it is useful to assign deadlines to each of the tasks on your plan to help you stick to the timescale and meet the final deadline for submission. Remember that this plan will be quite lengthy by the time you have finished it, especially if the larger tasks have subtasks attached to them.

Writing the thesis

As we noted earlier the sections of a thesis are not that different from a journal article or research report and we do not want to be repetitive. It may be useful at this point to go back to this section earlier in the chapter and remind yourself of the main headings. Furthermore it is essential that you consult the guidelines provided by your educational institution as they will have specific ways in which they want the thesis to be presented. As a general rule a thesis is broken into the following:

- *Title*: the title should be original, interesting and eye-catching while at the same time reflecting what the thesis is about.

- *Acknowledgements:* you may want to thank certain people who have helped you through the process such as your participants (although do not name them directly) and your supervisor.
- *Contents page:* your thesis should have a table of contents and potentially may contain a table of figures and tables too.
- *Abstract:* the abstract is an important section in the thesis and it is advisable to write this last.
- *Introduction/background/literature review:* this needs to be much more detailed than a journal article and should be divided up into key issues with signposts. In this section you need to convince your examiner that your research is contextualised within the broader evidence base and that there is a gap in knowledge which your research will help to fill.
- *Methods:* a particularly important chapter to convince the reader that the methods you have adopted for your child-focused project are both appropriate for the population and for the research question. You should outline all of your methodological choices in a sensible sequential order providing a clear rationale for the choices. This chapter will also contain your ethics discussion and some of the key procedural information.
- *Results/findings:* the length and breadth of this chapter will depend on whether your design was quantitative or qualitative. Some theses using qualitative designs will have more than one findings/analysis chapter. In this part of your thesis you will need to report on your main results/findings.
- *Discussion:* this is the chapter where you contextualise your findings within the broader context and the previous literature. You should summarise your main findings, demonstrate how your research fits with the wider literature, consider the contribution you have made, illustrate the limitations of your research in a constructive way and consider the future for this topic/issue. It is also useful to consider the broader implications of your findings in this section. There is an opportunity here for you to reflect on your role in the process, which is especially important in qualitative research where you include a section on reflexivity.
- *Conclusions:* your thesis should have a clear conclusion at the end which summarises the research clearly and makes a profound 'sign off' statement.
- *References:* you should have been making a list of all the sources you used for your project as you used them and therefore this part should be easy to compile. You simply list in alphabetical order all of the books, chapters, journal articles and web resources that you have utilised in your thesis.
- *Appendices:* it is likely that you will have an appendices section for your thesis which contains copies of your consent forms, information sheets, proposal, pilot study findings, letters of invitation and any other useful information.

Drafting chapters

During the process of your research it is advisable to start drafting chapters as you go rather than saving it all to the end of the project. This is especially important if there is a significant time difference between the different phases of the research. You cannot rely on your memory when it comes to writing up. The research diary that you have kept during the process will help you in the write-up but it is also a good idea to draft sections of your thesis as you go.

Plagiarism

Remember that plagiarism in your thesis is not acceptable. Your examiners will be mindful of this and are very likely to notice if you have plagiarised the work of others. Whenever you refer to what someone else has written, either in your own words or verbatim, you *must* credit the source and reference it appropriately. Note that if you are found to have plagiarised some work in your thesis then there are consequences and you may be thrown off your course and discredited (Murray, 2006).

Writer's block

Writer's block often becomes an excuse to procrastinate in the absence of any real barrier to writing and it can be difficult to get started. Remember that experiencing writer's block is a common experience for all writers and there may be several reasons why it occurs (Murray, 2006). Try to identify why you are feeling blocked. Take a break and come back to the thesis later and make sure that your environment is relaxed enough to allow you to write. Anxiety and tension may be preventing you from writing anything at all and therefore it is better to just get over the 'blank page' problem and write something, anything! Just make sure you get started. Do not expect perfection or even near perfection early on, especially if you are not used to writing up research. Also do not wait for an ideal time to begin, just begin, as that perfect opportunity may never arise. If you are following your plan properly you will be tackling small chunks of work and single sections so just try to write something from your notes.

Drafting, redrafting and proofreading

Remember that the first draft that you produce is not going to be the final draft that you submit. When you have all of the sections written try putting it together as a full chapter and read it all the way through to see if it makes sense, is not repetitive and addresses all of the main issues that the chapter should address. You might want to redraft it a couple of times before giving it to your supervisor for comments. Do not forget to proofread for typos and spelling errors.

The final version

Do not underestimate the amount of time needed to actually produce the final version and get it bound. You need to consult your institution's guidelines for submission. Sometimes they want ring binding, soft binding, hard binding and so forth and they are likely to require multiple copies. You will need a table of contents and figures for your thesis, page numbers throughout and to check that everything is in the right order before you get it bound.

Make a backup

Byrom (2007) notes that there have been occasions where single and only copies of students' theses have been destroyed in house fires. As you can imagine this can feel like a complete disaster for the student who finds that all their hard work has literally gone up in smoke. It is absolutely essential that you back up your work regularly (not just the final version). Use multiple formats such as memory sticks and CDs and try to keep the latest version in at least two locations. It may seem pedantic and hopefully the backup copies will never be needed, but it truly is better to be safe than sorry when dealing with such a volume of hard work.

Online dissemination

When we started in academic practice the internet was barely known and the notion of having such an accessible method of dissemination was beyond most imaginations. However, while there are several obvious advantages, there are also limitations which are probably greater for the audience than the disseminator. There are a number of reasons to disseminate online.

Cost: relatively cheap

Once a paper is posted online, it is widely accessible to a worldwide audience who can read it with no further cost to you, the producer. The credibility though may depend on how professional the website looks.

Potential unplanned new audiences

While not everyone has access to the internet, more people will be able to find and access your work if it is online as well as in print. The internet has made more information accessible to many more people and widened the potential audience for everyone's work.

It supplements and promotes your other dissemination methods

The internet enables access to people who may not be able to access journal publications or attend conferences. It can also help raise the profile of your organisation/team.

It is quick and flexible

Posting a piece of work online takes a lot less time than printing, so online dissemination can help your findings to be timely and fresh. Additionally, it is easier to update work and add further outcomes.

Funders

People who fund research are increasingly aware of the benefits of online dissemination as part of a good communication strategy. An online dissemination component is increasingly a key requirement of research funding and funders are likely to be attracted to organisations clearly committed to disseminating their knowledge to a wide range of end users. It is also helpful as funding bodies can provide links from their organisation to the outcomes of projects that they have supported.

Limitations

While all methods have limitations, there is to some extent some quality assurance through the peer-reviewed systems in place for journal publications. The internet is an unregulated way of presenting information, not only applicable to web-based publications but also other engines such as the widely used Wikipedia. It can often be difficult with web-based publications to be clear about the ethics and standards of the research, especially if there are no other methods to support the web dissemination. We are also a little wary of large projects that generate a book but without any pee-reviewed publications. However flawed the process therefore, it does ensure that people other than the research team have had an opportunity to review and comment. This is unlikely to be the case for online-only disseminations.

Press releases

In preparing press releases it is best to liaise with your organisation's media or communications office and in some organisations this will be mandatory. It is worth reviewing what the purpose is as poorly planned communications can backfire. It can be helpful to think about press releases serving the function of a lay abstract. Keep them short, clear and jargon-free.

Leaflets

Leaflets might usefully be prepared in a question and answer format, especially if intended for participants, as this will be consistent with most information leaflets when seeking their consent to participate (see Box 12.7). The skill is in conveying your message clearly and succinctly and making the leaflet attractive enough to engage potential readers. Think about the language you are using and avoid jargon and over-complicated terminology. Make sure you spell out all abbreviations as your reader may not be familiar with them. Most projects that involve participants will be expected to produce a participant information leaflet. These are often written using a question format, also shown in Box 12.7, and can be another useful format for disseminating findings.

Box 12.7   Potential format for a dissemination leaflet

Participant Information Leaflet	**Dissemination Leaflet**
• Project title	• Project title
• Background	• Background
• What are we doing?	• What we did
• Why are we doing this work?	• Why we did it
• How are we doing it?	• How we did it
• Are there benefits to you as a participant?	• What we found
	• The benefit of what we found
	• What our findings might mean for you

Posters

Posters are generally more difficult to create than most people realise, although advancing technology has increased the possibilities of what can be achieved. Most people tend to try and put too much information on them so think very hard about what the most important pieces of information are. It can be useful to have grades of information ranging from critical and desirable to optional. If everything is critical consider if a poster is the right vehicle.

Although posters are often the first method that new researchers use, as having posters accepted at conferences is generally easier, they can be challenging to do well and can also be expensive if you are not familiar with the relevant technology. They are generally considered less prestigious but again think about the message and the audience rather than ego!

Conferences usually have guidelines on the overall size of a poster but are more flexible on other aspects, leading to wide variability in the standards of posters produced. Remember that a poster is something that can be read from a distance so small fonts should be unacceptable. Avoid overdoing it with colour and font variation as that ultimately detracts from your message. The pitfalls of slide presentations discussed below apply equally to posters.

Mental health needs and service use in Indian and White adolescents in the UK

Authors
Dr Nadzeya Svirydzenka,*
Professors Nisha Dogra and Panos Vostanis
University of Leicester,
Department of Psychology,
Greenwood Institute of Child Health,
Leicester, United Kingdom

This project was funded by the NIHR Clinical Research Networks

*Corresponding author: ns280@le.ac.uk

Abstract

Current research on mental health needs of young people from ethnic backgrounds is limited and remains largely inconclusive, thus failing to offer guidance for policy and practice.

This research provides reliable evidence on mental health needs and patterns of specialist service engagement in UK adolescents from Indian and White ethnic backgrounds.

10% of children and young people in UK schools are likely to experience some form of mental health problem
(Green et al., 2005)

When untreated, these problems become disruptive to the lives of the child and their family. This is also likely to have long-lasting consequences for the child's personal and academic development (Broidy et al., 2003). Current policy points to the importance of reflecting ethnic awareness in provision of mental health services (Standard 9).

However, despite the increasing cultural diversity, current research is limited in providing reliable evidence for the mental health needs of local ethnic populations.

Therefore, it is not clear whether adolescents from ethnic minority backgrounds have different types or severity of mental health problems, and whether they are less likely to access mental health services than the general population.

Objectives

Establish the prevalence of mental health problems in and service use patterns in several meaningful ethnic groups.

Method

A school-based survey in Leicester and West London examined the prevalence rate of mental health problems (SDQ, SCOFF-short, MFQ-short) and service use in adolescents of Indian (N = 1049), White (N = 405) descent.

The questionnaire was administered in classrooms to groups of 20-30 students at a time.

Findings

5.6% Indian adolescents who will experience mental health problems

All ethnic groups present comparable gender patterns: girls score higher on total SDQ & MFQ & SCOFF

Factors associated with belonging to the Indian ethnic group also lead to fewer emotional problems

Young people in both ethnic groups show low levels of self-report of mental health problems and lower still is their level of use of specialist services (CAMHS)

6.9% Indian Adolescents who
14.5% White self-reported experiencing mental health problems

10.7% Indian Adolescents who
14.5% White self-reported mental health problems who also used CAMHS

Young people of Indian ethnic origin perceive and report lower rates of mental health needs than White young people attending the same schools.

Indian adolescents are more likely to first seek help from their siblings, extended family or teachers.

Accounting for differences in mental health needs, Indian adolescents have lower service contacts with mental health services.

Table 1: Ratios of abnormal and borderline scores in Indian and White subgroups and substance use (percentage of ethnic group in brackets)

ALL Scale	score range	Ethnic group Indian	White	χ2 (df in brackets)
SDQ total	normal	797 (82)	268 (70)	
	borderline	125 (13)	63 (17)	
	abnormal	48 (5)	46 (13)	
	total	970 (100)	384 (100)	30·80 (2) p < 0·001
SDQ prosocial	normal	884 (84)	312 (78)	
	borderline	104 (10)	59 (15)	
	abnormal	58 (6)	27 (7)	
	total	1046 (100)	398 (100)	8·14 (2) p < 0·05
SMFQ total	normal	818 (79)	276 (70)	
	abnormal	221 (21)	116 (30)	
	total	1039 (100)	392 (100)	10·95 (1) p < 0·01
SCOFF total	normal	927 (92)	356 (93)	
	abnormal	81 (8)	31 (8)	
	total	1008 (100)	387 (100)	0 (1) p = 1

Table 2: Comparison of Indian and White boys (percentage of ethnic group in brackets)

BOYS Scale	score range	Ethnic group Indian	White	χ2 (df in brackets)
SDQ total	normal	362 (84)	101 (75)	
	borderline	49 (11)	19 (14)	
	abnormal	21 (5)	14 (10)	
	total	432 (100)	134 (100)	6·73 (2) p < 0·05
SDQ prosocial	normal	356 (76)	100 (70)	
	borderline	73 (16)	28 (20)	
	abnormal	38 (8)	15 (10)	
	total	467 (100)	143 (100)	3·51 (2) p > 0·05
SMFQ total	normal	402 (85)	111 (79)	
	abnormal	72 (15)	29 (21)	
	total	474 (100)	140 (100)	2·40 (1) p > 0·05
SCOFF total	normal	429 (93)	132 (96)	
	abnormal	30 (7)	5 (4)	
	total	459 (100)	137 (100)	1·59 (1) p > 0·05

Table 3: Comparison of Indian and White girls (percentage of ethnic group in brackets)

GIRLS Scale	score range	Ethnic group Indian	White	χ2 (df in brackets)
SDQ total	normal	435 (81)	164 (67)	
	borderline	76 (14)	44 (18)	
	abnormal	27 (5)	33 (14)	
	total	538 (100)	230 (100)	23·23 (2) p < 0·001
SDQ prosocial	normal	528 (91)	212 (83)	
	borderline	51 (9)	31 (12)	
	abnormal	20 (3)	12 (5)	
	total	579 (100)	255 (100)	13·04 (2) p < 0·01
SMFQ total	normal	416 (74)	165 (65)	
	abnormal	149 (26)	87 (35)	
	total	565 (100)	252 (100)	5·63 (1) p < 0·05
SCOFF total	normal	498 (91)	224 (90)	
	abnormal	51 (9)	26 (10)	
	total	549 (100)	250 (100)	0·04 (1) p > 0·05

Figure 12.1   An example of a poster

Posters can, however, be an effective way of communicating with the community and can also serve as a legacy of their involvement with your project. These will generally be less structured than those for an academic purpose. A single format can, however, be used but with the contents tailored to suit specific audiences. Posters may also effectively support oral presentations: more and more conferences have question and answer sessions tied in with poster presentations to increase their credibility. If presenting a poster at a conference, be prepared to stand by your poster for some of the time to answer questions from viewers. Also ensure that the poster has contact details so viewers can contact you.

Activity 12.2

Figure 12.1 is an image of a recent project that we undertook on the prevalence of mental health problems in Indian children. It is one example of a poster format for disseminating research findings.

- Look at the poster and consider what works well on this as a poster.
- What could be done differently?

It might be useful to ask yourself:

- Is the poster clear in how the information is presented?
- Is it easily read?
- Is it likely to catch a passer-by's attention?

We provide some suggestions at the back of the book. You may want to refer to these after you have tried to address each of the questions.

Oral presentations

The chapter, 'How to give a lecture' (Dogra, 2011), is a very practical approach to disseminating research in a formal setting. Before we continue try the next exercise.

Activity 12.3

Think of 'good' and 'bad' presentations you have attended – these might be lectures at your university, conferences, training courses or leisure presentations. Now reflect on what from your perspective made them that way. Then:

- Make a list of the features of a good presenter/presentation

We provide a comprehensive list at the back of the book to compare your list to.

An oral presentation to a large group is effectively a lecture and you may find it helpful to read some teaching texts if this is an area that is unfamiliar to you. Unsurprisingly the advantages of a presentation are similar to a lecture in that they:

- Are an effective method for giving basic information rather than detailed synthesis or evaluation.
- Enable dissemination of information quickly to large audiences.
- Provide an overview.
- Encourage the audience to want to know more so that after the presentation they may visit your website or read your paper.

The advantage of presentations is that as a researcher you have great opportunities to receive feedback on your work, feedback that can be essential to planning further work and that also often helps with other dissemination activities. You may also get an opportunity to interact with the audience. Don't be put off by small audience numbers – quality is better than quantity as you may be better able to debate your research with the audience.

Effective planning and sometimes also rehearsal are key to effective presentations. Think carefully about the time you have and the number of messages you want to convey. If you remember nothing else remember that 'less is more' when it comes to presentations. Another mantra that still rings true is, 'Tell them what you are going to tell them, tell them and then tell them what you have told them!'

There are relatively few disadvantages from a presenter perspective of oral presentations except that they do require confidence and presentation skills. Both of these can be gained through practice. If going to a conference, have a rehearsal with colleagues you trust who will provide honest and constructive feedback. Make sure you stick to time as that always helps keep an audience on side. Prepare ahead and anticipate what questions you may be asked. It may be hard to do when ridden with nerves but do try and look like you are enjoying discussing your work. Typically presentations are performed with the aid of PowerPoint and it is useful therefore to think about how you use visual aids and how you prepare your slides for the audience. Consider Box 12.8.

Box 12.8   **Guidelines and pitfalls to slide preparation**

- Keep your slides simple.
- Use animation sparingly and for a clear purpose.
- Use a font that is easily read (such as Arial which does not have serifs).
- Use a colour scheme that offers good contrast.
- If you are using too small a font, it means you have too much on your slide.

It is important to make sure the number of slides and their contents fit the time allocated. Do not have one long presentation and hope that you can adapt it to fit the time. Leave plenty of time for questions and discussion, otherwise it may feel like a rather pointless exercise from both audience and presenter points of view.

Tailor your presentation to the audience you are speaking to. Think carefully about the language you use and the assumptions you may make about the audience. This is especially important when disseminating to children and young people. Box 12.9 is an example of a presentation aimed at 14-year-olds on mental health.

Box 12.9   An example of a slide presentation

Some factors that impact on young people's mental health include:

- Traumatic life events such as bereavement or abuse
- Not being loved or listened to, feeling left out
- Peer relationships
- Family problems
- Problems at school
- Having low self-esteem and/or confidence

Things to remember

- Children should be respected
- Children should be autonomous
- Children have the right to withdraw
- Give children space to ask questions
- Do not coerce your participants

The above are examples of fairly simple slides but simple is often more effective.

Attending conferences

Remember that conferences can be a useful way of learning about issues pertinent to children, keeping up-to-date with the latest research and networking with professionals with similar interests to your own. It is useful and interesting to present your own work at a conference (as this helps to lift your own professional profile), however, simply attending will afford you many opportunities to progress with your research and share anecdotal methodological stories.

Media dissemination

TV and radio interviews may be effective methods of dissemination. It is helpful to attend specific media training as a lack of confidence and/or communication skills may dilute your message. Again check with your organisation as to their guidelines on press interviews. Interviews can be tricky and nerve-wracking, especially if they are live. Consider carefully what function a live interview serves. The media can be very effective at raising your personal profile or the profile of the project. However, communications tend to be short so may not be an effective way of disseminating your findings. Recorded interviews where you have some editorial control can help you stay in charge of what information is shared and how it is shared.

Disseminating to children

If communities have reason to feel that they receive little feedback on research that they have participated in, it is likely that children have even greater grounds for complaint. It is important to think about what information is developmentally appropriate to share with children and how this might be effectively done. If the research took place with schools, it can be helpful to work with the school to think about how to disseminate your findings. An oral presentation in assembly with leaflets or posters to reinforce the message may be very effective. If you are new to working with children it can be helpful to have a practice run and ask children if they understood your key messages. Ask them to explain what you have just said as that can be very useful in establishing if they have actually understood the message.

Schools and parents are likely to want to know in advance what you are going to share with children so producing a leaflet children can take home with them may be useful. Posters may be a particularly useful way to communicate with children. Another possibility is sharing the findings with them and then asking them to produce a poster, as that will really tell you how they have understood your message.

An example

As we were writing this book, we were involved in some research exploring how school children understood the term 'mental health' and what they thought they could do to stay mentally healthy. Over 200 children attended over two days and participated in interactive workshops. The ideas generated from their small groups are being used to develop a CD entitled 'Staying mentally healthy', as well as some colourful posters, and we are also hoping to use the information to develop an interactive game. The CD, posters and hopefully the game will be made available to participating schools. This should be an effective way of showing them the outcomes of the work we did with them. The dissemination is being developed specifically for children so we will need to ensure that from the outset we bear in mind that the material is user-friendly and appropriate for the audience. These forms of dissemination are more likely to reach them than written reports or presentations.

Summary

In this chapter we have identified the reasons why dissemination is an important part of the research process. We have highlighted the different audiences that may benefit from dissemination as well as the different types of dissemination processes that might be effectively used. You should hopefully now also have some ideas about how to write a report and how to prepare for an oral presentation, as well as about the challenges both these types of dissemination present.

Further reading

Bonnett, A. (2001) *How to Argue*. Essex: Pearson Education.

Brink-Bugden, R. (2004) *Critical Thinking for Students* (3rd edn). Oxford: How to Books.

Byrom, J. (2007) 'How to write a thesis', in P. O'Brien and F. Pipkin (eds), *Introduction to Research Methodology: For Specialists and Trainees*. London: Royal College of Obstetricians and Gynaecologists, pp. 252–257.

EndNote Web's *Cite While You Write* (2010) www.knowledgecenter.unr.edu/instruction/help/citewrite.html (accessed 14/05/2011).

Murray, R. (2006) *How to Write a Thesis* (2nd edn). Maidenhead: Open University Press.

Silverman, D. (2005) *Doing Qualitative Research: A Practical Handbook* (2nd edn). London: Sage.

Swetnam, D. and Swetnam, R. (2009) *Writing your Dissertation* (3rd edn). Oxford: How to Books.

Answers to the Activities

Activity 1.1

Your experiences of working with, interacting with or communicating with children are likely to affect your perceptions of them. Your culture, social status, educational background, age and so forth will also affect how you think about children. Whatever your views on children they will affect the way you research children. Your opinions will shape the types of questions you are interested in, the ways in which you collect your data and the writing up of your research. You need to be aware of these as you do your research.

Perceptions and ideas about childhood vary. These perceptions tend to be shaped within personal, cultural, historical and social contexts. They emerge from the connections made with people, places, groups, communities and the larger world around us. A sense of belonging develops based on your experiences and notions of identity, relationships, acceptance and understanding. Therefore it is almost unavoidable that your research interests will be connected to your personal past experiences and the questions you may have about yourself. Rather than a disadvantage, a healthy combination of your experiences, questions about yourself and an area of research that needs to be better understood will keep you motivated and will help you to understand your participants' needs.

Activity 1.2

There are three main positions about children's legal rights. First are those who demand equal rights for children to tackle discrimination that children suffer by comparison with adults. A second view argues that children should have some but not all of the rights which adults have. Finally, there are those who think that children should not have any rights. This is an ongoing debate that presents conflicting approaches on how children achieve cognitive functions and whether or not they have capacity to make the right choices, versus the idea that giving rights to children will play an important part in their acquiring the qualifying capacity. In other words, the denial of children's rights of a certain age on account of their alleged incapacity is simply self-confirming and they cannot have rights because they are incapable, but they are incapable only because they do not have these rights!

Nevertheless, what is undeniable is that children are young human beings and, as such, hold a moral status. Perhaps the question is not whether children should or should not have rights, but rather what type of rights they should have. Most countries have ratified the 1989 United Nations Convention on the Rights of the Child (UNICEF, 1989), which established a wide range of basic rights including the right to have their 'best interests' be 'a primary consideration' in all actions concerning them (Article 3), the 'inherent right to life' (Article 6), and the right to form their own views, which are to be expressed freely in all matters affecting them. Those are recognised as moral rights that partially settle the question.

Activity 1.3

In addition to being intrinsic to their rights, the idea that children should be active participants in decisions that affect them is supported by a large body of evidence. It is argued that children's participation promotes the long-term development of citizenship and, more specifically, empowers them by providing a sense of local responsibility (Hart, 1997). Therefore while research with children validates their social role and rights, helping to understand their experiences or views, the process also brings children's issues to the attention of society. Essentially, child-led research enables mutual support, information-sharing and effective action.

On the other hand, it is important to consider cultural differences and the impact they may play in the way children feel about their participation. For example, in many communities, children are expected to be obedient and would expect adults to act as gatekeepers and to control them. In such cases, perhaps more importance has to be placed on parental involvement, making children feel at ease about their participation.

Activity 2.1

You should have written down many different ideas about race, ethnicity and culture. Any ideas you have had about these concepts should now be compared with the text in the chapter to see if they are similar or different. For example, we note that culture is defined as follows: 'Culture refers to the perspectives, practices and products of a social group' (Race Relations, 2009).

How close was your definition to this one? Do you think that this is a good definition of culture?

Activity 2.2

Potentially all the characteristics described could influence the research process. As a clinical child psychiatrist, she may have a vested interest in showing that CAMHS better meets the cultural needs of children than other services. However, her academic interests and experience might mean there is some vested interest in saying that CAMHS does not meet children's cultural needs and needs to hire someone like her to train their staff!

Of course, we all have vested interests; this in itself is not the issue. It only becomes an issue when they are not recognised and nor is their potential impact on the research process.

Activity 2.3

It is easy to compartmentalise our biases and think we only need to think about them at certain points, for example, in defining the research question. This is not enough and they need to be considered at each stage of the research process, that is in:

- undertaking the literature review
- defining the research question
- identifying the methods
- validating analyses and interpreting the findings
- writing up project reports and other forms of dissemination.

We need to think about all the factors that influence our thinking which include:

- our heritage (through race, ethnicity, language, country of origin)
- individual circumstances (age, gender, sexual orientation, socio-economic status, physical ability)
- personal choice (religious/spiritual beliefs).

These factors impact on our understanding of the world and influence a range of issues such as communication styles, health beliefs, and so on, which may then influence how we see research as a whole and also specific research questions. As this project is about how children and young people view their relationships, we would particularly need to think about how our views of children themselves, the value of their opinions and our own experience of peer relationships might influence the way that we carry out the research. For example, if we had experienced bullying our research might over-emphasise that aspect but not appreciate that many children have experiences different from our own. In some contexts peer relationships are viewed as less important than those of the family so again that might influence how we carry out and understand the topic.

Activity 3.1

Vignette 1

This research is important and over the last few decades, advances in medicine have saved thousands of children's lives. New medications and interventions mean that more children are surviving different diseases. Furthermore, medications have potential to improve quality of life and relieve symptoms in children who are suffering from painful illnesses. Without adequate tests these medications may never become fully available.

There are a number of key ethical issues with this study:

- As the doctor is Lucy's doctor the parents and child may feel coerced into taking part whether or not this is the case. The doctor has potential conflict of interest between delivering on the research project for which he is funded and also delivering care to his patient.
- There is a risk of the parents misunderstanding the value of the potential intervention to their daughter. That is, Lucy's parents may falsely believe that the medication may save her life.
- Obtaining true informed consent from distressed parents and a sick child will require very delicate management.
- Additional burdens of increased blood tests and hospital visits are required by Lucy and her parents.
- The drug may shorten Lucy's life.
- The drug may cause side-effects for an already sick child.
- Lucy's parents may find it difficult to withdraw, even if the additional demands become burdensome, because of the status of the doctor or fears that withdrawal may reduce other care opportunities for Lucy.
- Lucy's parents may believe that saying no to participation may affect their clinical care.

Vignette 2

This research is important as childhood obesity is increasing, placing additional burdens on medical care providers and parents. It is well known that children need to take care of their health, eat well and lead active lives. Children spend a considerable amount of time in education and therefore it is good for educational institutions to promote healthy eating and understand children's choices.

There are a number of ethical issues with the project:

- The researcher's own experiences may bias the research towards a particular slant.
- Healthy eating and obesity can be a sensitive subject and parents may feel criticised when asked about their child's participation.
- Schools may feel judged by the findings, or may fear the findings and thus be uncooperative.
- Children as young as 4 will require different considerations to young people of 16.
- The children may find the content of the interview upsetting.
- The children may find the content of the interview difficult to comprehend.
- Children may feel coerced into saying yes as a school setting is traditionally one whereby children do as directed by adults.
- Children may feel powerless to withdraw from the interview if they want to.

Activity 3.2

There are no answers to this activity as it is about you and your ideas.

Activity 3.3

There are a number of things that Cathy can do.

First she needs to talk to her supervisor about the alternative possibilities. For example is there a different recruitment strategy that could be used whereby she recruits young people whose parents know about the pregnancy. Perhaps she could interview young people who had given birth in the previous two months?

Cathy could consider only having institutional consent from the charity representatives, and from the young people themselves. She would need to consult the ethics committee about this issue before proceeding.

Cathy could consider internet interviews whereby the young people remain unidentified even to her.

Activity 3.4

Form 1
Good points:

- Uses the term 'young people'.
- Allows them to circle where they agree.
- Has the researcher's name on it.

Bad points:

- Long sentences.
- Complex terminology.
- Not child-friendly.
- No contact details.
- No title of the project.

You should have noticed that the first consent form was not as good as the second consent form. Hopefully you identified that there are a number of issues with the first consent form:

- There are no contact details for the researcher – these should be provided so that the child or the parents can contact the research team if they have any queries.
- The study title is not present on the consent form. This is quite a useful reference point and should be on the form.
- The language used on this form is not very child-friendly or accessible for the child, phrases like 'afforded the opportunity' and 'adequately' may not be understood by the child.
- The language is coercive in places – phrases like 'this very important study' suggest that the child ought to agree.
- There is no recognition or thanks at the end of the sheet.

Form 2
Good points:

- Has the term 'assent form' on it.
- Provides full contact details of the research team on it.
- Gives the title of the project on it.
- Tells the child they can have help from their parents.
- Is written in short statements.
- Is child-friendly.
- Has clear instructions.

Bad points:

- Not useful for all child age groups.

The second form is much better because:

- The researcher provides contact details so that the family can get in touch if need be.
- The study title is present on the form.
- The language used is child-friendly.
- The language used is not coercive.
- The researcher thanks the child.

Activity 3.5

Confidentiality not only ensures that individual autonomy is respected, but it is also a vital element of building trusting relationships. The law of confidence applies to personal information when the person who receives the information is expected to keep it confidential. This does not only apply to medicine or research, but to any other setting or professional relationship in which you are required to provide sensitive or personal information.

However, there are several circumstances when information given in confidence by someone can be disclosed – for instance, where there is a risk of serious harm to themselves or someone else, a risk of a serious crime being committed or when breaching confidentiality is in the public good. Personal information can also be disclosed if this is required by law.

Activity 4.1

Most evidence suggests that an essential element of children's ability to make decisions is their developmental stage. In ethical and legal terms, this means that when children are able to understand what is happening to them, they should be allowed to participate in discussions about their care, including making the decisions for themselves. Even though legally there is a presumption that young people above the age of 16 are competent, age is not a fixed parameter when considering their ability to make decisions about their care or participation in research.

In the case of competent children, because under 18-year-olds have not yet reached the legal **age of majority**, it is considered good practice to consult those adults who hold guardianship or parental responsibility in the case of competent children. However, when children of any age are deemed incompetent, there is a legal requirement to seek proxy consent from parents or guardians, and assent from children.

Parents or guardians have a role to play in consenting by proxy based on the principle of 'best interest' of the child, assuming that in most cases, a child's parents are the ones that care most about their children. Furthermore, since most medical decisions will also affect the child's family, parents can factor family issues and values into medical decisions about their children.

In addition to age, stage of development and views of parents or guardians, cultural factors are important because they might affect not only their understanding of what the procedure or research is about, but also views on children's moral rights to make decisions by themselves in different cultural settings vary significantly.

Activity 4.2

Parental responsibility is a legal concept that consists of the rights, duties, powers, responsibilities and authority that most parents have in respect of their children. This includes the parental right to give consent to medical treatment. On the other hand, parents also have a moral responsibility to make decisions in the best interest of their child.

However, there are limits on what parents are entitled to decide. For instance, they are not entitled to consent to inappropriate treatment for their children or to refuse treatment which is in the child's best interests. In those cases, medical caretakers have an ethical and legal duty to advocate for the best interests of the child when parental decisions are potentially dangerous, imprudent, neglectful or abusive to the child's health. When satisfactory resolution between parents and medical professionals cannot be attained through discussion and ethics consultation, seeking a court order for appropriate care might be necessary.

In previous chapters we discussed the different theoretical views for and against children's rights, which would affect their ability to make decisions about themselves. Examples include those who demand the same rights for children that adults have; those who see children as having some but not all of the rights that adults have; and finally those who think that children should not have any rights. However, following decades of discussion in support of children's rights, international and local legislation was developed conferring on children the right to be consulted and in some cases to decide for themselves, independently of their parents. This represented a change in the way children are socially perceived, from passive protagonists in what adults decided on their behalf, to active social actors that shape their place and role in society.

Activity 5.1

There are lots of reasons why research with children is important and these are dealt with in detail in the chapter. Your list could have included reasons such as:

- The need for developmental knowledge, to provide interventions for those who are developmentally delayed.
- To have a better understanding of children's feelings towards important issues in their lives.
- To improve children's services.
- To better appreciate how to design the education provided for children.
- Children have valid perspectives to inform policy.
- There are legal and moral obligations to include their views on their lives.

Activity 5.2

Risks specific to interviewing

- Unpredictable environments may make it difficult to mitigate risk. Just because you are interviewing a vulnerable group of participants does not mean that there are not risks related to their environment and you may not be aware of all of these before you attend the interview.
- There is a risk of physical or verbal hostility from members of the family or interviewees themselves without any access to colleagues. Interviewing vulnerable groups has potential to exacerbate this as the topic may be sensitive and evoke emotional responses in the adults; there is a co-morbidity between child mental health and adult mental health and therefore the adults may be more prone to aggression due to the nature of a specific mental health problem; if you are interviewing children who have witnessed domestic violence then the 'violent partner' may arrive during the interview; the parent (or the child) may have an infection that they pass on to you and so forth.

Broader environmental risks

- Unfamiliarity with the geographical area.
- Poorly lit streets.
- Risks related to own or public transport such as managing car breakdown or having unreliable public transport to help you leave.
- Area of high crime.

Activity 6.1

The answers to this activity will depend on the specifics of your own research project.

Activity 6.2

The answers to this activity will depend on the specifics of your own research project.

Activity 7.1

- There may be a need for an interpreter.
- The children may become distressed while talking.
- There are issues relating to culture and therefore Carmen should seek advice from cultural experts.

- The children may feel coerced because of her professional role.
- Terminology may not be suitable for this group of children.

Activity 7.2

Marcus faces a number of challenges in this research:

- There are a number of ethical considerations for accessing this population – informed consent being an important one.
- Marcus may have trouble gaining the trust of a population that tends to be suspicious of those in authority.
- Participants may be reluctant to talk about a delicate issue such as why they choose not to reveal information to the authorities.
- Participants may fear retribution.

Activity 7.3

- Mental health problem: mental health problems are those that can be classified by the diagnostic systems and reflect both neurotic problems and psychotic problems. While a person can have a positive state of mental health, a mental health problem is when the person's mental functioning is impaired by the presence of symptoms.
- Mental illness: mental illnesses are a subset of mental health problems and are also known as mental disorders. These are illnesses that interfere significantly with the day-to-day functioning of the individual. Mental illness refers to a diagnosable condition.
- Mental disorder: mental disorder is another term for mental illness and means that the person's normal functioning is impaired.
- Learning disability: learning disability is the term used by the government and is thus used in their documents. Learning difficulty is a term used more by service users to reflect their identity.
- Learning difficulty: learning difficulty is a term used more often in education. Learning difficulty and disability relate to the ability of the child to learn at a typical developmental rate – terminology varies across the world. Often the words used to describe such populations become derogatory terms such as 'mental retardation'.
- Disability: a disability is a condition which may affect the person's sensory, mental and/or mobility functions. There are many types of disability.

Activity 8.1

The answers to this activity will depend on the specifics of your own research project.

Activity 8.2

The answers to this activity will depend on the specifics of your own research project.

Activity 8.3

- Personal motivation.
- Previous experiences of being in research.
- Altruism.
- Coercion.
- Reciprocation.
- The view that research is not risky.
- Personal therapeutic benefit.
- Fear.

Activity 9.1

This is specific to your research project but the research question/hypothesis you develop should be answerable.

Activity 9.2

The answers to this activity will depend on the specifics of your own research project.

Activity 9.3

1 What do you think is on the supervisor's list of tasks?

- Sarah has no rationale for defining adolescence as 13–16 years. It makes sense to look at this age group if she is going to access the population through schools but more work needs to be done as to why and how this age group is appropriate to meet the aims of the study.
- Statistics in this subject are varied and produced by different organisations. Some evidence of this would be needed to provide a stronger rationale for the need for the project.
- There is no rationale for the qualitative design or the data collection method. Sarah has not thought about how or why this is appropriate for addressing the research questions and aims that she has.
- Sarah has no overall research question. In research it is the research question that drives methodological decisions and therefore a clear and strong research question is needed before she can make any other choices.

- The choice of perspective should not be driven by personal preferences.
- Sarah needs good relationships with gatekeepers and some formal communication in writing.
- There are issues with the 'opt in' approach to recruitment and Sarah seems to have failed to demonstrate what and how much information she gave the young people. Furthermore email is not always the most appropriate form of communication and perhaps other choices should have been given.
- The biggest problem with this study is that she has failed to obtain ethical approval. Sarah *cannot* start data collection until ethical approval has been secured. By going through the ethical process she will be required to construct information sheets for participants, have clear informed consent forms, and ensure the main ethical safeguards such as confidentiality, right to withdraw and debriefing are in place. There are additional ethical concerns when researching young people and these will need to be considered.
- A brief overview of a project is not sufficient planning. Planning a project of any nature is time-consuming and needs to be done properly and carefully. Sarah needs a full protocol in place before she goes ahead.
- Sarah should involve stakeholders to help with the research design and research process.
- Sarah needs to conduct a small pilot study to test her information sheets, interview schedule and technical equipment.

2 What advice would you give Sarah?

- Sarah should have a full supervision session with her supervisor to discuss her ideas and formulate a research question.
- Sarah needs to do more reading. She needs to read some basic methods textbooks to help her understand the approach and methods she plans to use and she needs to read around the subject more so that she can contextualise her topic within the evidence base.
- Sarah needs to do some reading around ethics in research with children and understand the core ethical principles and their application.
- Sarah then needs to develop a full protocol, information sheets, consent forms and an interview schedule.
- Sarah needs to obtain ethical approval for her project.
- Sarah needs to have regular supervision, send updated drafts of her work to her supervisor and consult with key stakeholders to inform the project.

3 How might this influence the supervisory relationship?

- Sarah has been upset by the long list of issues that have been raised by the supervisor and is concerned about the amount of time that these tasks will take. She is worried about paying for the PhD as she does not have external funding. As a result of the anxiety and stress she may feel annoyed at the supervisor and see the supervisor as blocking progress which will have a negative effect on their relationship. It is important that the supervisor goes through the advice list and shows Sarah how and why these things are important and supports her by reading through drafts.

Activity 10.1

Some possible questions for a questionnaire concerning children's attitudes towards dieting and healthy eating – try to think about which of these are good questions and which are bad:

- How often do you eat chocolate in a week?
- How often do you go out walking in a week?
- How often do you exercise in a week?
- Do you like your body?
- Do you worry about your weight?
- Does weight matter to you?
- How many pieces of fruit do you eat in a day?
- How many times per week do you have chips?
- What is your favourite food?
- Do you like sports at school?
- Do you think you are attractive?
- Do you read magazines?
- Do you think celebrities are too thin?
- Would you like to look like a celebrity? Which one?
- What is your favourite food?
- How often do you have fizzy drinks?
- How do you get to school?
- Does being fit matter to you?
- Do you do any after-school sports?
- What do you think is an ideal weight for someone of your height and gender?
- How often in a week do you weigh yourself?
- Do you know how many calories are in a Mars bar?

Activity 10.2

Which of these activities do you enjoy doing?

a Equestrian activities
b Angling
c Sculpting
d Genealogy
e Scuba diving
f Fossil hunting

This is a bad question as these are not especially child-friendly activities. Young children are not even likely to know what all of these activities are.

1 Which of these activities do you enjoy doing?

g Football
h Basketball

    i   Cricket
    j   Art and design
    k   Dancing
    l   Reading

This is a better question. The activities are more likely to be engaged in by children and children will know what they are. However, there should be an option to tick more than one activity.

2 Would you like to stay at school to do extra football or dancing?

This requires a simple yes or no answer. It would be better if there was room for them to say why they might like to stay after school, or why not.

3 Would you be prepared to stay in the school environment for an additional half hour on one of the days of the week to do an after-school club activity such as football or drama with one of the teachers in the main hall so that your parents could pick you up slightly later than is usual for you?

This question is far too long for young children to manage. It contains terms that they may not understand and it is too sophisticated for them to answer. It is also a yes or no question, yet is not as simple as the previous question.

Activity 10.3

In the modern age of technology most young children have a mobile telephone and by their teenage years nearly all children have one. They are familiar with the technology, but may be more used to using social networking sites or writing text messages, than making actual telephone calls. You will need to think about this if you consider telephone interviewing. While the general literature says that it makes very little difference to the quality of the data to do interviews over the telephone, it is more difficult to do participatory methods with children and more difficult to engage them. With a quantitative design (ticking boxes in a structured interview), however, there is less of a need to engage them in full conversation, and therefore depending on the child's age it may be useful.

Activity 11.1

This will be dependent upon the search you do.

Activity 11.2

Your list should be derived from the literature search that you completed.

Activity 11.3

- There is a need for caution if he uses children from his own school as he is a teacher and therefore there is the issue of power and role.
- Three focus groups may not achieve saturation or be representative. In qualitative research there is a need for transferability of findings.
- He is making assumptions that there will be fear about transition.
- There may be differences between boys and girls.
- He may find it difficult to stay neutral as he knows the children.
- There is the possibility that some of the children may become distressed during the focus group.

Activity 11.4

Potter and Hepburn (2005) note a number of problems with interviews:

- Deletion of the interviewer – the interviewee's talk can be taken out of context and rendered as an abstracted statement. Naturally occuring data manages to keep the talk in context and this means that you can see what each participant makes relevant rather than seeking it out from your frame of reference. However, you might not access what you want this way.
- A common problem, they feel, with the 'conventional orthographic' transcription is that 'it is often not clear what specific elements of the talk are being referred to' (p. 289). Naturally occuring data is usually subjected to detailed transcription but this is dependent upon the analytical approach that is to be taken.
- The failure to consider interviews as interaction. An interview is an interaction between two people and therefore if you use interviews you need to think about the voice of the interviewer as well as the participant and how this shapes the interaction. In naturally occuring data you would consider all of the different partcipants not just one.
- The interview reflects the researcher's agenda and concerns rather than the participants'. This may also be the case with naturally occurring in the sense that you chose the topic and you decide which aspects of the data to explore, but it is reduced as you can start from a more open position.
- Interviewer's and interviewee's stake and interest – interviewers often explicitly deny their own interest in the responses of the participant. If you are an interviewer you will be heavily involved in the collection of data and your vested interest may show through. By recording naturally occuring interactions you will be less physically and psychologically present in that interaction.
- They propose that qualitative interviews are overused and that they are actually difficult to perform and analyse well. This means that if you are going to use an interview you need a strong rationale, some training and experience and you need to recognise some of the limitations.

There is some value in interviews if they are performed well, reflexivity is assured, the interviewer's role is accounted for and quality markers are considered.

- They can provide a great deal of information and depth.
- They can be participant led if conducted appropriately.
- They should be driven by the perspective adopted.
- They do allow the participant to open up about a particular subject.
- They may be easier to set up than naturally occurring data.

Activity 12.1

Your answer will depend on your awareness and is personal to you.

Activity 12.2

- It has an easy to read and clear message.
- It is not so text-heavy or fussy that it distracts from the key message.
- The key messages are presented in text form and in text boxes which reiterate them.
- The poster is attractive.
- The figure 10 per cent (the finding from a national survey) is as large as the 5.6 per cent (our finding) and this may mean those reading the poster take away or remember the wrong number.
- Removing the abstract could remove some text without reducing the contents of the poster.

Activity 12.3

- Speaks with conviction and commitment.
- Speaks clearly.
- Makes good eye contact across the room.
- Checks that the audience is following the presentation.
- Relates the contents of the lecture to audience needs.
- Structures the presentation and has signposts so even if the audience loses concentration they can re-engage.
- Actively engages the audience through use of rhetorical or actual questions.
- Keeps to time.

Glossary

Age of majority – is the chronological threshold of legal adulthood as it is conceptualised in the law. Minors cease to be considered children, terminating the legal control and legal responsibilities of their parents or guardian over and for them.

Assent – sometimes children lack the competence or maturity to provide informed consent and therefore can provide assent, that is, agreement, to participate in research.

Anonymity – this is the removal of identifying features and characteristics.

Audit – generally a local activity to measure actual practice against some predefined standards.

Autonomy – this means treating the participant as an agent, in control of their own decisions.

Beneficence – this means that there is an aim of the research to benefit others.

Child-centred – a philosophy embedded in much policy that means work with children and families should be driven by the needs and interests of the child.

Closed questions – questions that restrict the participants' responses to yes or no, or a certain point on a scale.

Coercion – by virtue of your status, age or gender your participants may feel unduly pressured into taking part in your research.

Confidentiality – this means a protection of privacy through not disclosing what is shared with the researcher.

Confounding variables – these are variables that may be present in the research environment but unaccounted for by the researcher. Their presence may mean that the researcher misattributes the effect to the independent variable when it is actually the confounding variable that has led to the result.

Dependent variable – this is the variable you are setting out to measure. You are testing to see if the independent variable has any effect on the dependent variable.

Epistemology – this is the theory of knowledge and is concerned with how we can know what we know.

Experiment – this is a quantitative form of data collection, usually conducted in the laboratory with controlled variables and conditions.

Gatekeepers – these are the third parties with whom you will need to communicate to gain access to the population you want to study.

Generalisability – this is a quality criterion for quantitative research and refers to the ability to make generalisations about the broader population from the study population.

Hermeneutics – study of the theory and practice of interpretation. It is committed to understanding meanings.

Hypothesis – this is a prediction about the relationship between variables.

Independent variable – this is the variable that is manipulated between conditions by the researcher.

Informed consent – this means the active receiving of information and written willingness to participate in the research.

Justice – this means treating all participants equally and fairly regardless of age, ethnicity, social class, intelligence or economic status.

Likert scales – these allow the respondent to answer on a scale. Typically the respondent has several choices across a range. For example, strongly agree, agree, neutral, disagree or strongly disagree.

Methodology – refers to a system of the processes which are relevant to a particular field of inquiry and thus encompass the philosophy, epistemology and choices of methods.

Non-maleficence – this is a promise not to do participants harm.

Objectivity – the belief that quantitative research is value-free and thus objective.

Ontology – refers to the nature of reality and questions whether there is a reality which serves as a benchmark for the existence of phenomena.

Open questions – questions that allow the participant some freedom to answer the question in their own words.

Paradigm – this represents a world view that defines the nature of the world and the individual's place within that world. A paradigm is a framework containing the accepted assumptions and views about a subject.

Paternalism – refers to attitudes that exemplify a traditional relationship between father and child. The main features of paternalism are the interference with the liberty of a person but with a beneficent intention towards those whose liberty is interfered with (Dworkin, 1972).

Population – this is the broader population from which your sample is drawn. It refers to members of particular groups.

Positivism – the underpinning epistemology of quantitative research which aligns with the natural sciences. Positivism stipulates that human behaviour can be measured and cause and effect established.

Power calculation – refers to statistical power; as power increases the chances of a Type II error decrease. You need to use a statistical formula to determine your sample size to be sure that your study can detect a difference.

Qualitative – explores people's experiences, feelings and understandings and generally uses talk and text for transferability of findings.

Quantification – the process of reducing human behaviour to numbers.

Quantitative – reduces behaviour to numbers and statistically analyses the results to make wider generalisations about populations.

Rapport – building a positive relationship between people.

Reactivity – the way in which participants react to the presence of the researcher, the way in which the presence of the research interferes with the setting of the study and the possible ways it interferes with the behaviour of the participants.

Reflexivity – the active reflection on one's role and identity and the influence of the researcher on the research process; the process of reflecting back on the influences you have had on the research process.

Reliability – relates to the extent to which the study can be replicated.

Research – questions how things work, considers what the best thing to do is and explores important issues to advance knowledge.

Respondent bias – is a type of cognitive bias which can affect the results of the study as respondents answer questions in terms of how they think the researcher wants them to answer. This can be due to the wording of the question.

Response rate – this relates to the number of people who send back your questionnaire or agree to fill it in compared to the total number sent out.

Saturation – this occurs when no new ideas, themes or topics emerge during the data collection, so that data collection becomes repetitive. Signals a point to stop collecting data.

Semiotics – refers to a theory of signs and symbols and therefore analyses the relationships between signs in language.

Snowballing – this is when those who have already been recruited to participate in the research suggest other potential participants and they in turn may suggest others.

Stakeholders – these are people who are willing to be involved in the project in an advisory way and have a certain expertise; for example, parents of children with the condition, charity workers, policy-makers and so forth.

Subjectivity – the notion that research cannot be value-free and is always subject to the influence of the researcher.

Timeline or Gantt chart – this is a chart or graph which plots the timeline for a piece of work and illustrates the time slots that are to be devoted to particular chunks of the work.

Transferability – the extent to which qualitative findings can be useful beyond the study.

Transparency – the audit trail of a qualitative research project.

Validity – the extent to which the research measures what it intended to measure and is free of confounding variables.

Vulnerability – susceptible to harm.

References

ACT for Children (2012) *Terms Explained*. www.act.org.uk/page.asp?section=35&sectio nTitle=Terms+explained (accessed 07/02/2012).

Ainsworth, M., Blehar, M., Waters, E. and Wall S. (1978) *Patterns of Attachment: A Psychological Study of the Strange Situation*. Hillsdale, NJ: Lawrence Erlbaum Associates.

Alderson, P. (1993) *Children's Consent to Surgery*. Buckingham: Open University Press.

Alderson, P. (2004) 'Ethics', in S. Fraser, V. Lewis, S. Ding, M. Kellett and C. Robinson (eds), *Doing Research with Children and Young People*. London: Sage, pp. 97–112.

Alderson, P. and Morrow, V. (2011) *The Ethics of Research with Children and Young People: A Practical Handbook*. London: Sage.

Anderson, L., Scrimshaw, S., Fullilove, M., Fielding, J., Normand, J. and The Task Force on Community Preventive Services (2003) 'Culturally competent healthcare systems: a systematic review', *American Journal of Preventative Medicine*, 24 (3S): 68–79.

Annas, G. and Grodin, M. (eds) (1995) *The Nazi Doctors and the Nuremberg Code: Human Rights in Human Experimentation*. Oxford: Oxford University Press.

Ariès, P. (1962) *Centuries of Childhood* (trans. R. Baldick). New York: Jonathan Cape.

Armstrong, D., Gosling, A., Weinman, J. and Marteau, T. (1997) 'The place of inter-rater reliability in qualitative research: an empirical study', *Sociology*, 31 (3): 597–606.

Ashcroft, R. (2003) 'The ethics and governance of medical research: what does regulation have to do with morality?', *New Review of Bioethics*, 1 (1): 41–58.

Association of American Medical Colleges (1999) *Report III. Contemporary Issues in Medicine: Communication in Medicine*. Medical School Objectives Project. Washington, DC: Association of American Medical Colleges.

Aycicegi-Dinn, A. and Kagitcibasi, C. (2010) 'The value of children for parents in the minds of emerging adults', *Cross-Cultural Research*, 44 (2): 174–205.

Baker, S. and Edwards, R. (eds) (2012) *How Many Qualitative Interviews Is Enough? Expert Voices and Early Career Reflections on Sampling and Cases in Qualitative Research*. London: National Centre for Research Methods, Economic and Social Research Council.

Balen, R., Blyth, E., Calabretto, H., Fraser, C., Horrocks, C. and Manby, M. (2006) 'Involving children in health and social research: "human becomings" or "active beings"?', *Childhood*, 13 (1): 29–48.

Barbour, R. (1998) 'Mixing qualitative methods: quality assurance or qualitative quagmire?', *Qualitative Health Research*, 8 (3): 352–361.

Benjamin, H. and MacKinlay, D. (2010) 'Communicating challenges: overcoming disability', in S. Redsell and A. Hastings (eds), *Listening to Children and Young People in Healthcare Consultations*. Oxon: Radcliffe Publishing, pp. 151–168.

Bennett, J., Kalathil, J. and Keating, F. (2007) *Race Equality Training in Mental Health Services in England: Does One Size Fit All?* London: The Sainsbury Centre for Mental Health.

Biggs, H. (2010) *Healthcare Research Ethics and Law: Regulation, Review and Responsibility*. London: Routledge-Cavendish.

Black, D. (1996) 'Childhood bereavement: distress and long term sequelae can be lessened by early intervention', *British Medical Journal*, 312 (2): 4926–4927.

Bogolub, E. and Thomas, N. (2005) 'Parental consent and the ethics of research with foster children', *Qualitative Social Work*, 4 (3): 271–292.

Borzekowski, D.L. and Rickert, V.I. (2001) 'Adolescent cybersurfing for health information: a new resource that crosses barriers', *Archives of Pediatrics and Adolescent Medicine*, 155 (7): 813–817.

Boyatzis, R. (1998) *Transforming Qualitative Information: Thematic Analysis and Code Development*. London: Sage.

Bradby, H. (2003) 'Describing ethnicity in health research', *Ethnicity and Health*, 8: 5–13.

Braddock, D.L. and Parish, S.L. (2003) 'An institutional history of disability', in G.L. Albertcht, K.D. Seelman and M. Bury (eds), *Handbook of Disability Studies*. London: Sage.

Braun, V. and Clarke, V. (2006) 'Using thematic analysis in psychology', *Qualitative Research in Psychology*, 3: 77–101.

Brierley, J. and Larcher, V. (2010) 'Lest we forget ... research ethics in children: perhaps onerous, yet absolutely necessary', *Archives of Disease in Childhood*, 95 (11): 863–866.

British Medical Association and the Law Society (1995) *Assessment of Mental Capacity – Guidance for Doctors and Lawyers*. London: BMA.

British Sociological Association (2011) *Equality*. www.britsoc.co.uk/equality (accessed 14/05/2011).

Bryman, A. (2006) 'Paradigm peace and its implications for quality', *International Journal of Social Research Methodology*, 9 (2): 111–126.

Bryman, A. (2007) 'The research question in social research: what is its role?', *International Journal of Social Research Methodology*, 10 (1): 5–20.

Bryman, A. (2008) *Social Research Methods* (3rd edn). Oxford: Oxford University Press.

Byrom, J. (2007) 'How to write a thesis', in P. O'Brien and F. Pipkin (eds), *Introduction to Research Methodology: For Specialists and Trainees*. London: Royal College of Obstetricians and Gynaecologists, pp. 252–257.

Campbell, A. (2008) 'For their own good: recruiting children for research', *Childhood*, 15 (1): 30–49.

Canadian Health Services Research Foundation (2007) *Dissemination Strategies*. www.phcris.org.au/infobytes/dissemination.php (accessed 14/05/2011).

Christensen, P. (2004) 'Children's participation in ethnographic research: issues of power and representation', *Children and Society*, 18: 165–176.

Clark, T. (2010) 'On "being researched": why do people engage with qualitative research?', *Qualitative Research*, 10 (4): 399–419.

Closs, S. and Cheater, F. (1996) 'Audit or research – what is the difference?', *Journal of Clinical Nursing*, 5: 249–256.

Cocks, A. (2006) 'The ethical maze: finding an inclusive path towards gaining children's agreement to research participation', *Childhood*, 13 (2): 247–266.

Cole, E., Kriege, G. and Griffin, W. (2003) 'The family bereavement program: efficacy evaluation of a theory-based prevention program for parentally bereaved children and adolescents', *Journal of Consulting and Clinical Psychology*, 71 (3): 587–600.

Coyne, I. (2009) 'Accessing children as research participants: examining the role of gatekeepers', *Child: Care, Health and Development*, 36 (4): 452–454.

Creswell, J. (2002) *Research Design: Qualitative, Quantitative, and Mixed Methods Approaches* (2nd edn). London: Sage.

Cretney, S.M., Masson, J. and Bailey-Harris, R. (2003) *Principles of Family Law*. London: Sweet and Maxwell.

Crompton, L. (2003) *Homosexuality and Civilization*. Cambridge, MA: Harvard University Press.

Danby, S., Ewing, L. and Thorpe, K. (2011) 'The novice researcher: interviewing young children', *Qualitative Inquiry*, 17 (1): 74–84.

Davies, J. and Wright, J. (2008) 'Children's voices: a review of the literature pertinent to looked-after children's views of mental health services', *Child and Adolescent Mental Health*, 13 (1): 26–31.

Davis, J., Watson, N. and Cunningham-Burley, S. (2000) 'Learning the lives of disabled children: developing a reflexive approach', in P. Christensen and A. James (eds), *Research with Children: Perspectives and Practices*. London: The Falmer Press, pp. 201–224.

Del Carmen, M.G and Joffe, A. (2005) 'Informed consent for medical treatment and research: a review', *The Oncologist*, 10 (8): 636–641.

Dickson-Swift, V., James, E., Kippen, S. and Liamputtong, P. (2008) 'Risk to researchers in qualitative research on sensitive topics: issues and strategies', *Qualitative Health Research*, 18 (1): 133–144.

Dixon-Woods, M., Angell, E., Ashcroft, R. and Bryman, A. (2007) 'Written work: the social functions of research ethics committee letters', *Social Science and Medicine*, 65: 792–802.

Dixon-Woods, M. and Tarrant, C. (2009) 'Why do people cooperate with medical research? Findings from three studies', *Social Science and Medicine*, 68: 2215–2222.

Dixon-Woods, M., Tarrant, C., Jackson, C., Jones, D. and Kenyon, S. (2011) 'Providing the results of research to participants: a mixed-methods study of the benefits and challenges of a consultative approach', *Clinical Trials*, 8 (3): 330–341.

Dixon-Woods, M., Young, B. and Ross, E. (2006) 'Researching chronic childhood illness: the example of childhood cancer', *Chronic Illness*, 2: 165–177.

Dogra, N. (2003) 'Cultural competence or cultural sensibility? A comparison of two ideal type models to teach cultural diversity to medical students', *International Journal of Medicine*, 5 (4): 223–231.

Dogra, N. (2011) 'How to give a lecture', in J. Eagles and T. Brown (eds) *Teaching Undergraduate Psychiatry*. London: Royal College of Psychiatrists, pp. 85–96.

Dogra, N. and Davies, D. (2010) 'Clinical governance, audit and supervision', in N. Dogra and S. Leighton (eds), *Nursing in Child and Adolescent Mental Health*. Maidenhead: McGraw Hill, pp. 155–166.

Dogra, N., Singh, S., Svirydzenka, N. and Vostanis, P. (2012) 'Mental health problems in children and young people from minority ethnic groups: the need for targeted research', *The British Journal of Psychiatry*, 200: 265–267.

Dogra, N., Vostanis, P., Abuateya, H. and Jewson, N. (2007) 'Children's mental health services and ethnic diversity: Gujarati families' perspectives of service provision for mental health problems', *Transcultural Psychology*, 44 (2): 275–291.

DuBois, J.M. (2008) *Solving Ethical Problems in Ethics in Mental Health Research*. New York: Oxford University Press.

Dworkin, G. (1972) 'Paternalism', *The Monist*, 56: 64–84.

Dyregrov, K. (2004) 'Bereaved parents' experience of research participation', *Social Science and Medicine*, 58 (2): 391–400.

Elliott, R., Fischer, C. and Rennie, D. (1999) 'Evolving guidelines for publication of qualitative research studies in psychology and related fields', *British Journal of Clinical Psychology*, 38: 215–229.

Ellis, B., Kia-Keating, M., Yusef, S., Lincoln, A. and Nur, A. (2007) 'Ethical research in refugee communities and the use of community participatory methods', *Transcultural Psychiatry*, 44 (3): 459–481.

Emmel, N., Hughes, K., Greenhalgh, J. and Sales, A. (2007) 'Accessing socially excluded people: trust and the gatekeeper in the researcher–participant relationship', *Sociological Research Online*, 12 (2). www.socresonline.org.uk/12/2/emmel.html (doi: 10.5153/sro.1512) (accessed 23/07/2012).

Ennew, J. (2009) *The Right to Be Properly Researched: How to Do Rights-based, Scientific Research with Children. A Set of 10 Manuals for Field Researchers*. Oslo: Black on White Publications.

Farrell, A. (2010) 'Towards beneficence for young children in research: challenges for bioethics committees', *Medicine and Law*, 29: 389–402.

Finlay, L. (2002) 'Negotiating the swamp: the opportunity and challenge of reflexivity in research practice', *Qualitative Research*, 2 (2): 209–230.

Fisher, H.R., McKevitt, C. and Boaz, A. (2011) 'Why do parents enrol their children in research? A narrative synthesis', *Journal of Medical Ethics*, 37: 544–551 (doi:10.1136/jme.2010.040220).

Food and Drug Administration (2005) 'Medication guide about using antidepressants in children and adults'. www.fda.gov/downloads/drugs/drugsafety/informationbydrugclass/UCM161646.pdf. (accessed 14/12/2011).

Francis, J., Johnston, M., Robertson, C., Glidewell, L., Entwistle, V., Eccles, M. and Grimshaw, J. (2010) 'What is adequate sample size? Operationalising data saturation for theory-based interview studies', *Psychology and Health*, 25 (10): 1229–1245.

Fry, C. and Dwyer, R. (2001) 'For love or money? An exploratory study of why injecting drug users participate in research', *Addiction*, 96: 1319–1325.

Garth, B. and Aroni, R. (2003) '"I value what you have to say": seeking the perspective of children with a disability, not just their parents', *Disability and Society*, 18 (5): 561–576.

Garth, B., Murphy, G. and Reddihough, D. (2009) 'Perceptions of participation: child patients with a disability in the doctor–parent–child partnership', *Patient Education and Counseling*, 74 (1): 45–52.

Gattuso, J., Hinds, P., Tong, X. and Srivastava, K. (2005) 'Monitoring child and parent refusals to enrol in clinical research protocols', *Journal of Advanced Nursing*, 53 (3): 319–326.

Giordano, J., O'Reilly, M., Taylor, H. and Dogra, N. (2007) 'Confidentiality and autonomy: the challenge(s) of offering research participants a choice of disclosing their identity', *Qualitative Health Research*, 17 (2): 264–275.

Gortmaker, S., Must, A., Sobol, A., Peterson, K., Colditz, G. and Dietz, W. (1996) 'Television viewing as a cause of increasing obesity among children in the United States, 1986–1990', *Archives of Pediatric Adolescent Medicine*, 150: 356–362.

Grady, C. (2005) 'Payment of clinical research subjects', *The Journal of Clinical Investigation*, 115 (7): 1681–1687.

Green, H., McGinnity, A., Meltzer, H., Ford, T. and Goodman, R. (2005) *Mental Health of Children and Young People in Great Britain* (2004). London: ONS.

Greenstein, T. (2006) *Methods of Family Research*. London: Sage.

Guba, E.G. and Lincoln, Y.S. (2004) 'Competing paradigms in qualitative research: theories and issues', in S.N. Hesse-Biber and P. Leavy (eds), *Approaches to Qualitative Research: A Reader on Theory and Practice*. Oxford: Oxford University Press, pp. 17–38.

Hadley, E., Smith, C., Gallo, A., Angst, D. and Knaff, K. (2008) 'Parents' perspectives on having their children interviewed for research', *Research in Nursing and Health*, 31: 4–11.

Halcomb, E. and Davidson, P. (2006) 'Is verbatim transcription of interview data always necessary?' *Applied Nursing Research*, 19: 38–42.

Hall, L. and McGregor, J. (2000) 'A follow-up study of the peer relationships of children with disabilities in an inclusive school', *The Journal of Special Education*, 34 (3): 114–126.

Hardy, C., Phillips, N. and Clegg, S. (2001) 'Reflexivity in organization and management theory: a study of the production of the research "subject"', *Human Relations*, 54: 531–560.

Harris, M. and Butterworth, G. (2002) *Developmental Psychology: A Student's Handbook*. Hove: Psychology Press.

Hart, R. (1997) *Children's Participation: The Theory and Practice of Involving Young Citizens in Community Development and Environmental Care*. London: Earthscan.

Health and Safety at Work Act (1974) www.hse.gov.uk/legislation/hswa.htm (accessed 02/04/2012).

Heath, S., Charles, V., Crow, G. and Wiles, R. (2004) 'Informed consent, gatekeepers and go-betweens', paper presented at The Ethics & Social Relations of Research conference (Sixth International Conference on Social Science Methodology), Amsterdam.

Hedgecoe, A. (2009) '"A form of practical machinery": the origins of research ethics committees in the UK, 1967–1972', *Medical History*, 53: 331–350.

Hestenes, L. and Carroll, D. (2000) 'The play interactions of young children with and without disabilities: individual and environmental differences', *Early Childhood Research Quarterly*, 15 (2): 229–246.

HM Government (1989) *The Children Act 1989*. www.legislation.gov.uk/ukpga/1989/41/contents/enacted (accessed 08/09/2011).

HM Government ([1984] 1998) *Data Protection Act 1998*. www.legislation.gov.uk/ukpga/1998/29/contents (accessed 13/10/2011).

HM Government (1999) *Protection of Children Act 1999*. www.legislation.gov.uk/ukpga/1999/14/contents (accessed 10/08/2012).

HM Government (2004a) *Every Child Matters: Change for Children*. https://www.education.gov.uk/publications/eOrderingDownload/DfES10812004.pdf (accessed 15/08/2011).

HM Government (2004b) *Children Act 2004*. www.legislation.gov.uk/ukpga/2004/31/notes/contents (accessed 08/09/2011).

HM Government (2004c) *The Medicines for Human Use (Clinical Trials) Regulation 2004*. www.legislation.gov.uk/uksi/2004/1031/contents/made (accessed 10/08/2012).

HM Government (2004d) *Human Tissue Act 2004*. www.legislation.gov.uk/ukpga/2004/30/contents (accessed 10/08/2012).

Holder, B., Turner-Musa, J., Kimmel, P., Alleyne, S., Kobrin, S., Simmens, S., Cruz, I. and Reiss, D. (1998) 'Engagement of African American families in research on chronic illness: a multisystem recruitment approach', *Family Processes*, 37: 127–151.

Holland, J. (2001) *Understanding Children's Experiences of Parental Bereavement*. London: Jessica Kingsley.

Holliday, A. (2002) *Doing and Writing Qualitative Research*. London: Sage.

Horstman, M., Aldiss, S., Richardson, A. and Gibson, F. (2008) 'Methodological issues when using the draw and write technique with children aged 6–12 years', *Qualitative Health Research*, 18 (7): 1001–1011.

Hugman, R., Pittaway, E. and Bartolomei, L. (2011) 'When "do no harm" is not enough: the ethics of research with refugees and other vulnerable groups', *British Journal of Social Work*, 41 (7): 1271–1287 (doi: 10.1093/bjsw/bcr013).

Hunter, D. (2008) 'The ESRC research ethics framework and research ethics review at UK universities: rebuilding the tower of Babel REC by REC', *Journal of Medical Ethics*, 34: 815–820.

Hurley, J. and Underwood, M. (2002) 'Children's understanding of their research rights before and after debriefing: informed assent, confidentiality, and stopping participation', *Child Development*, 73 (1): 132–143.

Hutchby, I. and O'Reilly, M. (2010) 'Children's participation and the familial moral order in family therapy', *Discourse Studies*, 12 (1): 49–64.

Hynson, J., Aroni, R., Bauld, V. and Sawyer, S. (2006) 'Research with bereaved parents: a question of how not why', *Palliative Medicine*, 20: 805–811.

Irwin, L. and Johnson, J. (2005) 'Interviewing young children: explicating our practices and dilemmas', *Qualitative Health Research*, 15: 821–831.

James, A. (2001) 'Ethnography in the study of children and childhood', in P. Atkinson, A. Coffey, S. Delamont, J. Lofland and L. Lofland (eds), *Handbook of Ethnography*. London: Sage, pp. 246–257.

Jankowiak, W., Joiner, A. and Khatib, C. (2011) 'What observation studies can tell us about single child play patterns, gender, and changes in Chinese society: cross-cultural research', *Cross-Cultural Research*, 45 (2): 155–177.

Joffe, H. and Yardley, L. (2004) 'Content and thematic analysis', in D. Marks and L. Yardley (eds), *Research Methods for Clinical and Health Psychology*. London: Sage, pp. 56–68.

Kennedy, I. (1991) *Treat Me Right: Essays in Medical Law and Ethics*. Oxford: Oxford University Press.

King, N. (2004) 'Using templates in the thematic analysis of text', in C. Cassell and G. Symon (eds), *Essential Guide to Qualitative Methods in Organisational Research*. London: Sage, pp. 256–270.

King, N. and Churchill, L. (2000) 'Ethical principles guiding research on child and adolescent subjects', *Journal of Interpersonal Violence*, 12 (6): 710–724.

King, N. (2012) 'Template analysis', in G. Symon and C. Cassell (eds), *Qualitative Organizational Research: Core Methods and Current Challenges*. London: Sage, pp. 426–450.

Lansdown, G. (1994) 'Children's rights', in B. Mayall (ed.), *Children's Childhoods: Observed and Experienced*. London: Falmer Press, pp. 33–44.

Lapadat, J. and Lindsay, A. (1999) 'Transcription in research and practice: from standardization of technique to interpretive positionings', *Qualitative Inquiry*, 5 (1): 64–86.

Lo, B. (2010) *Ethical Issues in Clinical Research: A Practical Guide*. Philadelphia: Wolter Kluwer.

Lucas, K. (2010) 'A waste of time? The value and promise of researcher completed qualitative data transcribing', *Northeastern Educational Research Association Conference Proceedings*, paper 24. http://digitalcommons.uconn.edu/cgi/viewcontent.cgi?article=1008&context=nera_2010 (accessed 24/07/2012).

MacDonald, K. (2008) 'Dealing with chaos and complexity: the reality of interviewing children and families in their own homes', *Journal of Clinical Nursing*, 17 (23): 3123–3130.

Mauthner, M. (1997) 'Methodological aspects of collecting data from children: lessons from three research projects', *Children and Society*, 11: 16–28.

Mayring, P. (2000) 'Qualitative content analysis', *Forum Qualitative Social Research*, 1 (2). www.qualitative-research.net/index.php/fqs/article/view/1089/2385 (accessed 24/07/2012).

McPherson, A. (2010) 'Involving children: why it matters', in S. Redsell and A. Hastings (eds), *Listening to Children and Young People in Healthcare Consultations*. Oxon: Radcliffe Publishing, pp. 15–30.

Medical Research Council (2004) *MRC Ethics Guide: Medical Research Involving Children*. www.mrc.ac.uk/Utilities/Documentrecord/index.htm?d = MRC002430 (accessed 13/10/2011).

Mental Health Foundation (1999) *Bright Futures: Promoting Children and Young People's Mental Health*. London: Mental Health Foundation.

Millum, J. and Emanuel, E. (2007) 'The ethics of international research with abandoned children', *Science*, 318: 1874–1875.

Minkov, M. and Hofstede, G. (2012) 'Is national culture a meaningful concept? Cultural values delineate homogeneous national clusters of in-country regions', *Cross-Cultural Research*, 46 (2): 133–159.

Morgan, D. (1998) *Planning Focus Groups*. Thousand Oaks, CA: Sage.

Morley, C., Lau, R., Davis, P. and Morse, C. (2005) 'What do parents think about enrolling their premature babies in several research studies?', *Archives of Diseases in Childhood: Fetal & Neonatal Edition*, 90: F225–F228.

Mortimore, P. (1999) 'Does educational research matter?', Presidential Address to the British Educational Research Association Annual Conference, University of Sussex at Brighton, 2–5 September.

Moser, D., Arndt, S., Kanz, J., Benjamin, M., Bayless, J., Reese, R., Paulsen, J. and Flaum, M. (2004) 'Coercion and informed consent in research involving prisoners', *Comprehensive Psychiatry*, 45 (1): 1–9.

Munford, R. and Sanders, J. (2004) 'Recruiting diverse groups of young people to research', *Qualitative Social Work*, 3 (4): 469–482.

Murray, C. (2005) 'Children and young people's participation and non-participation in research', *Adoption and Fostering*, 29 (1): 57–66.

Murray, R. (2006) *How to Write a Thesis* (2nd edn). Maidenhead: Open University Press.

National Cancer Institute, Center for the Advancement of Health, Robert Wood Johnson Foundation (2002) *Designing for Dissemination: Conference Summary Report*, 19–20 September. http://cancercontrol.cancer.gov/IS/pdfs/d4d_conf_sum_report.pdf (accessed 10/04/2011).

O'Cathain, A. and Thomas, K. (2006) 'Combining qualitative and quantitative methods', in C. Pope and N. Mays (eds), *Qualitative Research in Health Care* (3rd edn). Oxford: Blackwell Publishing/BMJ Books, pp. 102–111.

O'Cathain, A., Murphy, E. and Nicholl, J. (2007) 'The quality of mixed methods studies in health services research', *Journal of Health Services Research Policy*, 13 (2): 92–98.

ONS (Office of National Statistics) (2011) www.ons.gov.uk/jobs/index.html (accessed 14/05/2011).

O'Reilly, M. (1999) '"Little angels and little devils": children's accounts of when the halo slips, negotiating conflict', unpublished MSc thesis, University of Derby.

O'Reilly, M. (2006) 'Should children be seen and not heard? An examination of how children's interruptions are treated in family therapy', *Discourse Studies*, 8 (4): 549–566.

O'Reilly, M. (2007) 'Who's a naughty boy then? Accountability, family therapy and the "naughty" child', *The Family Journal: Counseling and Therapy for Couples and Families*, 15 (3): 234–243.

O'Reilly, M. (2008) '"I didn't violent punch him": parental accounts of punishing children with mental health problems', *Journal of Family Therapy*, 30: 272–295.

O'Reilly, M., Dixon-Woods, M., Angell, E., Ashcroft, R. and Bryman, A. (2009a) 'Doing accountability: a discourse analysis of research ethics committee letters', *Sociology of Health and Illness*, 31 (2): 246–291.

O'Reilly, M., Karim, K., Taylor, H. and Dogra, N. (2012a) 'Parent and child views on anonymity: "I've got nothing to hide"', *International Journal of Social Research Methodology*, 15 (3): 211–224.

O'Reilly, M. and Parker, N. (2012) 'Unsatisfactory saturation': a critical exploration of the notion of saturated sample sizes in qualitative research', *Qualitative Research* (doi: 10.1177/1468794112446106).

O'Reilly, M., Parker, N. and Hutchby, I. (2011) 'Ongoing processes of managing consent: the empirical ethics of using video-recording in clinical practice and research', *Clinical Ethics*, 6: 179–185.

O'Reilly, M., Parker, N., Stafford, V., and Karim, K. (2012b) '"I think the university is doing some project": the challenge of convincing the NHS of the value of CA', paper presented at Discourse, Communication, Conversation: An Anniversary Conference, 21–23 March, Loughborough University.

O'Reilly, M., Taylor, H., and Vostanis, P. (2009b) '"Nuts, schiz, psycho": an exploration of young homeless people's perceptions and dilemmas of defining mental health', *Social Science and Medicine*, 68: 1737–1744.

Parker, N. and O'Reilly, M. (forthcoming) '"We are alone in the house": a case study addressing researcher safety and risk', *Qualitative Research in Psychology*.

Paterson, B., Gregory, D. and Thorne, S. (1999) 'A protocol for researcher safety', *Qualitative Health Research*, 9 (2): 259–269.

Paul, M. (2007) 'Rights', *Archives of Disease in Childhood*, 92: 720–725.

Peel, E., Parry, O., Douglas, M. and Lawton, J. (2006) '"It's no skin off my nose": why people take part in qualitative research', *Qualitative Health Research*, 16 (10): 1335–1349.

Piaget, J. ([1936] 1963) *The Origins of Intelligence in Children.* New York: W.W. Norton and Co.

Piercy, H. and Hargate, M. (2004) 'Social research on the under-16s: a consideration of the issues from a UK perspective', *Journal of Child Health Care*, 8 (4): 253–263.

Post, J.E., Preston, L.E. and Sachs, S. (2002) 'Managing the extended enterprise: the new stakeholder view', *California Management Review*, 45 (1): 6–28.

Potter, J. (2002) 'Two kinds of natural', *Discourse Studies*, 4: 539–542.

Potter, J. and Hepburn, A. (2005) 'Qualitative interviews in psychology: problems and possibilities', *Qualitative Research in Psychology*, 2: 1–27.

Punch, K.F. (2000) *Developing Effective Research Proposals.* London: Sage.

Punch, S. (2002) 'Research with children: the same or different from research with adults', *Childhood*, 9 (3): 321–341.

Race Relations (2009) *Ethnicity and Race.* http://racerelations.about.com/od/skills buildingresources/g/ethnicityrace.htm (accessed 22/06/2009).

Raymond, N.C., Chang, P.N., Crow, S.J., Mitchell, J.E., Dieperink, B.S., Beck, M.M., Crosby, R.D., Clawson, C.C and Warwick, W.J. (2000) 'Eating disorders in patients with cystic fibrosis', *Journal of Adolescence*, 23 (3): 359–63.

Rew, L., Taylor-Seehafer, M. and Thomas, N. (2000) 'Without parental consent: conducting research with homeless adolescents', *Journal of the Society of Pediatric Nurses*, 5 (3): 131–138.

Ribbens McCarthy, J. (2007) '"They all look as if they're coping, but I'm not": the relational power/lessness of "youth" in responding to experiences of bereavement', *Journal of Youth Studies*, 10 (3): 285–303.

Rice, M., Bunker, K., Kang, D., Howell, C. and Weaver, M. (2007) 'Accessing and recruiting children for research in schools', *Western Journal of Nursing Research*, 29 (4): 501–514.

Robert Wood Johnson Foundation (2008) 'Reflexivity', *Qualitative Research Guidelines Project*. www.qualres.org/HomeRefl-3703.html (accessed 27/12/2011).

Roszkowski, M. and Bean, A. (1990) 'Believe it or not! Longer questionnaires have lower response rates', *Journal of Business and Psychology*, 4 (4): 495–509.

Rothman, D.J. and Rothman S.M. ([1984] 2005) *The Willowbrook Wars: Bringing the Mentally Disabled into the Community*. New Brunswick, NJ: Transaction Publishers.

Rumsey, N. and Marks, D. (2004) 'Getting started: the practicalities of doing research', in D. Marks and L. Yardley (eds), *Research Methods for Clinical and Health Psychology*. London: Sage, pp. 21–38.

Sampson, H. (2004) 'Navigating the waves: the usefulness of a pilot in qualitative research', *Qualitative Research*, 4 (3): 383–402.

Sandelowski, M. (2004) 'Using qualitative research', *Qualitative Health Research*, 14 (10): 1366–1386.

Seale, C. (1999) *The Quality of Qualitative Research*. London: Sage.

Shaw, M. (2001) 'Competence and consent to treatment in children and adolescents', *Advances in Psychiatric Treatment*, 7: 150–159.

Shuy, R. (2001) 'In-person versus telephone interviewing', in J.F. Gubrium and J.A. Holstein (eds), *Handbook of Interview Research: Context and Method*. London: Sage, pp. 537–556.

Silverman, D. (2005) *Doing Qualitative Research: A Practical Handbook* (2nd edn). London: Sage.

Silverman, D. (2011) *Interpreting Qualitative Data* (4th edn). London: Sage.

Singh, I. (2010) 'Cryptic coercion', *Hastings Center Report*, 40 (1): 22–23.

Singh, I. and Keenan, S. (2010) 'The challenges and opportunities of qualitative health research with children', in I. Bourgeault, R. Dingwall and R. DeVries (eds), *The Sage Handbook of Qualitative Methods in Health Research*. London: Sage, pp. 696–713.

Speer, S. and Hutchby, I. (2003) 'From ethics to analytics: aspects of participants' orientations to the presence and relevance of recording devices', *Sociology*, 37 (2): 315–337.

Spencer, L., Ritchie, J., Lewis, J. and Dillon, L. (2003) *Quality in Qualitative Evaluation: A Framework for Assessing Research Evidence*. Government Chief Social Researcher's Office, Prime Minister's Strategy Unit, London. www.uea.ac.uk/edu/phdhkedu/acadpapers/qualityframework.pdf (accessed 24/07/2012).

Stevens, M., Lord, B., Proctor, M.T., Nagy, S. and O'Riordan, E. (2010) 'Research with vulnerable families caring for children with life-limiting conditions', *Qualitative Health Research*, 20 (4): 496–505.

Sturges, J. and Hanrahan, K.J. (2004) 'Comparing telephone and face-to-face qualitative interviewing: a research note', *Qualitative Research*, 4(1): 107–118.

Swartling, U., Helgesson, G., Hansson, M. and Ludvigsson, J. (2009) 'Split views among parents regarding children's right to decide about participation in research: a questionnaire survey', *Journal of Medical Ethics*, 35: 450–455.

Tarpery, M. (2006) *Why People Get Involved in Health and Social Care Research: A Working Paper*. Eastleigh: INVOLVE.

Taylor, H., Stuttaford, M., Broad, B. and Vostanis, P. (2006) 'Why a "roof" is not enough: the characteristics of young homeless people referred to a designated mental health service', *Journal of Mental Health*, 15: 491–501.

Taylor, H., Stuttaford, M. and Vostanis, P. (2007) 'Organisational issues facing a voluntary sector mental health service for homeless young people', *Journal of Integrated Care*, 15: 37–46.

Taylor, R. (2007) 'Reversing the retreat from Gillick? R (Axon) v Secretary of State for Health', *Child and Family Law Quarterly*, 19(1): 81–97.

Testa, A. and Coleman, L. (2006) 'Accessing research participants in schools: a case study of UK adolescent sexual health survey', *Health Education Research: Theory and Practice*, 21 (4): 518–526.

The Free Dictionary (2009) www.thefreedictionary.com (accessed 22/06/2009).

Tisdall, E.K. and Davis, J. (2004) 'Making a difference? Bringing children's and young people's views into policy-making', *Children and Society*, 18: 131–142.

Tong, A., Sainsbury, P. and Craig, J. (2007) 'Consolidated criteria for reporting qualitative research (COREQ): a 32-item checklist for interviews and focus groups', *International Journal for Quality Health Care*, 19 (6): 349–357.

Tracy, S. (2010) 'Qualitative quality: eight "Big-Tent" criteria for excellent qualitative research', *Qualitative Inquiry*, 16 (10): 837–851.

Truscott, Y.J. (1998) 'Chaucer's children and the medieval idea of childhood', *Children's Literature Association Quarterly*, 23 (1): 29–34.

Turkheimer, E., Haley, A., Waldron, M., D'Onofrio, B. and Gottesman, I. (2003) 'Socioeconomic status modifies heritability of IQ in young children', *Psychological Science*, 14: 623–628.

UCSF (University of California, San Francisco) (2008) *Use of Web-Based Outreach Strategies to Reach Teens: Findings from the TeenSMART Outreach Evaluation*. www.familypact.org/Files/Provider/Research%20Reports/TSO_Web-BasedOutreachStudy_FinalReport_1-16-09.pdf (accessed 05/02/2012).

UNICEF (1989) *The Convention on the Rights of the Child*. www.unicef.org/crc/files/Guiding_Principles.pdf (accessed 12/02/2012).

UNICEF (2012) *The Convention on the Rights of the Child*. www.unicef.org/crc/index_30229.html (accessed 11/01/2012).

United Nations High Commissioner for Human Rights (2002) *The Convention on the Rights of the Child*. www2.ohchr.org/english/law/crc.htm (accessed 18/11/2011).

US National Library of Medicine (2011) International Committee of Medical Journal Editors (ICMJE): Uniform Requirements for Manuscripts Submitted to Biomedical Journals. www.nlm.nih.gov/bsd/uniform_requirements.html (accessed 14/05/2011).

Weisner, T. (1996) 'Why ethnography should be the most important method in the study of human development', in R. Jessor, A. Colby and R. Schweder (eds), *Ethnography and Human Development: Context and Meaning in Social Inquiry*. Chicago: University of Chicago Press, pp. 305–326.

Weithorn, L.A. and Campbell, S.B. (1982) 'The competency of children and adolescents to make informed treatment decisions', *Child Development*, 53: 1589–1599.

Wendler, D. and Jenkins, T. (2008) 'Children's and the parents views on facing research risks for the benefit of others', *Archives of Psychiatry and Adolescent Medicine*, 162: 9–14.

Whyte, B. (2004) 'Effectiveness, research and youth justice', *Youth Justice*, 4 (1): 3–21.

Wilkinson, M. and Moore, A. (1997) 'Inducement to research', *Bioethics*, 11 (5): 373–389.

Willmott, A. (2010) 'Involving children: how to do it', in S. Redsell and A. Hastings (eds), *Listening to Children and Young People in Healthcare Consultations*. Oxon: Radcliffe Publishing, pp. 45–55.

Index